JOHN VASSOS

JOHN VASSOS

INDUSTRIAL DESIGN FOR MODERN LIFE

DANIELLE SHAPIRO

UNIVERSITY OF MINNESOTA PRESS
MINNEAPOLIS · LONDON

The University of Minnesota Press gratefully acknowledges the generous assistance provided for the publication of this book by the Margaret S. Harding Memorial Endowment honoring the first director of the University of Minnesota Press.

Frontispiece: John Vassos around age thirty (circa 1930), when he worked primarily as an illustrator and artist. Courtesy of Jayne Johnes.

Published by the University of Minnesota Press
111 Third Avenue South, Suite 290
Minneapolis, MN 55401-2520
http://www.upress.umn.edu

Book design by Laura Shaw Design, Inc.

Printed in the United States of America on acid-free paper

The University of Minnesota is an equal-opportunity educator and employer.

22 21 20 19 18 17 16   10 9 8 7 6 5 4 3 2 1

Library of Congress Cataloging-in-Publication Data
Names: Shapiro, Danielle, author.
Title: John Vassos : industrial design for modern life / Danielle Shapiro.
Description: Minneapolis : University of Minnesota Press, 2016. | Includes bibliographical references and index.
Identifiers: LCCN 2015037494| ISBN 978-0-8166-9340-5 (hc) |
ISBN 978-0-8166-9341-2 (pb)
Subjects: LCSH: Vassos, John, 1898–1985. | Industrial designers—United States—Biography. | Illustrators—United States—Biography. | Industrial design—United States—History—20th century. | RCA Corporation—History—20th century. | BISAC: ARCHITECTURE / History / Modern
(late 19th Century to 1945). | ARCHITECTURE / Individual Architects & Firms / General.
Classification: LCC TS140.V37 S53 2016 | DDC 745.2092—dc23
LC record available at http://lccn.loc.gov/2015037494

FOR BRUCE, MAYA, AND ARIELLE,
WITH LOVE

CONTENTS

Preface ix

Introduction: Creating Design We Can Live With xi

1. Drawing Modernity: Advertising and Book Illustrations 1

2. Becoming an Industrial Designer 55

3. Modernizing the Home through Radio 81

4. Designed for Electricity: Vassos's Architectural Interiors 109

5. Vassos and RCA: Money, Media, and Modernism 137

6. The TRK-12: RCA's First Mass-Marketed Television Receiver 165

7. John Vassos in Postwar America 183

Conclusion: The Legacy of John Vassos 213

Acknowledgments 223

Notes 227

Index 253

PREFACE

I was first drawn to the work of Greek American illustrator and industrial designer John Vassos (1898–1985) in 1994, while I was serving as a curatorial assistant at the Cooper Hewitt, National Design Museum, on *Packaging the New: Design and the American Consumer, 1925–1975,* an exhibition about American industrial design. The curator was considering including a powerful image by Vassos titled "Dromophobia: The Fear of Crossing the Street" from his 1931 book *Phobia.* The show examined the need for the application of style to daily life and included established industrial designers such as Henry Dreyfuss, Raymond Loewy, and Norman Bel Geddes. As a resident of New York City, I could relate to the point of view in Vassos's image of small people scrambling to avoid freakishly large speeding cars. On further investigation, I discovered that in the 1930s Vassos was a top industrial designer who designed many radio sets for the Radio Corporation of America (RCA), in addition to the company's debut television set presented at the 1939–40 New York World's Fair. I was intrigued that the same man who was critical of mass culture would build one of the first mass-produced television sets. In the end, after hundreds of drawings and designs were pared down for the exhibition, Vassos's illustration was omitted. Over time, his contribution to American industrial design was largely forgotten.

When I returned to investigate Vassos's career in 2002, I was surprised to discover there had still been little written about his work, despite vast growth in the field of American industrial design history. My effort to piece together his biography was accomplished primarily through research involving the two largest archives of his work: the uncataloged materials in more than twenty boxes at the Smithsonian Archives of American Art in Washington, D.C., and the neater but smaller John Vassos collection at the E. S. Bird Library at Syracuse University.

I began my unearthing at the Archives of American Art in March 2002 by diving into the disorganized boxes, including files and random objects from Vassos's home office in Norwalk, Connecticut. It was gritty, dirty, messy, and exhilarating work wading through thousands of documents, drawings, and letters spanning Vassos's multifaceted career from the Prohibition era to the computer age. To my delight,

I discovered not only the career of John Vassos but also an unfolding history of American industrial design and the story of modern style at RCA, the nation's major broadcasting and manufacturing company during this time.

Working my way through the materials, I found many important items, including manuscripts, a treasure of glass slides held in a rusted steel case, family photographs, numerous radio renderings, and sketches for a media-centered living room of the future. Other items included ribald jokes that Vassos shared with Ross Treseder, a vice president at Coca-Cola in the 1930s, Japanese pornographic prints, and, in the Syracuse archive, a telegram from Aristotle Onassis sent from the yacht *Christina* expressing gratitude to Vassos for sexual advice he had apparently offered. It read: "Many thanks for sending your secret aphrodisiac. *Stop.* It has made our honeymoon a success although Jackie is resisting some of our fine old Greek customs. *Stop.* However, I am sure she will get it in the end. *Exclamation Point.* Telis Onassis."[1] By the time I heard John Vassos's voice for the first time on an audiotape from a conference on design, I already felt very familiar with him.[2] I thought I even smelled his cologne as I opened his personal letters. After a while, Vassos's life story and major accomplishments began to take shape, and I recount them here.

INTRODUCTION
CREATING DESIGN WE CAN LIVE WITH

*Design should not be simply an embellishment of our lives,
something we enjoy on special occasions. It should be an
integral part of everything we do. It should be both physical
and spiritual enrichment.*

—JOHN VASSOS[1]

John Vassos has not received much attention in studies of twentieth-century design; his work does not
fit neatly into the categories that historians of design
have anointed in the past century. He significantly influenced the design of early
electronics—especially radios and televisions. Indeed, almost every kind of new electronic device that found its way into the modern home from the 1930s through the
1970s reflected Vassos's design influence. Since these objects were new additions to
increasing numbers of homes during this period, his designs helped to codify many
of the knobs, grilles, cases, and other features that came to be taken for granted in
twentieth-century homes and automobiles. His writings on social progress overturned the conventional expectations of a "company man" in a nation grappling with
mechanization in the decade after the Great Depression. While Vassos was on the
forefront as an artist and as an industrial designer, his most remarkable contribution is the way he blended art and industrial design into a new, well-thought-out
discipline. At a time when futuristic design was the dialect of avant-garde art and
science fiction, Vassos imagined futuristic machines in the average American living
room. His sensual Bakelite radios and television cabinets housed the ever-improving
media that allowed stories, music, news reports, and flickering images to enter the
home. With a keen eye and an intuition for how an average person can instinctively

control such technology, Vassos created a lasting legacy; he is still with us when we push a car radio button, swipe the screen on a mobile device, or find a screen to be perfectly proportioned for reading during a long airplane ride.

Just as people today grapple with the placement of their flat screens, designers at the dawn of the television age wrestled with where the television set should go and how it would appear. Should it look like a piece of furniture, so as not to interrupt the decor, or like a technical object that stands apart? Scholars of media have focused on the content rather than the housing of broadcast media. By explaining the ways in which Vassos's radios, televisions, and broadcast equipment redefined the user experience, I hope to broaden the conversation about the design of media technologies.

In a 1956 panel discussion with Arthur Drexler, director of the architecture and design department at the Museum of Modern Art, Vassos took issue with MoMA's "esoteric chair exhibit," stating that it lacked "any emphasis on the mass-produced unit which is intrinsic to our society and our objective—the thing that is well-designed with a feeling for the machine behind it."[2] While he deliberated over the human aspects of design—making sure that users do not strain their arms and that the lighting is appropriate—Vassos's designs put consumers directly in touch with modern electronics and the machine aesthetic.

More than a half century before the iPod, he enthused over the tactile experience of using a radio or a television. His drawings of hands touching knobs and his writings on the radio dial reveal his focus on the intuition of how we communicate with our machines. In the 1930s, tuning a radio dial was a new sensation that brought the gift of sound. Vassos understood that the act of radio listening engaged a broad ensemble of senses. Influencing what historian Andreas Fickers terms the "visualization of the hearing experience," he proposed the radical change from a circular station dial to a station scale that moves from left to right.[3] Vastly creative, Vassos harnessed his talents to make the abstract technologies of sight and sound tangibly real.

There is more at stake in this book than just the historical record of one industrial designer's career. By exploring the relationship between Vassos's work and American culture and by historicizing the birth of the media he designed, I hope to stimulate thinking about how these devices entered the home and the broadcast studio. Vassos's career spans the emergence of central new forms of mass media in the twentieth century and provides a template for understanding their success. This is Vassos's legacy—shaping the way we interact with our media technologies.

John Vassos began his career in New York City in 1921. Born to an affluent Greek family living in Constantinople (now Istanbul) in 1898, he escaped the oppressive conditions faced by Greek exiles in Turkey. He lived first on Barrow Street in bohemian Greenwich Village and worked with artists like photographer Margaret Bourke-White, abstract painter Jimmy Ernst, and radio personality Rudy Vallee. He spent time with intellectuals such as Harry Hopkins, who would join Franklin

Delano Roosevelt's brain trust, psychoanalyst Harry Stack Sullivan, and Edward Bernays, one of the first practitioners of public relations.

Revolutions in transportation and communication were transforming the world during this time. The proliferation of the assembly line had made mass-produced consumer goods readily available, and the new sales culture of advertising prioritized visual appeal. Vassos started his career as an advertising illustrator and later became a key participant in the growing field of industrial design. Industrial designers were versed in the display techniques used to sell consumer goods. As Vassos explained, a designer requires "a strong sense for mechanical design, an understanding of manufacturing limitations, a knowledge of wood, plastic, metal and glass"; a designer must be "a combination architect, draftsman and above all—a shrewd analyst."[4] In the age of mass production, marketing and design became increasingly important, as business owners had to move products off the burgeoning assembly lines and into the hands of consumers.

In the United States, modern design developed in a way that was different from that seen in Europe. Art deco had emerged in France as a luxurious mode and quickly morphed into something more pervasive and accessible.[5] In Germany, the Bauhaus school taught modern design with ideological foundations for affordable mass production. In the United States, modern design evolved in a plurality of styles, providing the look of the modern during the interwar years. This look referenced mechanization, electricity, and elemental shapes, as well as ancient motifs. Streamlining, a prominent vernacular American style, took its cue from the airplane, with bulbous shapes suggesting speed and lack of friction.[6] Calling his approach "functional modernism," Vassos drew on this wide visual vocabulary in the design of his prewar products.

Modern design meant more than exterior style. Following modernism's wider goals, it sought to break from the past and embrace technological advancement. Not a centralized movement, modernism embodied a range of ideas and styles, but a severance from antiquarian Victorian society was at its core. Vassos, as a Greek national escaping an oppressive political regime in Turkey, was drawn to the movement's resistance against the old order. Like many other modernists, he believed that a search for elemental truths and honesty of expression was appropriate for the machine age. Through his work on the radio, Vassos ushered in a style of modern design that was particularly suited for media receivers both in the home and in the studio. I call Vassos's particular aesthetic for broadcast products and equipment "media modern." While Vassos's designs for radio receivers echo the abstractions of cubism, the art retained enough realism to be successful with consumers. His work reflects a larger theme of industrial design and graphic design between the world wars—the casting of unpalatable modern styles in accessible forms that permitted ordinary folks to feel comfortable with disconcerting and often alienating modernity.[7]

Initially, Vassos appeared to be an unlikely figure to shape American mass media and consumer culture. A Greek immigrant with leftist politics, he was a trained artist who studied with artists John Sloan, a leader in the Ashcan school, and anatomical expert George Bridgman. Vassos was deeply conflicted about the machine age, which he found both transformative and tyrannical. His 1929 book *Contempo*, written by his wife, Ruth, with his illustrations, depicts frivolous commercialism alongside a dynamic urban tableau. Tabloids, movies, and advertising, characterized as "an edifice reaching to the skies and built on—BUNK," manipulate the public.[8] Even radio is depicted with ambivalence in Vassos's work. In his 1931 book *Phobia*, written in consultation with his friend Freudian psychoanalyst Harry Stack Sullivan, Vassos shows how the architecture, streets, and stores of urban life trigger psychological turmoil. The book allowed the designer to distinguish himself as an expert in the human mind and, more important, informed the way he empathetically approached design.

Vassos was most successful designing products for broadcasting, but he also made a mark in the consumer, leisure, and transportation markets. His design of a turnstile for the Perey Turnstile Company addressed the urban commuter's harrowing experience of moving through subway and train stations. Vassos enclosed the rigid mechanical parts of the turnstile to prevent clothes and fingers from getting caught, rounded the arms for a gentler nudge, and added a slight pedestal. Still sold today, this turnstile became the standard in the field and has been used everywhere, from subways to theme parks.

In the 1930s, Vassos and other industrial designers restyled restaurants to elicit particular responses from consumers, such as buying more food or not lingering too long, a novel concept at the time. At Nedick's, a popular New York City hot dog stand and one of the first fast-food restaurants, Vassos added curved freestanding Bakelite counters to increase capacity, softened the lighting to stimulate appetites and make customers more comfortable, and created matching server uniforms and menus, again a new idea, to convey continuity of the brand. In 1934, *Fortune* magazine listed Vassos as one of the top ten most important industrial designers in the country in a profile that included Walter Dorwin Teague, Raymond Loewy, and Henry Dreyfuss. Proclaiming that "his subject is psychoanalysis," the *Fortune* author wrote that Vassos's understanding of the psychology of consumers set him apart from other designers.[9]

At the time of the *Fortune* article, the Radio Corporation of America (RCA) had recently hired Vassos as a consultant designer to remedy the company's flagging sales of radio sets. Designing a radio was not like reinterpreting a table or a chair; rather, radio design involved creating a form for a new medium. There was little consensus among designers regarding what form the case, often called the receiver, should take. The shape of the receiver reflected larger questions about the role radio would have in modern life in the first half of the twentieth century. Historian Susan Douglas has argued that radio was "the most important electronic invention of the century," as it "revolutionized the perceptual habits of the nation," transforming time,

1. DRAWING MODERNITY
ADVERTISING AND BOOK ILLUSTRATIONS

John Plato Vassacopoulos was born of Greek parentage in Sulina, Romania, on October 23, 1898. His home was "on the north side of Mt. Olympus" in a small fishing village.[1] His father, Apostolos, worked as a principal at a Greek private school "overlooking the Bosphorus and Sultan Haimid's palace 'the Yildiz'" and was also the editor in chief of the Greek newspaper *Chronos* for five years.[2] He was an expert in national Greek life, the author of several books, and a strict father, according to Vassos.[3] John's mother, Iphigenia Mitarakis, a native of Constantinople and "a pure Byzantine," was very beautiful and an extremely talented artist.[4] Vassos characterized the Balkans as a crazy quilt of ethnicities: "You walk twelve feet and you are in another country—Bulgarians, Yugoslavs, Turks, Albanians, Montenegro, Serbians, Croatians."[5]

His family moved to Constantinople when Vassos was a boy, and there he attended the Gymnasium School and Robert College. It was "one of the most fascinating cities in the world," he later recalled. Like many Greek nationals living in Turkey, his family faced prejudice from the Turkish government. As Vassos wrote, "The Turks are systematically eliminating every nationality—one million Greeks have left—by a super taxation or seizure by some pretense."[6] At an early age, Vassos became an artist and used his drawings to criticize the Turkish government. Under the pseudonym "The Wasp," he published a drawing mocking the Turkish senate, which angered the government.[7] Fearing punishment, Vassos fled the country in 1914 by enlisting in the British army, which was moving troops from China, India, and Australia to the front lines as World War I began. Among other roles he played during the war, he served as a cabin steward on the Belgian steamer *Prince Albert,* the second ship to be torpedoed in 1915.[8] He ended up in the American transport service and finally landed in the United States in 1918.[9] Vassos worked briefly for the Virginia War Service Committee in Newport News and contributed art for the Liberty Loan drive. He worked

John Vassos's alien seaman's identification card, issued under the name Vasso when he entered the United States in 1918 at Newport News, Virginia. John Vassos Papers, Special Collections Research Center, Syracuse University Libraries.

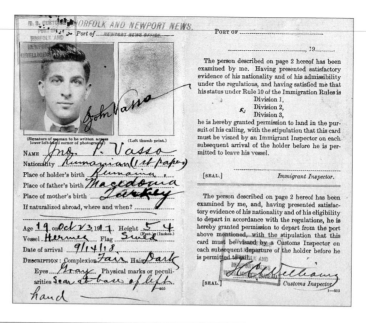

John Vassos's first business was the New York Display Service in New York City, 1922. John Vassos Papers, Archives of American Art, Smithsonian Institution.

in Boston before moving to New York City, where he was reunited with his father, his brother, Alex, and his sister, Ivi.[10] His mother, who stayed in Constantinople, died in 1919 of pneumonia.

While in Boston, Vassos studied under the artist John Singer Sargent at the Fenway Art School and the modernist set designer Joseph Urban at the Boston Opera Company.[11] He worked as a window dresser at the Columbia Gramophone Company, where he built dramatic window displays to promote "talking machines," or hand-crank phonographs, and musicians such as Enrico Caruso in the company's shop on Temple Street.[12] Vassos's vibrant personality won him favor among his employers. "He is a young man of sterling qualities, his character being very upright, his energy of the inexhaustible variety," wrote his manager, W. Blount Darden, in a letter of support for Vassos's naturalization.[13]

In 1921, Vassos moved to New York City, where he lived with his family for a short time before taking up residence in a studio apartment at 19 Barrow Street in the West Village. He designed sets for theater companies, including the Provincetown Players and the Berkshire Players, as well as for an unproduced Billy Rose musical production. The designer attended the Art Students League of New York in 1921 and 1922. He changed his name a few times during this period. When he first left Greece, his name was recorded incorrectly as John Wassocopoulos.[14] Then he changed it to Vasso, which was the name his brother used. He changed his name for a final time, adding the *s* to Vasso, when he was naturalized on January 30, 1924. Vassos was the original family name before the nineteenth century, when many Greeks created impressive names by elongating them.[15]

A handsome and charming young artist, with gray eyes and black hair, Vassos soon met the love of his life, Ruth Carrier (sometimes spelled Carriere), a successful fashion writer and stylist for Saks Fifth Avenue and Gimbels department stores. She advocated for modern design in her writings and fashion consulting. Vassos met Ruth at a party held at a hotel in 1921. "I sized up a stunning blonde and asked her to dance with me, her name, Ruth Carriere."[16] Ruth was five years older than Vassos and slightly taller, but they complemented each other, he an artist and she a writer. Both were seeking adult life in New York City and shedding their pasts, his in Greece and hers in upstate New York. They would collaborate on books and eventually build a life together in Norwalk, Connecticut. Soon after they met, Ruth moved into his Barrow Street studio after he "broke her bed," as he bawdily recalled, at the hotel for career women where she lived. They married in 1923 and were together until her death in 1965. They had no children. She was tolerant of his flirtations with other women and deeply supportive of his career.

The couple had a lot of friends, went to many parties, and had a huge social network. Vassos described their Upper West Side apartment as "a salon of drinking conversationalists. Ruth likes newspaper men and women, and I like artists. They mix compatibly."[17] The guests they entertained included Harry Hopkins (who became one of President Franklin Delano Roosevelt's closest advisers), Margaret Bourke-White, and Katherine and Nick Cassavetes (parents of the filmmaker John Cassavetes). Besides the contacts Vassos made through entertaining, he participated in the arts scene, putting on exhibitions in galleries and private homes around the city. American illustrator Willis Birchman described Vassos as "in Greenwich Village . . . part of the Max Bodenheim set. [He] wooed and married a Nordic blonde. The baby needed shoes to say nothing of an automobile and fur coat and Vassos turned out three national advertising campaigns for the cause."[18]

The enterprising young Vassos opened his first venture, the New York Display Service, in 1923, renting a studio at 46th Street and 6th Avenue. The business specialized in advertising and window design for department stores like A. I. Namm & Son in Brooklyn, Macy's in Manhattan, and Kaufmann's in Pittsburgh. He brought a modernistic style to advertisements for a range of products, from shoes to cars and department stores as well as theater sets and even an "exotic wedding cake in the futuristic manner."[19]

Vassos quickly rose from immigrant sign painter to the creative professional described in a 1930 issue of *The Bookman: A Review of Books and Life* as one of the top artists of the decade.[20] His most productive period as an illustrator and emerging artist overlapped with the swinging Jazz Age in New York and a new artistic aesthetic reflecting the fast pace of modern society. During the 1920s and early 1930s, he published three major books: *Salome* (1927 and 1930), his first and most popular book; *Contempo* (1929), a book of social criticism written by Ruth Vassos and illustrated by John; and *Phobia* (1931), which he referred to throughout his career as proof of his expertise in psychology. Vassos dedicated *Phobia* to his friend psychiatrist Harry Stack Sullivan. His other books, *Ultimo* (1929), about a futuristic underground city, and the lesser-known political critique *Humanities* (1935), along with his illustrations for periodicals such as *The Dance Magazine* and *Esquire*, solidified his reputation as a critically engaged and socially relevant artist. Vassos's publishers helped propel him to fame with public relations techniques, promoting the artist through print publications, lectures and other public events, and publicity photos. By the early 1930s, Vassos had become more mature and more self-aware, and he stepped assuredly into the public spotlight, taking on controversial issues like women's liberation and becoming an authority on modernism, a subject on which he lectured.

Vassos's work during this period offered a contradiction. He worked simultaneously as an advertising artist who embraced the machine age, individualism, and the consumer culture and as an independent artist who illustrated thirteen books between 1927 and 1946. Each type of work influenced the other. His advertisements featured a striking, highly patterned visual style. As historian Stuart Ewen points out, over time the goal of advertising changed from selling a product to selling a lifestyle, and the advertising industry had begun to recognize the power of imagery to make emotional appeals and reach the unconscious, a concept that Freudian psychology

Painting of a New York City subway by John Vassos, circa 1921. Courtesy of Jayne Johnes.

had introduced.[21] Vassos's drawing style developed under the influence of these new ideas. His illustrations for Packard cars, for example, use striking futuristic borders to convey movement and tempo; they celebrate the progress and excitement of the modern age. On the other hand, his books reflect an attitude highly skeptical of modern culture. For example, in *Contempo*, the text of which was written by Ruth Vassos, the perspective on the intestinal clog of the modern city is bleak. Traffic is a "Frankenstein that is choking our cities," Ruth writes. "More and more powerful it grows, insidiously, it uncoils its length. It belches smoke, our lungs are filled with its poisonous breath. Our cities are disfigured."[22]

In the drawings made for *Phobia*, Vassos also used the surrealistic juxtapositions deployed in his modernistic advertising to convey extreme emotions. *Phobia* was his best-known and most publicized book. It informed his understanding of human psychology, and the success he gained as a modernist illustrator gave him a taste of the stability and gratification that was to come in 1933 when he started working for the predominant media company in the country, RCA.

His earliest art illustrations show a process of creative discovery and mastery of skills in a range of artistic approaches. These works include impressionistic water-color paintings of his experience on the torpedoed ship during World War I. At the Art Students League, Vassos had studied with the artist John Sloan, who influenced his early drawings of New York City, such as his atmospheric series of the subway system. However, the figure-drawing expert George Bridgman, also at the Art Students League, had the greatest impact on Vassos. Numerous sketches of nude bodies and body parts in the Vassos archive reflect Bridgman's unique technique for capturing anatomical details and gestures, exemplified in his 1920 classic book *Constructive Anatomy*. Bridgman, who influenced a generation of illustrators, including Norman Rockwell, inspired Vassos to observe the body carefully, although the young artist never strove for realism except in his renderings of three-dimensional objects for industrial design purposes. Vassos finally found his unique style, which he described as "pure clear color with sharp defined lines, subject matter current in concept," in the mid-1920s.[23]

Vassos drew inspiration from the larger modern art movement in the use of reductive forms and essential geometries and the incorporation of decorative imagery. These techniques were part of contemporary modern design, which relied on dynamism, asymmetry, and surprise to convey messages. Major tropes of modernistic advertising clearly informed Vassos's illustration style. As identified by Roland Marchand, these tropes include the repetitive shapes borrowed from the assembly line, the off-center layout, dissonant juxtapositions of montage, and expressive distortion. Vassos incorporated all of these as well as simplicity, which, as Marchand notes, was part of the modernist advertising vernacular. Vassos focused on the product, cutting out the extraneous realism that marked the oil paint medium of older advertisements.[24] His illustrations sought to convey the "tempo and feeling" of the time "in a simple and direct manner" with the "utmost economy and simplicity of line and shade."[25] Accordingly, his chosen color palette was black, gray, and white. He appreciated filmmakers' use of wide shots to capture large groups "like mobs and masses . . . and infuse them with emotion as in Dr. Caligari landscapes" (referring to the 1920 German expressionist horror film *The Cabinet of Dr. Caligari*). He felt urban life—"a stream of movement in futurist rhythm, an abstract result of the modern age"—could be best captured from a distance.[26] Such a view of the city, seen as if from a helicopter, is depicted in an advertisement for the Sherry-Netherland hotel. Vassos incorporates towering skyscrapers, a bridge, even a cruise ship, to create a kinetic urban landscape.

Beyond inspiration from film, Vassos took advantage of innovative printing methods, such as the Ben Day process in his advertisements and the Knudsen process in the book *Ultimo*. He ambitiously claimed to have developed a new school of illustration that could represent the movement and perceptual shifts that characterized modernity. Vassos lectured often on modern illustration (for example, in a presentation titled "The Art of Graphically Portraying Emotions and Ideas") and published in writer's magazines.

Vassos's advertising output was prolific, including work in the fashion industry for department stores like Bonwit Teller, Wanamaker's, and Best & Company; for Cammeyer Fashion, a shoe company; and for cosmetics companies such as Armand

"Piver Announces Modern Perfumes," Piver advertisement with illustrations by John Vassos (signed in bottom right corner), 1927. Private collection.

and Piver. He created more than nine illustrated advertisements for the French Line ocean liner company, which was so pleased with his work that it offered him a European cruise. Vassos also was confident of his strengths in illustration. He wrote, "With my command of black and white and the flights of imagination in this acclaimed style of mine, I can dominate the pages of any magazine in which my ads may appear."[27]

Vassos illustrated more than a dozen advertisements for the luxury Packard motorcar that appeared in the *New Yorker* magazine in 1931–32. Many featured the handsome automobile, dubbed "the aristocrat of the metropolis," amid sweeping,

"Aristocrat of the Metropolis." Packard Motor Car Company advertisement with illustrations by John Vassos, which appeared in the *New Yorker*, March 19, 1932. John Vassos Papers, Archives of American Art, Smithsonian Institution.

impressionistic views of New York City. Other industrial designers, such as Walter Dorwin Teague and Raymond Loewy, also worked in advertising. Teague's black-and-white pen-and-ink advertisements, including some for the Packard Company, contrast sharply to Vassos's modern ones. While Teague began illustrating for commercial print in the early 1900s, he began to employ classical motifs in the 1920s as ornate framing devices, a feature that became known as the Teague border.[28] Loewy also created modernistic ads but focused on fashion illustration. Vassos contributed advertising illustrations for a range of products. He expanded beyond fashion advertising to work with the automobile and cruise line industries, where his aerodynamic fantastical drawings were welcomed. To create dramatic effects in his illustrations, Vassos would emphasize a singular element, such as an arm or a shoe, by elongating the body part or product or using repetition to make the scene visually interesting. In one advertisement for Packard, cars on a curving highway create a futuristic border while the Packard in the center of the page stands out. It is "distinguished," as the text of the ad claims. The automobile was one of the most conspicuous new mass-marketed products in the 1920s and 1930s and was associated with a range of meanings, such as mobility, leisure, and prestige.[29]

An advertising brochure for Artcote papers features another Vassos illustration that conveys the thrill of mobility. In this work Vassos creates a soaring vista of transport, no doubt to illustrate the accompanying text that refers to the "importance of modernism" to "transport your message." Layers of transportation modes are packed into the frame: a plane is hovering over a ship poised to fall over a towering waterfall; the outline of a bridge takes shape; a tiny human figure, in the bottom left corner of the image, walks toward an unknown destination. Indeed, many of Vassos's drawings of transportation include aerodynamic forms taken from airplanes: the ad for Artcote papers, many Packard ads, and, most vividly, the illustrations for the book *Ultimo,* where streamlined architectural forms dominate.

At the same time Vassos was creating illustrations for advertisements, he continued his involvement in the performing arts, including designing the set for the 1929 experimental dance drama *The Sixth Sense* by Demetrious Vilan and Margaret Severn at the Guild Theater.[30] His modern art served as the backdrop for events like the "Abstract Ball" at the Plaza Hotel alongside the work of other artists such as Childe Hassam and Vassos's mentor John Sloan.[31] Vassos contributed trenchant illustrations to *The Dance Magazine* that proposed dance performances intended to reveal the mechanizations of capitalism and urban life. In "Traffic Dance," traffic is visualized as an ensemble of bodies moving rapidly but "getting nowhere."[32] A soloist dancer attempts but fails to break free from the ceaseless, ever-increasing flow. Similarly, in "Mass Production," the image and accompanying acerbic text describe a futile effort by a rebellious dancer to reject the suffocating conformity:

> Men move in unison; they produce the same thoughts, the same objects.
> Before them dances a single figure, moving in the stereotyped measure
> that the mass demands. Behind him, dances his soul, the invisible soul ever
> protesting, fighting, striving in vain to break the bonds of mass production
> and mass demands, in vain, for the man himself is only a product of the
> machine.[33]

These works reveal Vassos's response to inhumane forces of modernity, where people become like cars traveling on predetermined pathways, devoid of individuality. With repetitive patterns that suggest motion and the mix of clarity and indeterminacy, the illustrations follow the avant-garde style of such artists as the French painters Fernand Léger and Robert and Sonia Delaunay.[34]

The Spring mode is expressed by Cammeyer in intertwined straps on two distinctive models. Spring fashions by Cammeyer will be shown in many cities. We shall be pleased to tell you where you can see them and mail you a brochure of new styles.

SALON de LUXE FIFTH AVENUE at FIFTY THIRD NEW YORK

Modernistic advertisements for Cammeyer shoes illustrated by John Vassos: the spring collection, *Harper's Bazaar,* April 1927, and selections from the summer collection, *Vogue,* June 1927. Private collection.

By JOHN VASSOS

MASS PRODUCTION

Men move in unison; they produce the same thoughts, the same objects. Before them dances a single figure, moving in the stereotyped measures that the mass demands. Behind him, dances his soul, the invisible soul ever protesting, fighting, striving in vain to break the bonds of mass production and mass demand. In vain, for the man himself is only a product of the machine

This illustration, "Mass Production," with text by John Vassos, appeared in *The Dance Magazine*, February 1931. Private collection.

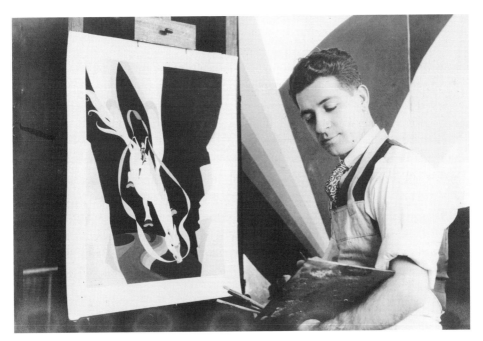

Vassos completes the artwork "Icarus" in his Upper West Side apartment, circa 1929. Courtesy of Jayne Johnes.

Vassos's written signature appears in many of the ads he illustrated. As art historian Michele Bogart argues, an artist's signature drew the viewer's attention to an ad, imbuing the ad with the aura of a fine painting; the appearance of such signatures reflected advertising directors' own creative aspirations for their burgeoning industry.[35] Vassos's signature is most prominent in the dreamlike series of advertisements he illustrated for Cammeyer shoes. In one advertisement, shoes seemingly float in bubbles while a horse with a long ribbon tail runs across the top of the page, its image reflected in a series of rounded evocative shapes composed of graduated shades of black and gray.

The use of artistic illustration proved to be short-lived, as advertising executives grappled with whether advertising should be a realistic representation or an artistic expression of a product. Modernistic advertising was controversial among advertising executives particularly since it lacked broad appeal.[36] In one article criticizing modernistic art in advertising, the author found these ads positively offensive, saying they "look like something that had been inspired by a night out in Greenwich Village."[37] Voicing a common complaint that modernistic advertising held little appeal outside New York City, the writer called for the use of appealing artistic images rather than jarring "puzzles." Vassos's ads for Best & Company, which asked the question "to be or not to be—Chic!" and featured an androgynous woman dressed half in a gown and half in a tuxedo, were the focus of this kind of critique.

Advertising as an expression of modern art and creativity lost favor by the early 1930s as photography began to dominate. Most consumers preferred to see ads that featured romanticized realistic imagery in familiar settings rather than jarring perspectives. By the 1930s, photography had become a widely used medium for entertainment, information, and persuasion. Advertising agencies, once wary of photography, embraced this new modern art as it was increasingly executed by skilled professionals who created enticing compositions for magazines. According to Bogart, illustrators' authority in advertising diminished in part due to a shift that solidified the position of professional photographers. Pioneers like Edward Steichen, whose work combined portrait, commercial, and artistic imagery, convinced advertising agencies to take photography seriously.[38] The persuasive power of photography was also being recognized in politics. Columbia professor Roy Stryker of the Farm Security Administration hired a team of photographers to document American life in a campaign to "sell" New Deal programs to the American people. The rise of color photography strengthened the format's claim to realism and further helped usher in the dominance of the medium.

With the decline in demand for advertising illustrations by the early 1930s, Vassos began focusing on the production of illustrated books and murals. Employing the same persuasive techniques and graphic psychological effects, he developed logos, brand identities, and corporate iconography for clients as part of entire design packages. He did not return to contract illustration work until decades later, after he had moved on to establish himself as an artist and designer.

SALOME

Salome was Vassos's first foray into art illustration. Columbia University's 1926 production of Oscar Wilde's 1893 play was produced by the Greek Letters and Arts Society and apparently performed in Greek. Vassos created illustrations for the playbill and poster and designed the stage and lighting effects. The play was presented at the International House at 500 Riverside Drive, Manhattan.[39] The play's music, by Richard Strauss, was performed by the Commodore Orchestra directed by Bernard Levitow. The illustrations for the play marked a transition in Vassos's illustration style, as he was becoming more comfortable with expressing internal emotional states rather than realistic but superficial images. As Ruth Vassos (writing as Ruth Carriere) wrote in the introduction to the playbill, "John Vassos has so perfectly and beautifully portrayed the feeling and nuances of Salome."

Unbeknownst to Vassos, a major book publisher was tracking his work. A week after the *Salome* performance at International House, John MacCrae Jr., son of the founder of E. P. Dutton and soon to become co-owner of the company with his father and brother, invited Vassos to bring the three illustrations for the *Salome* program to his Fifth Avenue office. At that meeting, MacCrae commissioned Vassos to do twelve to fourteen illustrations for the Oscar Wilde text. He further promised to award Vassos a contract for two more Wilde texts, creating a trilogy, if these drawings were compelling.

GREEK LETTERS AND ARTS SOCIETY

JOHN VASSOS

ΣΑΛΩΜΗ

SECOND ANNUAL
MUSICAL AND DRAMATIC
FESTIVAL

AUDITORIUM
INTERNATIONAL HOUSE
NOVEMBER FOUR
NINETEEN TWENTY SIX

"Bearing on a silver shield the head of Jokanaan." Illustration by John Vassos from the cover of the program for the play *Salome* at Columbia University, 1926 (slightly different from the image that appeared in the book). Private collection.

This request marked the beginning of Vassos's career as a serious illustrator. Ann Douglas points out that the solidification of New York City as the center of culture was due, in part, to the movement of American publishing to New York from Boston and Chicago in the nineteenth century, as well as to the new participation of immigrant authors like Vassos.[40] Certainly John MacCrae Jr. hoped to be courting a new illustration star when he invited Vassos to illustrate Wilde's *Salome.* Later Dutton highlighted the ethnicity of its "young Greek" illustrator and emphasized his work in advertising, providing evidence of his success in the realm of modern commerce. The timing was right, Vassos later recalled: "By that time I had enough advertising in my system and wanted to get out of it."[41] Vassos worked quickly to create illustrations that expressed the story but in a decidedly modern way. As he noted years later: "A voluptuous young Jewish girl is the model. I did not make life drawings of her, I just 'drank' the movement for a week and made only notations, the last day I invited John Jr. to take a look and he was speechless."[42]

E. P. Dutton was known for its close relationships with authors and its investment in modernist art through high-quality book production.[43] The company, which started in Boston as a small bookshop in 1865, moved to 23rd Street and Madison Avenue in New York in 1906, where it catered to a specialized market. Dutton sought to cultivate an elite book market in reaction to the rising mass marketing of books in ventures like the Book of the Month Club, which John MacCrae Sr. considered to be lowering artistic standards in book production. Dutton focused on specialized artists' books and limited press runs that kept the prices high. This was "an ideal mode of cultural production" in the elite publishing world, since the limited edition book turned the methods of mass production into a patron's craft.[44] The patron collector, a new kind of consumer who was elite yet still engaged in the marketplace, was the target of the marketing campaign.[45]

Dutton gave Vassos a lot of editorial control, as was the practice in small publishing houses for artist-made books. He was reimbursed in a way typical of these firms, given a small advance against royalties, which were split 50 percent for the author and 50 percent for the illustrator.[46] In a manner unique to this era, the author dealt directly with the publisher, without a literary agent. This reflected a fundamental philosophy of Dutton—to respect the author's integrity. "A publisher must believe deeply that some of the books he publishes will inspire them to better living and to the building of a better world."[47] Vassos even changed the title of his role in the book's production; rather than naming him as illustrator, the cover announces "inventions by John Vassos."

A range of modernist visual tropes are evident in the Oscar Wilde trilogy he illustrated for Dutton. Some of these include the swirling rhythmic dances and costumes of the Ballets Russes and the strong lines of Japanese art. Vassos's use of thickly layered lines pulsating obliquely around bodies is reminiscent of Sonia Delaunay's Orphist drawings and costumes, although without her vivid use of color. Vassos's

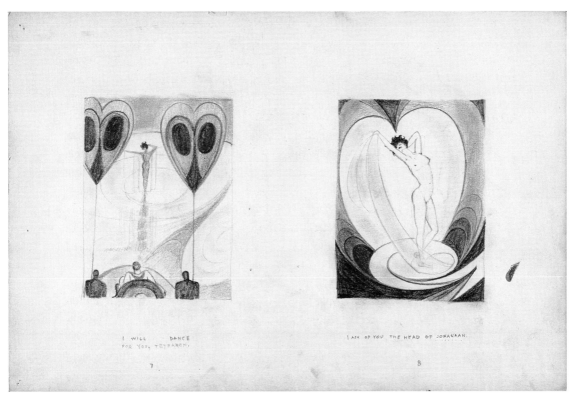

Sketches by John Vassos: "I will dance for you, Tetrarch" *(left)* and "I ask of you the head of Jokanaan" *(right)* from a draft of the book *Salome,* circa 1926. John Vassos Papers, Archives of American Art, Smithsonian Institution.

sketches for the book show his use of lines to depict emotional states. Disturbing angles and dizzying lines with strong contrasts of dark and light dominate the illustrations. Salome's naked body emerges from a circular pool of lines in the illustration "I will dance for you, Tetrarch." Significantly, the only straight line in this image is the one depicting the Tetrarch's sharp gaze at his object of desire. This penetrating gaze is mirrored in the long handles of the heart-shaped fans held by the men flanking the Tetrarch.

These densely packed images echo the work of surrealist painters. The vibrations emanating from the severed head of Jokanaan (John the Baptist) in the background of the playbill's cover image suggest a surrealistic world in which reality has been replaced by passion. Salome, an emblem of dangerous female desire, dominates the image, glancing seemingly deliriously at the prize she has earned by performing the dance for her lecherous uncle: the severed head of Jokanaan brought to her from the cistern in which he was murdered. Her huge eyes rimmed with layers of makeup and her open lips suggest her voluptuous and perverse sensuous appetite for Jokanaan, who had rejected her.

JOHN VASSOS

Courtesy of the "Greek National Herald"

JOKANAAN

"Jokanaan." Illustration by John Vassos from the program for the play *Salome.* In the book this illustration was titled "The executioner goes down into the cistern." Private collection.

John MacCrae maintained a close relationship with Vassos during the years the artist published with Dutton. They were friends and saw each other socially, even if they had their disagreements. Indeed, Vassos listed MacCrae as his emergency contact on his 1929 passport application. Vassos's art and exuberant personality excited the publisher, and MacCrae strongly supported his firm's rising star. Vassos was well known and apparently well liked at the firm, even after the publication of his last book for Dutton, *Dogs Are Like That,* in 1941. A colleague, commenting on the ladies at Dutton, wrote that "they idolize him, walk into this publishing house, you'll see how his pictures, his large originals [dominate] the walls."[48] His drawings were regularly displayed, starting with the 1927 publication of *Salome,* which Dutton proudly featured in its big window on Fifth Avenue.[49]

Despite their small audience, publishers like Dutton used innovative packaging to compete for readers.[50] As a method of enhancing commodity value, Dutton varied the covers of books to increase their worth and launched quick press runs. The first edition of *Salome,* for instance, featured an elaborate gold frontispiece and endpapers with gold-and-black abstract patterns. It was limited to five hundred copies signed by John Vassos. The second edition had two variations in the color of the book cloth.[51] This edition featured a dramatic hot-pink dust jacket with gold accents and an erotic graphic suggesting a pair of breasts. More than one reviewer commented on the magnificent printing and cover of *Salome.* One wrote, "The jacket is quite as rich as the book itself—all of which is a high tribute to the bookmaking of the Messrs Dutton."[52] Inside, the book revealed its visual treasures, with its gold leaf inlays and sharply reproduced images overlaid with protective transparent paper.

Dutton also allowed Vassos to experiment with the Knudsen process, a new form of image reproduction that resulted in a crisper image. This process involved the creation of lithographic plates for printing that were produced photographically and without ruled screens. It achieved the accuracy of gravure reproduction technologies like woodcuts and lithography and was faster than the prior offset dot-related printing process.[53] The Ben Day process enabled printers to add shaded or tinted areas by overlaying fine screens or patterns of dots.[54] Although Vassos's illustrations were sharp, most of them were reproduced unevenly in his books because, according to conservationist Peter Verheyen, the technology was so new.[55] Although the resulting reproductions were not as clear as they might have been, these processes did represent a modernization of the press.

Vassos's choice of font was the sans serif Futura, which was created by the German modernist typeface designer Paul Renner and commercially released in 1927. Futura has been noted as the most important geometric sans serif font; it was influenced by the simple clean lines prized by Bauhaus designers and is still in use today. Renner hoped to expose the geometric basis of letterforms, according to biographer Christopher Burke.[56] Vassos's choice of Futura marked one of the earliest uses of the font in American book publishing.

Dutton was smart to choose Oscar Wilde's most controversial play as the first opportunity for Vassos to show off his skill at rendering erotic, emotional imagery. The story itself was incendiary and twice a scandal, first with its production and later with its book illustrations. The 1894 English edition of the play, with belle epoque illustrations by Aubrey Beardsley, shocked Victorian audiences. The play expressed Wilde's disdain for tradition and his entanglement with the themes of dangerous desire (and the women who represented it), wealth, and power.[57] As Dutton had

THE DANCER'S REWARD

Aubrey Beardsley's illustration "The Dancer's Reward" from *Salome* by Oscar Wilde (New York: Halcyon House, 1950).

hoped, many reviewers compared Vassos's work to that of Beardsley. Part of Vassos's success stemmed from his ability to Americanize an important British book, thus contributing to the burgeoning role of the United States in literature, the arts, and industrial design. Reviewers picked up on Vassos's uniquely American twist on the imagery. As one of them wrote, "Here was America's own Aubrey Beardsley."[58] Reviewer Edwin Bjorkman went so far as to write, "Had Wilde seen Salome and her environment with the vision of John Vassos, his play might have been a bigger one than it is now."[59] As another commentator put it, Vassos "need concede nothing to the famous Beardsley editions of the same play [since] Vassos has developed a medium all his own. It is futurist without the preposterous stuff that often masks as futurism."[60] Both Beardsley and Vassos were artists who embodied the spirit of an era on the verge of radical change in sexual politics and social power.

Vassos's and Beardsley's editions shared a few stylistic similarities. Vassos emulated Beardsley's open display of sensual detail and his drawing style of strong black-and-white patterns. Vassos also evoked sex and death through rich shading, voluptuous curves, and gruesome detail, although he chose not to include full frontal male nudity, as Beardsley did. In both, Salome's wild hair, her massive eyes, and the backgrounds pulsated with eerie detail. But there were also major stylistic and narrative differences. Vassos's illustrations were filled with narrative detail and emotional economy, unlike Beardsley's stark backgrounds and singular details. Illustrating the story almost thirty-five years after Beardsley, Vassos focused less on Salome's sexual depravity and more on the narrative, illustrating the scenes of Herod's kingdom of Judea with a vivid subjective landscape. Vassos painted an unflattering portrait of the leaders, Herod, Herodias, and all the court, most clearly in the image "The Jews." Arguably, Vassos was more concerned with the dangers of authoritarian rule than with the dangers of female sexuality. Vassos also refused to demonize Salome's breasts or other parts of her body, presenting her in a sultry way rather than as a castrating witch, as Beardsley had. Her sexuality invigorated the pulsating scene rather than destroyed it, the flowing waves of her hair echoing behind her, filling the frame with her voracious desire. Indeed, Vassos himself was disappointed that his work was compared with Beardsley's, as such comparison undercut his modern treatment. He wrote: "I was hoping for a discussion and evaluation of what I tried to do in the simplest most direct manner to introduce a setting for Wilde's play. Beardsley saw it in a totally different way, decadent, sophisticated."[61]

Reviewers praised Vassos's reinterpretation of the "voluptuous drama of Salome and her mad longing." In advertisements, Vassos's illustrations were referred to as "decorations" and "realizations" of the tragedy, with the story "pictorially interpreted."[62] Commenting on the uniqueness of the images and the relationship of image to text, another reviewer noted, "Vassos seems to evoke them literally out of his imagination . . . and set them down here in black and white; it is almost a verbal reproduction."[63] The art, yet another reviewer wrote, adequately captures "the over-ripe beauty, the subtle fragrance of decay, the luxuriance and ferocity of Wilde's tragedy."[64]

Critics appreciated Vassos's highly original imagery. Herschel Brickell wrote: "Another contribution of Dutton's to fine book-making is a new edition of Oscar Wilde's *Salome* with inventions by a young modernist named John Vassos. . . . The Vassos illustrations are highly symbolical and for the most part freshly original and quite striking."[65] A review of the second printing in 1930 with four new "inventions" by Vassos described the "sophisticated, erotic touch to the illustrations, which are wholly in keeping with the text."[66] Another writer focused on the formal elements of the drawings, noting the strength of Vassos's imagery coming from the use of black and white and a range of intermediate tones as masses to create a sense of color, rather than line.[67]

Vassos's graphics were part of a growing movement toward the increased status of mass-produced illustrated arts. Graphic artists began to realize that their work could be the focal point. The American Institute of Graphic Arts chose *Salome* as one of the fifty best illustrated books of 1927. The institute, born in 1914 and later renamed AIGA, was formed to stimulate and encourage those engaged in the graphic arts and to promote the significance of the profession in the new age of print. Book designers were increasingly considered creative equals to authors rather than subordinate to them. This new image of the graphic artist as cutting-edge rather than as someone whose work merely got reproduced was part of a growing movement to consolidate the profession of graphic design and to recognize the artist's value in the machine age. Graphic artists sought to clarify the relationship between words and images, suggesting that words and images were not equal. As the program for the institute's second annual exhibition asked: "Is it conceivable that one man should express a certain mood in words and another should find forms expressing an identical one? . . . When the writer is an artist and the illustrator is an artist there must be divergence."[68]

In part, the organization was responding to shifts in the field such as the growth of photography; illustrators, edged out by photographers, sought to find a new place for themselves in book, magazine, and newspaper illustration. In their work, they

"... the holy hands that took The Thief to Paradise." The dramatic final illustration by John Vassos from *The Ballad of Reading Gaol* (New York: E. P. Dutton & Company, Inc., 1928). Private collection.

emphasized typography, and they defined their art in opposition to photography while using some of its forms of reproduction, such as halftone photoengraving. Using sophisticated tools of graphic presentation, these artists aimed to reduce the visual clutter that defined nineteenth-century newspapers and other print publications. They used a "varied assembly of reproductive processes," acknowledging their debt to both the creativity of advertising illustration and the European avant-garde.[69] This widening appeal of graphic arts occurred alongside the rise of sensational photography, which was published in tabloid newspapers and distributed across the photographic wire services that were launched in 1929.[70]

Vassos followed *Salome* with illustrations for *The Ballad of Reading Gaol,* Oscar Wilde's indictment of the Victorian prison system told from the perspective of a prisoner condemned to die. The book probed the emotional depths of a condemned prisoner, magnificently depicted in the sixteen drawings, or "conceptions," by Vassos. Dedicated "to all prisoners," the book rendered Wilde's poem relevant to American audiences. As research for his illustrations, Vassos visited prisons around New York City and even interviewed a prisoner on death row "in the shadow of the electric chair." The poem's gruesome story connected to contemporary issues such as lynching and fulfilled a public desire to know the "terrible" truth, even from a murderer's perspective.[71] The images in the book are among Vassos's most powerful, disturbing, and socially resonant.

The final book in the Wilde series was *The Harlot's House and Other Poems,* for which Vassos interpreted each poem with a single image. The most gripping illustration was that for the obscure 1885 title poem, which featured a "harlot" in a see-through shirt gazing out of the image as men pound vigorously at her door. It is a sympathetic image of the prostitute, who is clearly miserable, in contrast to the "horrible marionette" that Wilde describes. This book was the least popular of the series. Critics found the poems not substantial enough to warrant illustration. As one reviewer wrote, "In a number of cases, Mr. Vassos' ideas are radically different from Wilde's—and considerably more interesting."[72] Vassos was ready to move on to creating his own books.

CONTEMPO

Vassos's first original book, *Contempo,* was produced in collaboration with his wife, Ruth, who wrote the text after seeing the drawings. Vassos was the leading force in the book's construction, which marked an innovation in illustrated book production by inverting the typical order of creating text before illustrations.[73] Vassos hoped this book would widen his reputation beyond that of an artist to that of a public intellectual and profound thinker. As he explained, *Contempo* is "my first book of commentary on our Society, in which all our misconceptions and dead-ends come [under] scrutiny. . . . The book evokes criticism and controversy."[74] In this book, he critiqued the major institutions of American life—mass media, transportation, banks, and religion—in a sweeping dismissal.[75]

The book expressed his disillusionment with American life after the Wall Street crash that led to the Great Depression. Following his 1929 trip to Europe, he and Ruth returned to find "the crash . . . in full bloom":

> [I am] wondering if unchecked capitalism is a good thing for the people. Many hard-earned fortunes are wiped out, including a couple of stocks I owned. Capable men are selling apples in the streets. The Russians are having a picnic with their propaganda; intellectuals are the biggest audience the Soviets have: all sorts of "front" organizations are springing up.[76]

Vassos was clearly ambivalent toward American culture. He both celebrated the "certain sharp staccato rhythm almost like a riveting machine that exists nowhere else in the world" and recognized the treacherous dynamics and commercial interests that fueled this machine. In their essay for the catalog accompanying the 2003

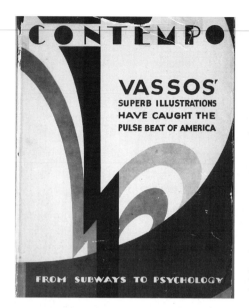

The dynamic dust jacket of *Contempo* (1929) announces that "Vassos' superb illustrations have caught the pulse beat of America" and adds the subtitle *From Subways to Psychology*. Private collection.

art deco exhibition at the Victoria and Albert Museum, Charlotte Benton and Tim Benton observe that the *Contempo* illustration titled "Commercialism" embodies the art deco style, which reflected a "contraction of new values with old, and the hint of fragility and tragedy that often lurks behind its glitter."[77] The illustration "The Market" openly shows the damage wrought by economic greed: the ticker tape of Wall Street lashes the backs of the workers scrambling up a ladder as destitute men gather in a dark corner, their heads hung low.

In *Contempo*, Vassos's depiction of the human form, with the subjects broken down to geometrical components, exhibits the influence of cubism. Vassos's work resonates with the deserted urban scenes of the Italian painter and theater designer Giorgio de Chirico, who had designed the costumes for the Ballets Russes dance *The Ball* in 1929. De Chirico's dramatic use of shadows to create a distorted pictorial space in "The Uncertainty of the Poet" (1913) and "The Song of Love" (1914) are echoed in Vassos's *Contempo* drawings. Indeed, Vassos admitted that de Chirico was a major influence. Vassos is agnostic about modern art in *Contempo*. The section "Modern Art" criticizes the "designs born in an insane asylum. Poetry with no meaning." Its illustration shows a jumble of styles while the text lists them: "Impressionism, futurism, cubism, surrealism. Cézanne to skyscrapers . . . an expression of this age—our own. Our desire to break away from the photographic, the orthodox. Machinery set the key—and we experiment."[78]

The book, subtitled *This American Tempo*, is a scathing examination of modern life. John and Ruth Vassos welcomed the American machine age, with its "sharp staccato rhythm," but feared the consequences of unrestrained technological and economic growth.[79] In *Contempo*, Vassos intended his drawings to be heavily symbolic and linked to sound and structure, each image a metonymy of society as a whole, transforming a city into a paper pile, for instance, in "Advertising," or a swirl of buildings, or a mess of cars. In these experimental images, Vassos also tried to link the idea of sound to image, starting with the title of the book. He borrowed the increasingly popular rhythms of jazz to express the feelings of disconnection, speed, and solitude that the city evoked. As he wrote in the preface, the book presented

The ticker tape of Wall Street lashes men as they climb upward. One man "escapes into the light" at upper left. Faceless people gather in the shadows in lower left corner. "The Market" from *Contempo*. Private Collection.

each element of modern society on its own page with a description: "Emblazoned symbolic drawings interpret modernism through modernistic rhythm/appreciation of the symbolism of the imagery making living things of electricity, advertising, sky-scrapers, the subway, Prohibition, the radio."[80]

"An edifice reaching to the skies, and built on—BUNK" proclaims the text adjacent to the illustration titled "Advertising" from *Contempo*. Private Collection.

Vassos softened *Contempo*'s skewering of modern society when he called it "that satiric panorama of the American scene," as did his publisher, E. P. Dutton, in a promotional brochure that noted the "twinkle in Vassos's eye." Critics, however, were clearly moved by the book's emotional force and groundbreaking style. They commented on both the book's politics and its unique visual style, both of which reflected a modern spirit in theme and in expression. It was, one wrote, a testament "not only to Vassos's reputation as an artist but to the body of achievement in modern design . . . a remarkably beautiful book it is besides the first pictorial judgment of our time."[81] Another reviewer wrote, "The Vassos team swings superbly free of convention in *Contempo*."[82] Beyond the politics, critics commented on his graphic style, saying that "probably no artist today uses gray and black as effectively as he does. The gradations of black in his drawings give them depth and luminosity. Invariably, he is best when he most nearly approaches photography."[83] Another argued that this work brought Vassos into the modern art canon: "The book as a whole adds considerably not only to Vassos' reputation as an artist and an individual but to the body of achievement in modern design."[84]

Interestingly, no reviewers commented on the illustration of "The Jew" and its accompanying text. Vassos may have been primed by the openly anti-Semitic text of *Salome*, in which the despotic Jewish royals murder a Christian. Scholar Yeeyon Im discusses that story's Orientalist clichés of harems, excessive sexuality, and backwardness,[85] all of which the Vassoses draw from in the image and text for "The Jew." The illustration features a dark-haired, big-nosed man wielding seemingly unobstructed power; presumably he is a Hollywood mogul, creeping into the "sacred edifices of banking" with "rings on his fingers and bells on his toes," his "plump and Oriental women" by his side.

Popular anti-Semitic notions regarding the Jewish control of Hollywood certainly influenced Vassos's caricatured image of the parasitic Jew. In the United States, the myth of this omnipotent Jew was articulated most notably through Henry Ford's publication of the first volume of *The International Jew* in 1920. According to scholar Harold Brackman, the image of Jewish mogul was solidified by the simultaneous publication of F. Scott Fitzgerald's *The Last Tycoon* and Budd Schulberg's *What Makes Sammy Run*, both of which featured Jewish movie producers.[86]

Vassos's participation in the propagation of the ugly stereotype of the greedy Jew is inconsistent with his involvement in Jewish organizations and his work for prominent Jews. Around the time *Contempo* was published, Vassos was asked to give a lecture to the Junior Federation for the Jewish Philanthropic Society and also began working for RCA, whose president, David Sarnoff, was a Jew.[87] Vassos had productive relationships with Jewish artists and business associates throughout his career. He was also openly attracted to Jewish women, including the voluptuous woman who served as the model for the illustrations in *Salome* and the "lovely petite Jewish girl" he met in his camouflage course.[88] Further, there is no indication in his art or writings that he expressed racism toward other groups. His image of "Emancipation" in *Humanities* and the accompanying text reveal his disgust at the treatment of African Americans—from the denial of education, jobs, and economic opportunity to the horror of lynching, vividly depicted in the image. Vassos was angered by the depiction of himself in an army newsletter as "John the Greek" and penned a scathing letter to the editor. In 1933, a few years after the publication of *Contempo*, brothers Isaac and Leon Levy, prominent Jewish broadcasters who later founded the Columbia Broadcasting System, hired Vassos to paint murals at their Philadelphia radio station, WCAU. Given that anti-Semitism was never part of his rhetoric, at this or any other time, it seems likely that the imagery of "The Jew" was a youthful mistake and not the expression of long-term bigoted beliefs.

The illustrations for *Contempo* and their ambiguous meanings continued to have resonance in Vassos's professional life. The image "Radio" was repeated as a mural in the background of a recording studio at WCAU (which is discussed in more detail in chapter 5). The mural, like the illustration, features a nimble, godlike creature flying through the ether, chasing a large ball that represents the world. It shows a fast-paced, transformative medium that dominates society, as the "god" rips through the center of the image. On either side of the kinetic "god," swirls, modern geometric buildings, and a radio tower electrified by a surging bolt of energy can be seen, but the point is unclear. This vague view of radio is reflected in the text as well, which describes it as having the power both to save lives and to stupefy listeners with commercial messages. Radio's possible impacts are as yet unknown: "His wings are still untried, his powers not yet gauged."[89] In 1929, radio was still young. It was not until 1933, when Vassos used this image as a backdrop in the WCAU studio, that the importance of the medium was becoming clear, nationally and in Vassos's own career.

ULTIMO

Vassos continued exploring the theme of the physical landscape transformed by the forces of modernity in *Ultimo*. Subtitled *An Imaginative Narration of Life under the Earth*, "with projections by John Vassos and the text by Ruth Vassos," the book portrays the future human race driven by a new ice age to live beneath the surface of the Earth in a society dominated by streamlined architecture and out-of-control scientific rationality. Told in the present tense, the book features a first-person narrator who is trapped in this claustrophobic dystopia. Scientific progress, unable to help the human race, is presented ambiguously. For example, there is rigid eugenic control, but there is also the possibility of escape through the use of a rocket-type car.

The book refers to contemporary debates concerning building height and density. It offers a caustic response to the contemporary discussion of urban growth, which included Hugh Ferriss's influential book *The Metropolis of Tomorrow*, published in 1929.[90] Unlike Ferriss's utopian vision, Vassos's futuristic New York is a case of urban crowding in its extreme, forcing humans to flee to an underground city. This dismal city is inhuman and crippled my human-caused climate change, but Vassos sees beauty in the decay. The book presents a critique of urban growth without planning, which leads humans to lose their personalities and express only the mechanical features of their society.[91]

authorial credit, he openly associated himself with the book and lectured with Vassos. This collaboration began a lifelong friendship between the artist and the psychoanalyst.[103] Vassos admired Sullivan. He designed an emblem of two interlocked horses' heads that apparently held great meaning for Sullivan, who asked that the insignia be included on all his published works.[104] Vassos wrote movingly of Sullivan in a text accompanying an exhibition of his work held at Hofstra University:

> *Phobia* has been out of print for many years—the original book is dedicated to Harry Stack Sullivan, the eminent psychiatrist and friend who also guided me to the realization of *Phobia,* and the man who had a profound influence on my life. Although *Phobia* was a disturbing subject, I found it an excellent vehicle for graphic and intellectual exercise and expression.[105]

Vassos's imagery in *Phobia* was influenced by the dreamlike narrative depictions of the surrealists. Urban settings are the backdrop and the stimulus for debilitating fears, as in "Acrophobia: The Fear of High Places," in which a man in a suit tumbles from a precipice as high as a nearby skyscraper. There is no immediate identification of the people in the image; rather, the illustration is a parable of pain in which the victims are in distress from their phobia. The falling man's suit and tie, however, mark him as a professional, likely an urban dweller. In "Astrophobia: The Fear of Storms," a storm terrorizes a smartly attired man whose jacket flares slightly as he flees. Indeed, the image is a projection of the individual's painful subconscious; the phobic person's inner landscape shapes what he actually sees in the world around him. Vassos's empathy toward the phobic sufferer inspired him to show us the world as seen through the eyes of that sufferer.

Vassos's fixation on the external manifestation of internal suffering—the urban scene infused with pain—can also be read through an analysis of what Michael Leja calls "the contemporary discourse of modern man." In his book *Reframing Abstract Expressionism: Subjectivity and Painting in the 1940s,* Leja argues that rumination about the self and its primitive and unconscious aspects was central to literature and art during the first half of the twentieth century as a response to the horrors of war.[106] Political scientist David Harvey similarly provides a historical context for understanding Vassos's concern with the inner life of humans. Harvey notes a middle stage in modernism, spanning from 1918 to 1945, when the arts began to explicitly examine the nature of modern people.[107] One of the key questions uniting European and North American art at the time was whether humanity could survive the terrors of modern society. This theme was conveyed in expressionistic renderings of the decaying, corrupt metropolis and the scientifically twisted world. It forced some modernist artists to use abstraction as a response to such a confused world. Vassos rejected abstraction, preferring vivid tableaux that illustrated fundamental tensions in human society. His imagery tells a blunt story that the viewer is meant to grasp

"Acrophobia: The Fear of High Places" from *Phobia*. John Vassos Papers, Special Collections Research Center, Syracuse University Libraries.

quickly; greed, fear, and the desire for power are raw emotions that Vassos wanted to show. In *Phobia*, although the text can be heavy-handed at times, the artist presents humanity confronting eternal emotional struggles in the theater of daily urban life. Freudian psychology is tied to a search for the truth, for "terrible honesty," no matter how ugly.[108] Suggesting a widespread awareness of Freudian theories, critics

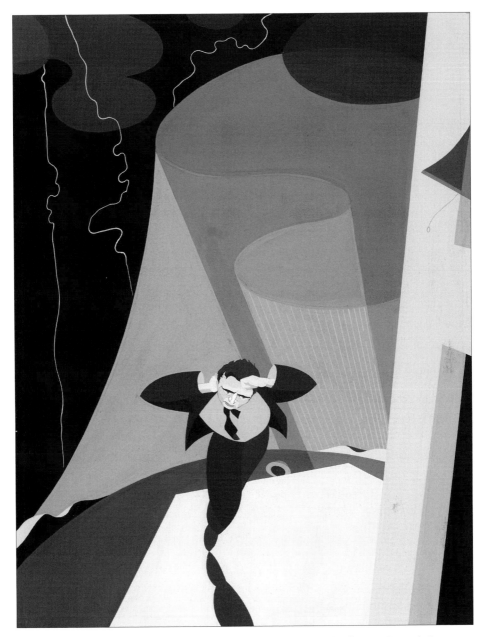

"Astrophobia: The Fear of Storms" from *Phobia*. John Vassos Papers, Special Collections Research Center, Syracuse University Libraries.

noted Vassos's portrayal of "supernatural horror, with Freudian symbols and ghostly skyscrapers."[109]

With *Phobia*, Vassos achieved his stated goal of evoking the subjectivity of the German expressionists. As one reviewer wrote, "Vassos's illustrations for Phobias [*sic*] are in the vein of 'The Cabinet of Dr. Caligari.'"[110] Critics thought the subject suited Vassos's evocative graphic style. As one explained, "*Phobia* supplies him with perfect material, for its mood is his favorite one . . . well-fitted to his adaptation of the well-known double and triple exposure of the photographer."[111] Other reviewers gently mocked the premise of the book, suggesting that it could lead to "optiphobia," the fear of pictures; "reviewersphobia," the fear of books; and "John Vassosphobia," which one described humorously:

> Watch out for the symptoms of this one. If you find yourself slouching over a copy of *Phobia* and pursuing a strange gent, intent on compelling him to read it, you've got John Vassosphobia. It is believed that authors deliberately spread this dreaded phobia. It has many names—Sinclair Lewisphobia, and so on. The only way to avoid it is to say, "I read nothing but detective stories"—and that's nearly as bad.[112]

As part of a campaign to publicize the book, Covici-Friede requested that people send in ideas for new phobias; the responses included "aquaphobia" (fear of washing) and "radiophobia" (fear of loudspeakers).[113] The book inspired a 1932 dance performance by the dance company of Gluck-Sandor and Felicia Sorel called *Dream Phobias,* written and designed by Vassos with music by Lehman Engel.[114] *Phobia* reached its widest audience when an article by Vassos, "A Case of Acrophobia," was published in the February 1937 issues of *Esquire.*[115] The article was rich with sexual imagery and descriptions of how desire leads to many of the psychological maladies pictured. *Phobia* was widely popular; even Vassos's colleague and competitor industrial designer Raymond Loewy requested a copy.[116]

Vassos noted that he was "the only artist who ever made a study of psychiatry and then presented a graphic presentation of the fears and phobias that harass mankind, *Phobia.*"[117] The ideas expressed in *Phobia* influenced Vassos's design practice for the rest of his career. In a letter to theatrical and industrial designer Norman Bel Geddes, he stated, "My book *Phobia* is a basic treatise on human fears and conflicts of today"—symptoms of modern life that, he eventually believed, could be alleviated through modernistic designs for daily living.[118] This belief formed the basis for his use of design as a balm for modern life and as a way to mitigate the fear of the machine in mechanized society. In the book's introduction, he revealed that he too did "not have a so-called normal mind" and appreciated the "tremendous imaginative power" that the subconscious offered.

HUMANITIES

The dangers of mechanistic and unchecked power, greed, and bureaucracy also are at the core of *Humanities,* Vassos's final major book for E. P. Dutton. The images in this book are Vassos's most didactic and reveal the stark contrasts between wealth and poverty in Depression-era America. Published in 1935, the book was Vassos's most

"Waste" from *Humanities* by John Vassos, text by Ruth Vassos, copyright 1935 by E. P. Dutton & Company, renewed 1963 by Ruth Vassos and John Vassos. Reprinted by permission of Dutton, an imprint of Penguin Publishing Group, a division of Penguin Random House LLC. John Vassos Papers, Special Collections Research Center, Syracuse University Libraries.

radical, and, surprisingly, it remains one of his least well-known works. The book uses illustrations and brief accompanying text (by Ruth Vassos) to expose the damage that unchecked greed and authoritarianism inflict on human lives. Vassos explains in the introduction that he was inspired to participate in this "clear exposition" of society by the muralists and artists of his time:

> The coming of Orozco and Rivera to this country, plus the efforts of such native muralists as Thomas Benton, James Daugherty, Boardman Robinson and a few others, is bringing about a consciousness of a more virile expression and has brought out the necessity of art participating in the portrayal of our present scene. This consciousness is evidencing itself on all fronts—in the theatre, in literature, painting, sculpture and music.[119]

In this book, all aspects of society are interrogated, and hypocrisy is revealed in religion, education, international politics, labor, and science. Unlike *Contempo*, which presents modern institutions with ambivalence, *Humanities* has an overall tone of dark despair. Even the rich who claim to do good are criticized; the text accompanying the illustration "Philanthropy" skewers the "noble" philanthropist who "erects in the slums a costly library" while caring little for the poor who live there.[120] The accompanying illustration shows a man in a suit entering a formidable building while at the base of the image a policeman hauls away an impoverished-looking man.

Each of Vassos's illustrations in *Humanities* juxtaposes related scenes in a single "frame," to use a cinematic term. In most of the illustrations, Vassos incorporates exaggerated architectural features to symbolize the physical divide between the victors and the victims. In the image "The Machine," a line of workers beg to enter a guarded factory belching smoke, while beyond its walls lies a halcyon scene of wealth, with horseback riding, race cars, and mansions. In "Homo Sapiens," a massive tank provides a physical framework on which solders stuff young men into the guns and on which mothers clutch their children and cry. The powerful illustration "Waste" contrasts empty factories and train cars with jobless men gambling and slumped against the wall that visually divides the image. The text reads, "Idle men and women are gradually going to pieces as their physical and mental powers rot from lack of opportunity."[121]

As in *Contempo,* Vassos skewers the media industry, in which he had recently begun employment as a consultant designer (for RCA) in 1933. In "The Leaders" and "Nationalism," demagogues at the top of the images' "frames" spill their vitriol on mounted microphones (which Vassos would soon be designing) while the masses below suffer. In "Enlightenment," propaganda is transmitted over the radio while rich people whisper lies into the ears of a blindfolded journalist. The so-called freedom of the press is also interrogated in the accompanying satirical text: "Is it freedom to distort facts, to decide how much of the truth shall be deleted, to incite

Men are violently kept outside the factory walls by military personnel in gas masks as industrialists gather safely inside in "The Workers." From *Humanities* by John Vassos, text by Ruth Vassos, copyright 1935 by E. P. Dutton & Company, renewed 1963 by Ruth Vassos and John Vassos. Reprinted by permission of Dutton, an imprint of Penguin Publishing Group, a division of Penguin Random House LLC. Private Collection.

race prejudice, to fight child labor legislation, to hide its latent Fascism under the cloak of patriotism?"

Visceral violent illustrations abound in this book. In "Education," a teacher in cap and gown force-feeds students, putting material into funnels placed in their gaping upturned mouths. In "Emancipation," a lynched African American man burns. In "Nationalism," Jews are rounded up and whipped while Hitler rouses the crowds. In "Ethics," a man is sprawled on an operating table, his intestines exposed while doctors look away from the gruesome scene and hold their fingers to their lips to signify silence. These wrenching portraits of sharp inequality express what historian Joseph Entin calls "sensational modernism." This mode of representation, which emerged during the Great Depression, used visceral imagery to comment on the violence of class distinctions, racial discrimination, and industrial injury.[122] Vassos's illustrations reveal the preoccupation with social boundaries, aesthetic experimentation, and blurring of "high" and "low" cultures that Entin identifies as marks of this style. Vassos's images also share this movement's fascination with physical disfigurement.

The sobering look at the nation's economic realities presented in *Humanities* was typical of the era; during this period, magazine editors and writers felt obligated to critique the excesses of capitalism that had led to the market crash. Historian Michael Denning calls this new era of American populism in the arts, which flowered around 1934, the "cultural front."[123] Although it was largely associated with the "popular front" strategy of the Communist Party, the movement had wide aesthetic resonance. Vassos's political allegiance was decidedly progressive and critical of power in a way that would fit the New Deal's ideology, if not that of the Communist Party. Vassos openly rejected communism's idealization of the worker, although "The Workers" in *Humanities* presents a sympathetic portrait of men who are "underpaid, discarded and thrown on the junk heap."[124] Vassos explained in a letter to the wife of George Throckmorton, his boss at RCA, "I certainly hold no brief for the dictatorship of the proletariat (the worker) but neither do we want the machinations of slick politicians, exploiters and demagogues running the country."[125]

P. K. Thomajan, an artist and friend, put Vassos's work in a larger historical context in his introduction to a compilation of the artist's work, noting, "Vassos was among the traditions of the 1920s when arts cut loose from the apron strings of binding traditions."[126] Thomajan was a poet who had known Vassos since the early 1930s; the two collaborated on various projects and had similar political views.

A 1995 exhibition at the University of Toledo, *The Ardent Image: Book Illustration for Adults in America, 1920–1942*, included Vassos among more politically left-leaning illustrators such as Aaron Douglas, Rockwell Kent, and Lynd Ward. Vassos disliked Kent's image-making style, but this exhibition demonstrated that they were both artists who used illustration as a way to criticize social systems. Vassos's politics often confused his contemporaries, however. "His conservative friends think he is a red, and his red friends think he's pink," wrote Willis Birchman and James Flagg in 1937.[127]

Regardless of the politics of *Humanities,* reviewers were disappointed that the illustrations strayed from the style of Vassos's typical work. As one reviewer commented early in the book's production, "For Vassos' style is now well known, and people will look for advance and expect to find it. If they don't, they may turn sour."[128] Nonetheless, Vassos was proud of *Humanities,* expressing in a letter to John MacCrae that the book "is fearless, it is timely, it is necessary, and I believe it will have wide appeal."[129] The book was not as popular as his others, however. Its anti-fascist theme did resonate to a degree, and the book's illustrations were used to complement articles on related topics. MacCrae had certainly hoped that *Humanities* would sell better, given the two thousand copies printed and the hefty advance— three hundred dollars—paid to the authors.

Following *Humanities,* Vassos published a few personal, quirky books that did not receive the wide attention of his earlier works. The satirical cartoon *Beatrice the Ballerina,* published by E. P. Dutton in 1941 under the pseudonym Ivan Vassilovitch, was not for children. In it, a bisexual dog named La Chienne Fatale ruthlessly uses men for her own pleasure. Vassos later noted that he wrote this humorous tale about a seductive dancing dog out of his distress at the end of an affair with prominent ballet dancer Catherine Littlefield.[130] Vassos described their relationship as an "open battle ground of two strong willed individuals."[131] Apparently, Ruth knew about that affair and others. One critic described *Beatrice the Ballerina* as not "anything more than a New York comic strip."[132] Faber distributed it in Europe in 1942. Vassos tried unsuccessfully to sell a screenplay version of the story to Hollywood executives.

In 1945, Vassos provided the background decorations for the proverbs in *A Proverb for It: 1510 Greek Sayings.* In their nostalgic depiction of rural Greek life, these drawings are uncharacteristic of the artist's other work but are in keeping with the book's focus on folk life and wisdom. *Dogs Are Like That* and *Rex and Lobo,* his final books, focused on upland game hunting and dog training.

PROMOTING VASSOS

E. P. Dutton promoted Vassos heavily through brochures, public events, book signings, and exhibitions at the publisher's offices and throughout New York City. His image appeared in magazines internationally. The public relations fanfare around Vassos appears contradictory to his own critiques of the commercial and publicity-oriented mechanizations of the mass media. *Contempo* featured indictments of the "media" and of "advertising" while actually relying heavily on them for promotion. Literary theorist Lawrence Rainey suggests that this presumably contradictory practice was common among modernist artists and writers such as James Joyce and Ezra Pound.

Analyzing the promotion of modernist writers and their texts, he reads these efforts as part of the larger set of formal principles and ideological constellation that he calls modernism. His definition goes beyond the aesthetics of modernism to include a set of social practices that he characterizes as uniquely modern: "new strategies of reputation building involving theatricality, spectacle, publicity, and novel modes of cultural marketing and media manipulation."[133] Rainey's method suggests a way to analyze Vassos's promotional campaigns.

As part of its effort to win public attention for its new artist, Dutton scheduled numerous appearances for Vassos in a wide range of venues, including book fairs, publishers' conventions, parties, exhibitions, political discussions, and debates. To create wide exposure, the publisher promoted Vassos's persona through the publication of his images in numerous magazines. In order to prepare for this media attention, Vassos had to develop what Rainey calls techniques of "authorial self-construction," which entailed particular attention to his wardrobe and even the depiction of his home. Vassos's modernist apartment on the Upper West Side, the site of many promotional parties and book launches, served as the backdrop for the playboy artist's emergence in the urban art world. Journalists picked up on the resonance between his home and his art; as one writer commented, Vassos had "achieved that haven that all city dwellers sigh for, a penthouse with broad veranda overlooking the Hudson river and within the last word in modernist furniture, his own design."[134] An article in *Pencil Points* magazine described the apartment as a "small modern" one, but the generous terrace, proportional furnishings, and Vassos's artwork must have made it feel luxurious. In another dramatic sign of having achieved success, Vassos relocated his office to a newly built luxurious art deco skyscraper, the French Building at 555 Fifth Avenue in 1928.

Another aspect of his self-construction was the improvement of his voice. Vassos recounted this process in his autobiography, in particular his efforts to master public speaking. This may have been a challenge for the thickly accented Vassos. As he recalled in a speech he gave in 1973: "I was careful to study other speakers. . . . I must say, some of our literary giants were indeed very bad speakers: they stuttered, hesitated, and the most distracting habit was the 'errr'" sound."[135] He became increasingly interested in the dynamics of public speaking, choosing a style with which he felt comfortable.

Vassos spoke publicly on all sorts of topics, beyond merely promoting his books, and he was touted as an expert on modern art. Although it is hard to measure the intentions behind these lectures, certainly his public speaking brought more people in touch with his work, garnered press attention, and eventually helped him expand his interior and industrial design practice as he gained scholarly credentials as a lecturer. His lectures were held at venues throughout New York City, including the Plaza Hotel and the Barbizon Plaza.[136] Among his other engagements, he participated in a debate on the rights of women held at the Pierrepont Hotel, along with

Vassos reviews copies of his art at his Upper West Side apartment in New York City around 1928. In the background is a vibrant art deco screen he painted in his signature style. Courtesy of Jayne Johnes.

Ralph Borsodi, economist and foe of the modern woman, and Margaret Kilkes of *Collier's*.[137]

Framed images from Vassos's books were exhibited in galleries at the Art Center, the Hellenic Craft Shop, and the Advertising Club of New York, which held a show featuring images from *Contempo*.[138] In November 1930, Dutton sponsored an exhibition of original drawings from *Ultimo* to promote the publication of the new book. A publicity brochure listed Vassos's lecture subjects and included a brief autobiographical study titled "The Odyssey of John Vassos," which boasted that "he made an instant success with his first illustrative work, Oscar Wilde's *Salome*, which has sold over fifteen thousand copies. Today he is accepted as the founder of a new school of illustration."[139]

Many staff members at Dutton were involved in promoting Vassos, including company head John MacCrae, suggesting the importance of these public events to the publishing house. In a 1929 letter to Vassos, MacCrae told the artist,

"Wanamaker's would like to have you give a little talk on the Thursday program, Nov. 14, during their book week"; this appearance is confirmed by an ad for Wanamaker Book Week.[140] In 1931, Dutton hosted a big party at the Rismont, a restaurant for which Vassos had served as designer; the event was attended by ninety-two people, who dined on such Turkish and Greek specialties as shish kebab, baklava, pilaf, and special Turkish coffee.[141] Vassos invited guests who represented different parts of his life, such as Harry Stack Sullivan and prominent Greek American friends like theater owner George Skouras and Adamantios Polyzoides of the Greek-language newspaper *Atlantis.* Also invited were a range of journalists from publications such as *The Bookman* and *The Dance Magazine* and newspapers such as the *New York Times* and the *Brooklyn Eagle.*

Dutton took pride in its author's crossover achievement in interior design and cleverly saw that success as a way to sell books. In its press release, Dutton enthusiastically described the new restaurant as an excellent example of "modernism gone wild" and thus an extension of Vassos's work as an illustrator who also had "the last word in modern art."[142] The press, as hoped, reported on the party and Vassos's

E. P. Dutton produced this promotional brochure of the "famous illustrator and modernist" with images from *Salome, Elegy in a Country Churchyard,* and *Contempo,* circa 1930. John Vassos Papers, Archives of American Art, Smithsonian Institution.

accomplishments in design and book illustration, including his newest book. One reviewer wrote that Vassos "designed [the Rismont] between books, since he has just turned over to his publisher, E. P. Dutton, the illustrations for *Gray's Elegy in a Country Churchyard,* which they will publish this fall."[143] Other public events and exhibitions included a show featuring works from *Phobia* on display at the home of Mrs. Walter Hoochchild.[144]

Vassos offered an impressive variety of lectures on various themes, from which a prospective host could choose. A lecture titled "The Predicament of Modernism" included a comprehensive summary of the various "isms" in painting, with a discussion of the contemporary scene and American contributions to each particular art movement. Another talk, "Phobia—Its Whys and Wherefores," featured a study of the fears that harass civilized man and the underlying causes for the existence of these phobias. The announcement for this lecture proclaimed, "This psychiatric discussion is for advanced groups."[145] The talk "Is Modern Design Permanent Expression?" broadly examined design's value in industry, in architecture, in advertising, in decor, and in daily life. "The Art of Illustrating" covered Vassos's theory of illustration, and "The Art of Graphically Portraying Emotions and Ideas" demonstrated the true function of the modern illustrator.[146] The latter lecture was linked to a book launch, Vassos's forthcoming interpretation of Coleridge's "Kubla Khan."[147] It was alternatively titled "Illustration and Its Function in Our Time," which was also the title of a talk that Vassos gave with Ruth Vassos.[148] For presenting these lectures, which were illustrated with slides, Vassos received a small honorarium to cover expenses.[149]

Requests for lectures came from groups throughout New York City, including philanthropic organizations such as the Junior Federation of the Jewish Philanthropic Societies,[150] arts organizations like Rebel Arts (a socialist group whose invitation Vassos declined),[151] and the College Art Association.[152] Other markers of Vassos's success included heavy press coverage and acclaim. In its "Chronicle and Comment" section, the January 1930 issue of *The Bookman* summarized the literary achievements of the past decade and listed Vassos among the great authors of the 1920s.

Dutton's publicity photographs show Vassos carefully dressed, posing with his books and illustrations. Some photos from the 1920s show Vassos with a pipe. As Vassos became more established, later publicity photographs reflected a more hip person dressed in baggy suits, socializing with well-known people. In one such photo, Vassos is hanging out with the singer Rudy Vallee on the rooftop of his apartment. The group shot, taken at an E. P. Dutton press party in 1928, includes Ruth Vassos as well.[153]

The announcement of Vassos's plan to build the largest skyscraper in Athens was the most elaborately staged of all his public relations events. Vassos was to design the building on behalf of the American Legion in Athens. This announcement, which took place in his Upper West Side apartment, was mentioned in many major newspapers just in time for the release of the second edition of *Salome* in the summer and of *Ultimo* in the fall of 1930. The announcement led to a string of articles covering the angry response by Athens residents who were opposed to the plan. In some publications, stories about the heavily publicized project were accompanied by a caricature of Vassos by Wolf Kska.[154] The *New York Times* reported that the cost of the sixteen-story skyscraper, one million dollars, would be defrayed by Americans of Greek origin and that more than three hundred thousand dollars had already been collected. The article noted, "The architect [Vassos] explained yesterday that in design, it would tend toward the modernistic."[155] The project was never mentioned again after that, suggesting it was more a fabrication for publicity than a realizable plan. Indeed, the fact that Vassos was not an architect seems to have gone unnoticed in the national press.[156]

The announcement of the Athens skyscraper plan, which occurred on the eve of the release of *Ultimo*, Vassos's dystopian urban story, was well timed to substantiate

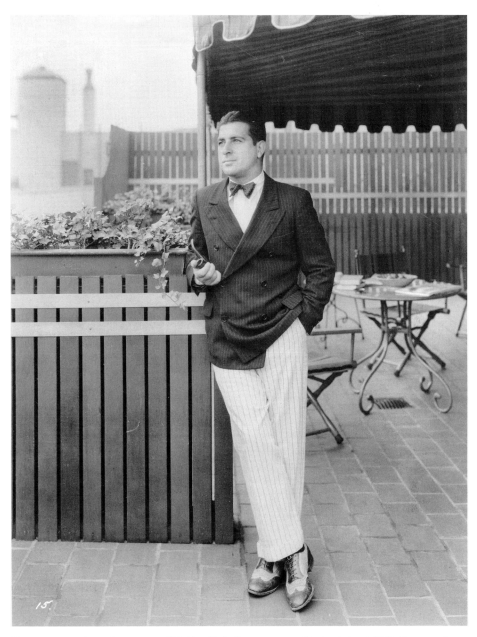

Vassos poses on the rooftop terrace of his New York City apartment with pipe in hand, 1930. Courtesy of Jayne Johnes.

his participation in debates surrounding the heights of skyscrapers and their impact on light. This elaborate publicity event connected the artist with great architecture, attracted reporters to his apartment, and drew attention to the forthcoming *Ultimo*.

During Vassos's book promotion periods, magazines sometimes printed his work to illustrate articles by other writers. Editors appreciated that Vassos's readily accessible and bold images complemented the growing numbers of articles on urban ills.[157] For example, "Mechanophobia: The Fear of Machinery" from *Phobia* was used with an article titled "Taking Heart against Our Perils in the Machine Age."[158] E. P. Dutton encouraged editors to use the graphics, offering to "supply mats (65 screen cuts)" at no charge through the publicity department at Dutton.[159]

Beyond gaining wide exposure for Vassos through the publication of his illustrations in the print media, Dutton used innovative packaging and price scales to increase sales of his books. Vassos, labeled "a certain artist of importance," topped the Dutton Christmas list of authors with books that had been "selected because of their gift qualities, because of their 'good press' and because of the versatility of their appeal."[160] Dutton smartly bundled his first three books interpreting Oscar Wilde—*Salome, The Ballad of Reading Gaol,* and *The Harlot's House*—offering them for sale together for a savings of about one dollar.[161]

Vassos's other literary affiliations helped expand his social network and subsequently increased his visibility in the modernist art world. He worked closely on the "little" literary magazine *Contempo,* of North Carolina, which took its name from Vassos's 1929 book with his permission. Published by Milton Abernethy and Anthony Buttitta, the magazine was short-lived, running only from May 1931 to February 1934.[162] It featured contributions by major modernist writers and journalists, and it openly took a stance against traditional literature, which its editors described as "a violent tonic for that haberdashery of current bourgeois literature." The editors of *Contempo* aimed to "carry on the pioneering spirit of Margaret Anderson's 'The Little Review'" by identifying and publishing emerging creative writers as well as established ones such as Ezra Pound, Sinclair Lewis, Nathanael West, Langston Hughes, and William Faulkner.[163] Vassos helped design the magazine and also contributed writings and reviews.[164] His innovative cover design, which used the Futura typeface, met with resounding approval from Buttitta, who wrote to Vassos:

> You can't imagine how much I like the cover design you made for our magazine. It's goddam good . . . it adds so much to the magazine. You don't realize what a difference it makes. I couldn't get Futura Bold. . . . I got Bernard gothic . . . had to buy some for this print shop . . . they didn't have it. . . . That is as good as Futura . . . they didn't even know what Futura is.[165]

Letters between Vassos and Buttitta reveal the artist's stature in the modern art scene. In a letter to Abernethy regarding a dispute over the ownership of a Vassos illustration, Buttitta wrote that "Vassos doesn't need publicity nor promotion; he is too big and too much of a genuine creator for that."[166] After the magazine folded, Vassos maintained his connections with modernist writers through the Silvermine Guild of Artists.

Retrato por Andrés Vigneaux, París.

Caricatura por Riverón, New York.

JOHN VASSOS

67

Vassos with his book *Contempo,* with a caricatured picture by Cuban artist Enrique Riverón in the lower left corner. *Social,* September 1931. John Vassos Papers, Archives of American Art, Smithsonian Institution.

Despite all of his publisher's promotion efforts, most of Vassos's books (*Phobia* aside) did not sell out their print runs. According to letters from Elliott Beck Mac-Crae, treasurer at Dutton, by 1932 the press had overstocks: "In looking at our inventory records, I see that we have on hand at least 2,000 extra copies each of *Ultimo* and *Contempo*."[167] There were 167 limited numbered copies signed by both John and Ruth Vassos to be sold at twenty-five dollars each, of which only 56 were sold between October 29, 1929, and April 30, 1930.[168] MacCrae hoped to unload the copies by selling them to Vassos at a cheap price. A letter to Vassos detailing the financial arrangements revealed that Vassos was actually overpaid, as, according to the letter, he had received an advance against royalties of one thousand dollars on both *Contempo* and *Ultimo*.[169]

Vassos's publishing career dwindled after World War II. However, he always came back to illustration. In the postwar era he moved toward abstraction, the style he used for his murals at RCA's Washington, D.C., office. He continued to paint until the end of his life, even doing covers for magazines, experimenting with form and color. It was to these roots he would return again and again, even when he was stationed in the Middle East working for the Office of Strategic Services creating illustrated manuals for spies.

THE VASSOS ILLUSTRATION STYLE

Despite Vassos's short career as a book illustrator, his books have become synonymous with the prewar modernist style. His unique style of illustration and relative obscurity as an illustrator and industrial designer have left contemporary curators confused about how to characterize and understand Vassos's work. Usually, it is categorized as social criticism and included in major exhibitions on the machine age and the art deco era. Occasionally, his original illustrations come up for auction; for example, a gouache from Barbra Streisand's art deco collection was offered by Christie's in 1999.

His style, as described by Vassos himself, sought to capture subconscious life, to strip illustration of its allegiance to realism and let it be influenced by modernity.[170] He felt strongly that art should reflect the influence of its culture and move the viewer. His choice to create illustrations and books, which are reproducible, reflects his commitment to mass society and his excitement about new forms of distribution. Rarely seeking to create one-of-a-kind works, he intended his art, including his murals, to be enjoyed by a wide audience. His uncommon imagery borrowed from a range of ideas, fusing such disparate styles as high art, surrealism, and Orphism. Vassos drew from a multiplicity of sources and was fueled by the energy of modern art and life. As he wrote, "Stravinsky, Respighi, Ravel among others in music, James Joyce, D. H. Lawrence, Robinson Jeffers in literature, Brancusi, Epstein, Bourdelle in sculpture—and our bathrooms and kitchens, all our comforts and conveniences of daily life, are direct expressions of this so-called modern feeling."[171] Even in the 1930s,

John and Ruth Vassos strike a silly pose at the Silvermine Guild, circa 1940. John Vassos Papers, Archives of American Art, Smithsonian Institution.

no one really knew how to characterize Vassos's style. Reviews of his work tended to make wide artistic connections to describe this fusion. One reviewer wrote, "As a graphic artist, Mr. Vassos discloses a kinship with such unlike personages as Blake, Beardsley, and Picasso."[172]

Vassos positioned himself as both a producer and a critic of mass culture. He recycled themes and artwork so much that an image from the social criticism of *Contempo* found its way into an ad he created for Packard. Indeed, his advertising work gave him more than cash—it also provided him with stylistic ideas that germinated into complete books. The futuristic images in *Ultimo,* the scenes of swirling traffic that he reused in the social criticism text *Contempo,* and the pulsating backgrounds of *Salome* were all influenced by motifs found in his advertising illustrations. In this fluid movement from artist to advertiser and back again, he was similar to many other creative figures who navigated between the worlds of art and commerce.[173]

Vassos was committed to nurturing the Connecticut artists' community he helped create, the Silvermine Guild. He regarded the guild as a great source of inspiration, a place where he could effectively make things happen, perhaps in contrast to the red tape he encountered at RCA. He served ten terms as president of the guild between 1936 and 1955. Under his leadership, the guild became an art center of national status.[174] He designed the guild's logo to reflect its unifying mission—a broad tree with five branches representing painting, sculpture, drama, music, and dance.[175] Vassos sought out the support of his colleagues from RCA-owned NBC to produce the Silvermine Music Festival, which included a performance by the New York Philharmonic in 1938. He wrote to NBC president Robert Sarnoff in the hope that the network would produce a show about the Silvermine Arts Center, noting, "Our members' work is in practically every museum in the United States and the artistic standards of the Guild are the highest possible."[176] He did a tremendous amount of fund-raising for the Florence Schick Gifford Hall complex, completed in 1951, and was instrumental in creating a sculpture and ceramics building for the center, which was named John Vassos Hall in his honor in 1953. He frequently participated in the annual "Silvermine Sillies" theatrical event by designing sets or writing plays with titles like *Audio Video Smellio Dough* and *Radioactive Art.* He expressed his commitment to community arts at Silvermine. As he wrote, "I firmly believed the Arts have a definite place in our society. The big cities do an excellent job . . . but the suburbs, no matter how close to the city both the young and old don't have enough exposure to creative arts."[177] He also enjoyed erotic liaisons with members there, particularly in the late 1930s. He later recalled, "Romances keep happening every day—love affairs surprise everybody (no homosexuality) but lots of dynamic screwing—another manifestation of the feverish times that swept the world."[178]

Vassos felt that art should be narrative and have political and emotional meaning for the viewer. This commitment was most vividly expressed in Vassos's paintings exhibited by the Silvermine Guild. Its 1939 *Social Democracy* exhibition was held at the Riverside Museum in New York City while Vassos was guild president. This show, accompanied by a symposium titled "Art in Democracy," expressed a view that contrasted with the corporate "World of Tomorrow" being presented at the 1939–40 New York World's Fair. The guild differed sharply from the world's fair in its process for selecting art for its exhibition, which had no jury, no hanging committee, no competition, and no refusals; *Social Democracy* also emphasized themes of social inequity and the dangers of militarization.

The well-received show, which included works by Drexler Jacobson, Leslie Randall, and David Robinson, had thirty thousand visitors during the guild's music festival, before it was moved to the Warwick Galleries in Philadelphia.[179] One reviewer commented on the scope and power of the show, observing that it drew its "vigor [from] the pictorial propaganda of the Russians" to show the dangers of modern society. Indeed, the guild acknowledged its debt to the Works Progress Administration for stimulating artists to express their political views openly.[180]

In his introduction to the second show of the guild's Social Statement Series, also held at the Riverside Museum, Vassos wrote that it was "the obligation of the creative person to sustain cultural values in a time like this . . . through his talent to crystallize, to unify, to keep alive and to advance the vital hopes and aspirations of a people."[181] In his contribution to the show, the sarcastically titled "Everything Is Hunky-Dory," Vassos incorporated the symbols of the 1939–40 World's Fair—the Trylon and Perisphere—in the background of the image to express the theme of humans being forced to go underground while machines take over the Earth. In this frightening image, the huddling, wounded human figures, reduced to primordial shapes with giant heads and big eyes, retreat helplessly from the machines.

At Silvermine, Vassos found another outlet for his artistic practice and social criticism. While he did not continue publishing books, beyond homages to his beloved hunting dogs, his experience as an illustrator influenced and informed his industrial design practice. In particular, it made him attuned to the relationships between people and machines and between individual bodies and the settings they inhabit. He continued to examine the emotional impact of graphic imagery through the design of logos, which were visually integrated composites of the image and the word. In the postwar period, he returned to his role as a muralist. He was prolific, creating murals in diverse settings, including a 120-foot marine mural for Condado Beach Hotel in Puerto Rico, a mural at Grauman's Egyptian Theatre in Los Angeles telling the story of wide-screen cinema, and one titled *Cosmosynthesis* at RCA's Washington, D.C., headquarters in 1960, an ambivalent depiction of atomic energy. These murals were largely abstract, more evocative of midcentury artistic styles than the madly original swirling "projections" found in his 1920s and 1930s work.

As an illustrator, Vassos achieved fame and celebrity in the late 1920s and early 1930s, which led him to the emergent field of industrial design. Multidisciplined artisans versed in the language of modernism were welcomed by business owners who were seeking to compete in thriftier times. Vassos was favorably poised to transition into the new profession. His multidimensional talents as an interior designer, artist, and book illustrator were already well established, and his name was widely recognized. His private and restaurant interiors were celebrated by the important architectural journal *Pencil Points* and in other magazines. By 1934 he was profiled in a *Fortune* magazine article, alongside his colleagues Walter Dorwin Teague, Raymond Loewy, and Henry Dreyfuss, as a rising and prominent member of the budding industrial design profession.

Vassos's first industrial design assignments grew out of commissions to do commercial illustrations for Armand, a cosmetics company. Following that, he received the prestigious commission to paint the murals at the newly built art deco WCAU radio station in Philadelphia. At this spectacular, groundbreaking skyscraper devoted to radio production, he started to think about how to dramatize the largely invisible medium of radio through his vivid murals. While there, he met the heads of RCA, who were interested in hiring a designer to modernize the radio sets the company sold for use in American homes. Vassos easily made the leap from decorating the walls of the radio station to shaping the look of modern radio receivers.

Other enterprising artists who began in advertising illustration, such as Teague and Loewy, gravitated toward product design. Unlike these colleagues, Vassos maintained his identity as an illustrator and painter throughout his career. He put his skills to use creating product drafts and sketches, and later, in the postwar period, he returned to mural making for RCA and other large corporations. Never again, however, did he achieve the fame he enjoyed in the 1930s for his artwork.

2. BECOMING AN INDUSTRIAL DESIGNER

The field of industrial design emerged in the late 1920s.[1] Individuals from various professions, including graphic design, stage design, and advertising illustration, offered their services in bundled packages, providing materials for improving their clients' profits from sketch to sale. During this time, along with his illustration and interior design work, Vassos branched out into industrial design. He cultivated a client base through contacts and promotional letters that resulted in his being hired in 1933 by the country's largest manufacturer of radios, thus solidifying his position in the new field. This chapter presents Vassos's major early industrial designs for various manufacturers and reveals the networks of power, authority, and influence in which Vassos worked. His archival papers, which contain detailed letters between Vassos and his clients, reveal the enormous effort and collaboration involved in the realization of a single product. Industrial design required more than creating a new product or sketching out an idea for restyling an old one. Vassos's letters show the complicated process of balancing, compromising, and sorting out the disparate demands of all involved. A design could come to market only after a series of negotiations and trade-offs with manufacturers, engineers, materials companies, and sales forces. Despite this complexity, Vassos quickly achieved success in industrial design.

In the United States, industrial design was slow to take hold among manufacturers, who were not convinced of its merits. Typically, engineers determined the style of a machine-made object based on ease of production rather than on the beauty of the final product.[2] Held in Paris in 1925, the Exposition Internationale des Arts Décoratifs et Industriels Modernes, from the title of which the term *art deco* was derived, marked the international awareness of a new design style. As Steven Heller and Seymour Chwast note, this style "universally affected architecture, furniture, clothing, and graphic art between the world wars" as art nouveau began to wane.[3] In the graphical ornamentation of art deco, which drew from sources as varied as Egyptian hieroglyphics, stylized peasant art, machinery, and nature, designers found a

Fig. 1

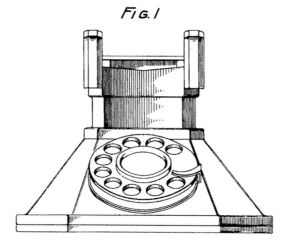

Fig. 2

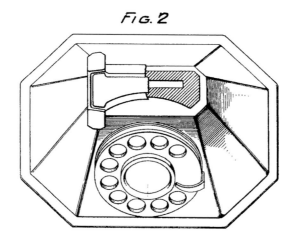

INVENTOR
J. VASSOS
BY
Walter C. Kiesel
ATTORNEY

John Vassos, Desk Stand for a Hand Telephone, U.S. Design Patent No. 81,562, filed May 10, 1930, and issued July 8, 1930.

more pleasing style for the public than the increasingly abstract modernism. The layered geometric form, strong lines, and skyscraper shape of Vassos's 1930 telephone for Bell Telephone Laboratories is an example of this style.[4] The 1925 Paris exhibition brought together thousands of designs from all over Europe and beyond. With more than sixteen million visitors, it marked the high point of the first phase of the art deco style. Modern American design was still in its infancy, however, and not part of the exposition. Herbert Hoover, who was U.S. secretary of commerce at the time, concluded that the United States had no examples of modern design, and thus American products did not fit the exhibition's parameters. In the later 1920s, however, American museums and artists began to embrace the commercial value of the art deco movement as a sales tool and advocated for the production and display of beautiful mass-produced objects.[5] Museums, in particular, played a valuable role in promoting the alliance of industry and design. The Newark Museum, the Metropolitan Museum under the leadership of Richard Bach in the newly formed industrial arts department, and the Museum of Modern Art, founded in 1929, all promoted new mass-produced objects as modernity's art. In an effort to draw attention to the beauty in mechanical production, they displayed these products as artworks in newly formed "decorative arts" departments.

Designers brought aesthetics into the boardroom and forced companies to think about how consumers used their products and services. Their work became indispensable for industries seeking to rationalize the user experience and gain greater control over sales at the point of purchase. Industrial designer Paul Frankl described himself as the modern artist who brought art to the masses.[6] Business theorists such as J. Gordon Lippincott proclaimed that designers were "pioneers in art" who recognized the profit potential of design style that offered economic value to manufacturers while providing beauty and function to the consumer.[7] Beyond the bottom line, critics hailed the alliance of industry and art as revolutionary expression. Sheldon and Martha Cheney's influential book *Art and the Machine* praised the new field as one of the most vital expressions of the new age.[8]

Advocates of industrial design also touted its democratizing effects, since it was agreed that well-designed products could function as vehicles of social uplift and express the inclusiveness of democratic society.[9] Designers envisioned themselves as more than just stylists—they were also philosopher/practitioners serving the common social good. Walter Dorwin Teague's 1940 book *Design This Day: The Technique of Order in the Machine Age,* Norman Bel Geddes's *Horizons* (1932), and Henry Dreyfuss's *Designing for People* (1955) all make the point that the designer's job is more than making the product look pretty; the designer should also seek to improve public taste and public life.[10]

The relationship between form and profit was firmly established by the early 1930s, when everything seemed to undergo restyling.[11] Other changes as well contributed to the rise of industrial design. Expanding forms of visual mass media, such as advertising, magazines, and film, gave consumers a new awareness of the importance of style and made it accessible. The migration to urban centers and the rise of factory work transformed daily life. The ties that had bound rural communities together came undone, leaving individuals isolated and vulnerable to the growing influence of consumerism. Products once made at home were now replaced with store-bought items. These shifts facilitated the rise of an image-driven consumer culture in which people and products became valued for their external appearance rather than their intrinsic qualities.[12]

Similarly, industrial designers helped manufacturers disguise the true nature of their products, divorcing the external shell from the internal object; that is, form no longer followed function but rather hid it. According to historian Adrian Forty, because consumers are resistant to innovation, design is used to alter the way we see products by disguising the shape of what we take to be reality. Forty describes three types of disguises used in design: the archaic, the suppressive, and the utopian. Archaic design disguises the newness of an object by presenting it in an old-fashioned form, thus referring to the past. Suppressive design presents the new object as part of some other established form that serves an entirely different purpose—for example, a pen that looks like a lipstick. In this case design makes a product marketable by adding recognizable form to it that makes it palatable to consumers. Utopian design suggests that the object belongs to a future and better world. The exterior style of the product has little relationship to the product within.[13]

Art deco and the futuristic aesthetic of streamlining became the dominant look of the era. Designers, inspired by aerodynamic engineering used to reduce wind resistance for airplanes, applied streamlining to stationary objects from pencil sharpeners to houses. Although many commented that the application of such design to grounded objects was silly—why would anyone need a wind-resistant refrigerator or radio?—streamlining nonetheless proliferated alongside the zigzagging ornamentation of art deco. It was an ideal American aesthetic in some ways: sleek, appealing, and shiny, not as harsh as Bauhaus modernism. Besides looking futuristic, streamlined objects reflected the utopian social values of the era, particularly a desire to speed effortlessly into the future and away from the Great Depression.[14]

ENTERING THE INDUSTRIAL DESIGN FIELD

Vassos's diverse output, ranging from the Perey turnstile used in subway systems to a kitchen utensil rack, was typical for an industrial designer at the time. His work also included adding cosmetic details and artistry to full-scale redesigns. For the Wallace Company, he created the Ultra line of silver-plate flatware. The rather severe appearance of the utensils, pared down to their basic form, was lightened by a decorative single stalk of wheat on each piece.[15] For Remington, he designed a dramatic series of lighter, versatile shotguns. Some of his designs are collector's items today, such as the "Hundred Year" Lucite pen he created for Waterman in 1940 in four jewellike colors. This was among the first uses of plastic in a fountain pen. Vassos improved the basic pen by adding a "sure grip" of symmetric corrugations and a clip with decorative streamlined detailing, which was widely copied by other manufacturers. The company was so confident in the pen's construction that it guaranteed each one for a century.

Vassos's earliest commissions taught him valuable lessons about working with clients and established his reputation as a serious industrial designer. Although he went to work for RCA in 1933, he continued to solicit clients throughout his career, adding to his income and his client base. Designers used heavily promotional pitch letters to attract potential clients and to stand out against their competition. These letters reveal the process of soliciting new work and the networks that united designers and manufacturers. For example, in a letter to a potential client, Walgreen's Pharmacy, Vassos wrote as if he had been involved in industrial design for decades, stating that by 1933, his work included

> redesigning and bringing up to date the entire line of Armand Products; revolutionizing the turnstile industry by the creation of a turnstile for the Perey Turnstile Company; Coca-Cola dispenser and sterilizers; a modern stove for Montgomery Ward—and many minor objects too numerous to mention.[16]

At first, Vassos considered himself primarily an illustrator and display expert. As he strove to bundle all his talents and recognized that he worked well with three-dimensional models, however, he realized he could package these skills into the profession of industrial designer. In later years, Vassos would be instrumental, along with Alexander Kostellow, in solidifying the educational curriculum for industrial designers. But in the beginning, the definition of industrial designer was wide open. Also, although Vassos was well known as an artist, he needed to establish his credentials as a designer. By 1934, he had made enough of a name for himself as a designer of architectural interiors to be featured by Listerine in a dental powder advertisement.

Vassos's pitch letters show how broad the category of industrial designer was during this period. They also reveal the high priority that manufacturers placed on reaching the wealthiest consumers. In his earliest letters, Vassos associated his products and therefore himself with institutions of status and prestige, and he tended to list companies whose products were aimed at high-end markets. Vassos sought to align himself with prestigious firms, although most of his associations were through illustrations and window design rather than product design. He wrote:

> My style has been associated with nothing but the finest products. Cammeyer shoes 1927–1929, French line 1929–31, Piver perfumes 1920, Bonwit Teller, Saks Fifth Avenue, Lord & Taylor, Wanamaker . . . Curtis Wright Transport service, and for the past five years the Packard motor car; this

"A Sensational New Pen!" Advertisement for the jewel-colored "Hundred Year" Lucite pen guaranteed for a century, "created by John Vassos, famous designer." From *Sunday News,* December 3, 1939. Private collection.

outside of my industrial design, which has all been for class products. My style is definitely associated with class products and class advertising.[17]

Vassos also began to note his accomplishments as an interior designer among the skills he offered. For example, in one letter he wrote, "I devoted my talents and energies for the past four years to . . . modern decor."[18] Vassos was not the only industrial designer using vanity to promote his fledgling business. Norman Bel Geddes was similarly boastful. In one of his pitch letters, he described himself as "a man of great versatility and dynamic qualities. Norman Bel Geddes has through the medium of design found himself in the midst of innumerable vastly different fields and in each one of them has left his mark."[19] The newly minted designers turned to unchecked self-promotion to sell themselves in a field that was not yet clearly defined in the open market.

These pitch letters demonstrate the way in which designers promoted the versatility of their skill sets: the more skills they had, the more they could offer their clients. At the same time, designers sought to differentiate themselves from their competition by choosing specialties. From 1927 to 1934, Vassos's descriptions of himself shifted from a man associated with "class"—as expressed in his associations with Packard and Bonwit Teller—to a man who was knowledgeable about psychology. He increasingly emphasized this claim, especially following the publication of a 1934 *Fortune* magazine article in which this unique talent was mentioned. This special skill enabled him to stand out among the other designers, none of whom had Vassos's intense association with psychoanalysis.

Vassos had a strong start in the field of product design. His first successful design was for the cosmetics giant Carl Weeks, who owned the Armand Company. As historian Kathy Peiss notes, Weeks was a significant entrepreneur who helped develop the mass-market cosmetic industry in the early twentieth century, starting with a long-wearing face powder. With its iconic package evoking French elegance and an elaborate advertising campaign by N. W. Ayer, the company boomed until 1927, when American women's tastes in face powders changed.[20] Weeks tried different strategies to stay relevant, including tying his makeup line to fashion, marketing to men, and also apparently bringing Vassos on board to develop modern packaging.[21]

Vassos initially just designed labels for Armand, but then he observed that the company's premier skin rejuvenator, a cream astringent, was packaged in a medicinal-looking bottle and set out to improve it. His ideas to replace the cork cap with a plastic screw top and to enhance the glass bottle with deco styling were quickly adopted, and the product became a successful item for the struggling company. The bottle—which could fit easily into a pocket—could be repurposed as a flask, making it popular during Prohibition as a way to smuggle liquor into restaurants. Its curved shape and leakproof cap also looked stylish on a makeup table. Vassos described the bottle years later, perhaps with some exaggeration:

Whiter Teeth *QUICK!*

that's even more important than the 25¢ price

When you try Listerine Tooth Paste, you'll discover why so many people prefer it. You'll discover, for one thing, the speedy way this dentifrice cleanses. We use a modern polishing agent. It gets film and stains off the teeth with surprisingly little brushing. Teeth become whiter after only a few days' use. Soft and gentle, this polishing agent cannot possibly harm the teeth in any way.

Then—this 25¢ dentifrice certainly does give teeth a handsome lustre and polish. Again and again, people—particularly women — remark upon the way it makes teeth glisten.

Also—Listerine Tooth Paste has an unusually refreshing effect upon the mouth and gums—in this respect it is just what you'd expect of a Listerine product. After you brush your teeth with it, your mouth feels thoroughly "washed"—assurance of a purer, sweeter breath.

Begin your test of Listerine Tooth Paste soon. Results are what count! If you find this tooth paste better than the one you are using now, you'll welcome the saving it brings you. Try either the 25¢ size—or the new 40¢ size containing *twice* as much. Lambert Pharmacal Company, St. Louis, Mo.

**(above)
FORMER LEAGUE
BALL PLAYER,** Curtiss W. Scoville is now a business man of Albany, N. Y. He likes Listerine Tooth Paste because "it gets the stains off my teeth quickly."

"KING KONG" AND "SON OF KONG" added to the reputation of Edward Linden, their chief cinematographer. "I have used Listerine Tooth Paste in my travels and at home," he says. "It has always satisfied me because it cleans quick."

A HARD WORKER, John Vassos likes a dentifrice which gets prompt results—Listerine Tooth Paste. Mr. Vassos is a designer whose architectural interiors have won wide recognition.

"Whiter Teeth QUICK!" This 1934 advertisement for Listerine toothpaste features John Vassos, "a hard worker." *American Magazine*, June 1934. Private collection.

We were at the height of the so-called noble experiment. Meaning the prohibition days and all of us used to make bathtub gin. We mixed it in the bathroom with gin, always good alcohol, juniper, and glycerin. But we had no way of carrying it to nightclubs, no flasks. . . . Sales [went] up.[22]

Vassos's design exhibits the subversive use of mass production to undermine legal restraint. This first design taught Vassos the power of the package to convey a range of meanings to the customer, meanings related to status, convenience, eye appeal, and association with a reputable company. Vassos was also thinking about ergonomics and the way humans interact with objects. A sketch that he created in the late 1920s examines finger and hand movements, particularly the motion of grasping a bottle that looks like one he designed for the Armand Company.

Vassos's friend Margaret Bourke-White took dramatic photographs of the astringent bottle. The designer, from the first stages of the design process, had to consider how the package would be displayed. The archives show that Vassos's mass-produced packages for Armand were photographed as if they were works of art. Vassos, who knew Bourke-White from the Art Students League, appears to have exchanged services with her, his interior design work for her photography; the two also shared job leads and props with each other. He designed the modern furniture for her penthouse office in the Empire State Building.[23] They built a strong friendship that continued for many years.[24]

Bourke-White's monochrome photographs of the Armand bottles feature her characteristic dramatic lighting and heightened attention to form. As design historians Tim and Charlotte Benton have noted, Bourke-White's work shares qualities of art deco photography in that it is "commercial, decorative, innovative and in love with the same shining materials of modernity—chrome, silver," and also glass favored by the movement's architects and designers.[25] To create emotional portraits of the packages, Bourke-White added lighting and texture; soft curtains provide a backdrop, and a black, sensuously shiny surface provides a reflective pool of light, revealing narcissistic bottles in love with their image. Bourke-White was in many ways the ideal person to photograph Vassos's architectural designs. With her groundbreaking modernist style, she captured the heroic optimism of the machine age in the portrayal of a single object.[26] Her style bears the imprint of her mentor, pictorialist photographer Clarence White, who argued that photographers should apply artistic principles to even the most utilitarian objects. Advertisers found this modernistic artistic style appealing.[27]

The promotional use of packaging—that is, as a way of selling an item beyond advertising—reveals the industrial designer's job as more than that of mere package designer. As Vassos wrote: "The styling and designing of a product is not where the work of the industrial designer stops. Promotion and presentation after the styling and designing have been done are equally important and are a very definite part of the industrial designer's job."[28]

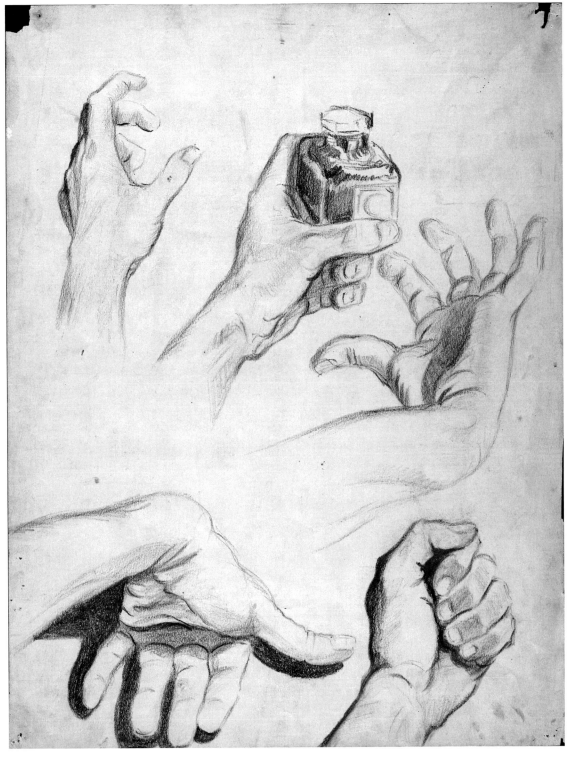

ABOVE Sketches by John Vassos exploring how hands grasp a bottle, circa 1920s. John Vassos Papers, Archives of American Art, Smithsonian Institution.

OPPOSITE John Vassos's glass bottle for a cream astringent with a screw-off cap for the Armand Company. The bottle doubled as a flask. John Vassos Papers, Archives of American Art, Smithsonian Institution. Copyright Estate of Margaret Bourke-White. Licensed by VAGA, New York, NY.

Vassos knew from experience that modern marketing techniques were needed to sell modern products. Indeed, he was frustrated when the Wallace Silver Company refused to let him get involved in display and marketing. After designing three separate lines in metals of sterling, plate, and functional alloy over a six-month period, including flatware, a tea and coffee set, and serving bowls, the company let him go, as they were not "progressive enough to continue [his] programs" of marketing. They apparently didn't appreciate Vassos's belief that he was more than a draftsman; he was also a publicist. The "Ultra" pattern, his elegant design for silver-plated flatware with a subtle wheat strand on the edge, sold successfully however. Other designers with similar backgrounds were also involved in merchandising and all areas of product presentation. In 1936, Henry Dreyfuss noted that, "a second important change in industrial design is the way it is breaking into new fields . . . the designer must be able to understand merchandising."[29]

The bottle for D.A. tooth powder is another example of Vassos's designing product packaging for photography as well as for retail display. Thick green and ivory strips encircled the bottle's base, creating a striking exterior that fused letters and shapes. The double-boxed geometric frame in the advertising photographs emphasized the package's graphic design. Vassos bragged in a letter to the manufacturer that his package had enough photographic appeal to "dominate the pages of any magazine."[30] So while these photographs were used to sell the design to Armand's owner, Carl Weeks, Vassos also anticipated how the product would look in the modern ad layout of a magazine.

Vassos applied "styling" to a stream of consumer products, from toothpicks to vacuum cleaners to cars. This wide-ranging application of style by industrial designers, regardless of the significance or cost of the product, remains a topic of great interest to scholars. For example, the title of industrial design historian John Heskett's 2002 book *Toothpicks and Logos: Design in Everyday Life* reflects a fascination with industrial design's scope and also echoes the title of a chapter in Raymond Loewy's 1951 book *Never Leave Well Enough Alone*: "From Toothpicks to Locomotives."[31] Vassos and his contemporaries brought to industrial design enormous versatility and perhaps arrogance in their claim that they could style any consumer product regardless of size, use, and materials. As Vassos wrote, somewhat theoretically, "Industrial design consists of styling an object from the point of view of form, of color, and of functionalism in order to make the object of more appeal to the buying public, *no matter what that object might be.*"[32]

In the 1930s, "styling" was synonymous with streamlining. Streamlining was the second major aesthetic to shape mass production in American consumer society, after the art deco or zigzag moderne of the 1920s. Streamlining replaced the earlier style of "exuberance and easy money . . . like something in a motion picture"; it removed the "curlicues and reduced forms to clearly logical lines."[33] Reviewers such as the one who offered this description, who was responding to a Metropolitan Museum design show, appreciated the simple forms of machine art that would both fit Depression-era budgets and complement the furnishings already occupying consumers' homes. Although modernistic furniture started with one-of-a-kind works created by elite designers like Walter Dorwin Teague and Norman Bel Geddes, the forms of those works were well suited to the limitations of machine manufacture and the demand for low prices.

Like most designers in the 1930s, Vassos participated in the streamlining craze. According to scholars of design, the aerodynamic streamlined aesthetic was massively popular because the sleek style embodied Depression-era hopefulness. Streamlined forms, with their horizontal speed whiskers and "curious ornament of parallel lines," symbolically glided away from the Depression, heading toward a prosperous future thanks to technological advances.[34] It was a democratic style—applied to products and packages across categories as well as to public spaces and transportation. Streamlining also fit with the production mandate of planned obsolescence, as companies encouraged consumers to ditch their conservationist impulses and buy more. Another advantage of streamlining was that it was suited to new production methods. For instance, in assembly-line production a die-stamped skin of material could be used to cover a product in a seamless shell. A seamless sheath of plastic or metal could hide the internal parts of new machine-driven products and make them look less threatening. It also served the useful role of encasing potentially dangerous mechanical bits and protrusions.

For some scholars, the streamlining craze epitomizes the wastefulness of consumer society and a technocracy of style that culminated in the architecture displayed at the 1939–40 New York World's Fair. Australian cultural theorist Tony Fry calls this style "dreamlining": "a convergence of factors culminating in the rise of mass desire, the mass design of a new product as well as a poverty of mind, with no assessment of use and impact."[35] Industrial designers defended their use of streamlining, drawing from science to support the style as particularly hygienic. Henry Dreyfuss referred to it as "cleanlining," referring to the easy-to-clean jointless sheathed skins.[36] Clearly, the embrace of the style by manufacturers was driven significantly by sales. As Vassos joked, the new style not only looked more aerodynamic but also "eliminated a great deal of sales resistance."[37] In letters to clients, he proposed to streamline and "modernize their [products'] design, to give [them] more eye appeal and sales value."[38] More seriously, he was happy that "designers are beginning to be recognized as a radical necessity in industry" and quick to maintain that they also contributed mechanical improvements to products "in many instances."[39]

Vassos was commissioned to streamline a range of products, including the Paragon Company's ticket punch, a bicycle, and plumbing equipment such as the Quimby screw pump.[40] He designed a series of streamlined harmonicas for the

Hohner Company, a musical instrument manufacturer based in Trossingen, Germany. His improvements made the harmonicas easier to hold and curved for the lips. Vassos designed the Hohner Echo Elite and two other models for which he received design patents in 1939.[41] Hohner's factory was converted to munitions production during World War II, severely limiting the manufacture of harmonicas during the war. After the war, the company worked quickly to regain its international market and reestablish its supremacy among harmonica makers.[42]

Among Vassos's more profitable product redesigns were a kitchen paring knife and the turnstile. For the Paragon ticket punch, Vassos also suggested a snappy name—"Shur punch"—to reflect the new efficient design.[43] Transportation vehicles were obvious choices for the application of the streamlined style. For this reason, Vassos was enthusiastic about his design for a streamlined bicycle, the "aerobike," for which he received two design patents.[44] Although it is unclear whether the aerobike was produced, Vassos's study of the market was hopeful, as he revealed in a letter for the project:

> I read with extreme interest the bicycle market data. . . . It will be very wise for us, even if we don't manufacture the two sketches submitted to copyright or even patent the designs or certain elements. Thus, we can at least prevent others from going into the market with a streamlined bicycle . . . constructed on aeropolane [sic] studies where stresses of resistance and wind resistance were minimum.[45]

While it is unknown how much the streamlined design might have affected the bicycle's speed, the bulbous forward-directed shape shown in Vassos's sketches suggests that it would have gone faster than a regular bike.[46]

Vassos also streamlined kitchen appliances and tools, such as a stove for Montgomery Ward and a paring knife, entering the feminine domain of the kitchen for one of the few times in his career. (Later, he specialized in designing furniture for the living room.) Vassos had the tricky job of streamlining the coal stove, making it modern despite the certainty that the final product would get filthy. He stylistically cleaned up the stove by removing the control buttons behind the back burners, highlighting the simplicity of the design, and adding a single button on the side, presumably where the user would open a door to insert coal. With its squared-off base and decorative horizontal lines creating the illusion of an abstract grid, the stove was a classic reinvention of a familiar item according to the principles of streamlining.[47] In the carefully constructed sketch that sold the idea, Vassos added a geometric shape—a slightly twisted black rectangle—on which he blocked the image, adding depth and motion to make the drawing more visually interesting.

THE HUMBLE TURNSTILE, BEFORE AND AFTER THE **VASSOS** TOUCH—EMPIRE STATE BUILDING, NEW YORK CITY —NOT ONLY IS THE NEW DESIGN 15 PER CENT CHEAPER TO MANUFACTURE, BUT ITS SALES HAVE INCREASED 25 PER CENT OVER THE OLD DESIGN

The Perey Turnstile Company turnstile installed in the Empire State Building, before and after Vassos's redesign. *Broadcast News,* February 1934. Courtesy of the Hagley Museum and Library.

Vassos's sketches as he worked on the project reveal his process and priorities. In the sketches, he responded to the concerns of the manufacturer, visualizing new features. Specifically, he addressed the turnstile's size and its ability to move the body quickly and efficiently. He improved the casing by placing the turnstile in a silver body and adding streamlined details that suggested movement. Vassos's design transformed the turnstile, making it more functional, compact, and safe. The addition of a semicircular standing platform and attractive styling certainly contributed to this model's enduring popularity as the industry standard for many years. Vassos took credit for the most significant alteration, the changing of the orientation of the arms from a propeller-like form into a sort of "milk stool on its side," as Vassos described it. Company owner John Perey and Conrad Trubenback received a utility patent for the three-legged turnstile in 1932.[56]

Vassos used his book *Phobia* to explain the psychology behind his design, which took into account the range of experiences of customers who would pass through the machines. In particular, Vassos wanted phobic people to feel more comfortable as they passed through the turnstiles at subway stations. He explained, "Here my knowledge of the aicmophobic's reaction—fear of pointed objects—guided me, and I produced a simple contrivance with gently curving surfaces, with any disturbing design around the feet of the user eliminated."[57] The Perey Company was proud of Vassos's contribution, stating in its newsletter, the *Perey Pioneer*: "Hardly any detail in the old order of things is safe from the radical changes originating in the mind of John Vassos. The humble turnstile which we have always regarded as a just and ugly commonplace necessity in the commercial world of today suddenly takes on a new individuality pleasing in appearance and miraculously harmonizing with its surroundings."[58]

The Perey Passimeter became one of Vassos's best-known designs. It remained one of the best turnstile models long after streamlining went out of style, used in stadiums and public transportation systems across the country. The popularity of the design revealed Vassos's skill in designing for urban spaces. Vassos was happy with the design, as he wrote after the turnstile's premiere at the 1933 Chicago World's Fair, where it was chosen for use at the official entrances: "I have always felt that it is one of my best pieces of industrial design. . . . The attendance at this exposition is . . . thousand[s] of people a day."[59] The product was hugely successful for the Perey Company almost immediately, with orders from the Brooklyn–Manhattan Transit Subway System, the Bronx Zoo (then called the New York Zoological Park), and the Santa Anita Park racetrack near Los Angeles.[60] With the new tripod, the turnstile allowed subway stations to gain 66 percent in entrance capacity without structural change. This turnstile, complete with streamlined details, is still manufactured today. In 2007, the president of Perey Turnstiles, Ed Hendrickson, said that Vassos "designed the overall shape and character of the single most prevalent turnstile on the planet; our Model HD."[61]

Industrial designers who were innovative in their use of materials in product designs and displays needed to be knowledgeable about the chemistry of materials and manufacturing processes. Materials industries wisely began to court the designers, recognizing that they could influence manufacturing decisions. They created marketing campaigns targeted to designers in an effort to gain favor and create cross-promotional opportunities. For instance, the Bakelite Corporation invited Vassos, along with "the only ten living designers in America (the rest having all starved to death)" to a special lunch to engage their help in promoting better design through a series of ads uniting the designers and the Bakelite product.[62] Vassos in turn became a spokesperson for Bakelite, and he used the material in the radios he designed.

Vassos also employed new technologies in exhibition displays, such as the "artificial" lighting he used in the Packard Company booth in an exhibition held at the Roosevelt Hotel in New York City. This innovative use of lighting garnered Vassos attention in magazines such as *Signs of the Times, Edison Magazine, Lighting,* and the General Electric Company's *Nela Park Magazine*.[63] In his displays of commercial products, Vassos was able to experiment with many new materials—materials that he would continue to draw on during the 1930s, particularly Formica and brushed

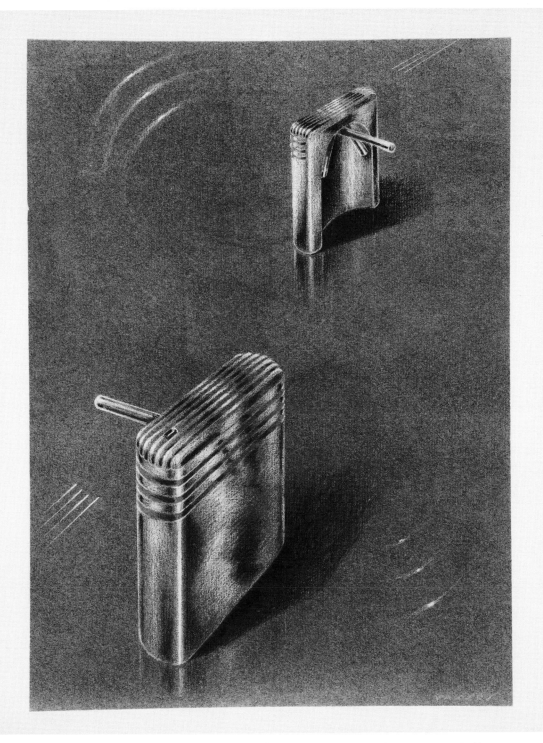

Rendering of turnstile in motion for the Perey Turnstile Company, circa 1932. John Vassos Papers, Archives of American Art, Smithsonian Institution.

Turnstile from the main lobby of the Brooklyn Museum, circa 1932. John Vassos, designer; Perey Company, New York, manufacturer. Iron, enameled and chromium-plated steel, 38¾ × 27 × 24 inches. Reprinted with permission of The Wolfsonian–Florida International University, Miami, Florida, The Mitchell Wolfson, Jr. Collection, TD1989.50.1. Photograph by Silvia Ros.

aluminum. He also was fond of Fabrikoid, an artificial leather made of cotton that was durable and easy to clean. He later incorporated all of these materials into his modern office at RCA's plant in Camden, New Jersey. In a 1932 letter, he described how he melded such modern materials and techniques in a display for the Packard Company: "The background is treated as three separate units, and the materials used are the most modern, celloglass for the lights, Formica and Fabrikoid to add color, brushed aluminum for the metal trimmings, and the entire display wired to meet the lighting requirements."[64] Vassos frequently used plastics, which were becoming increasingly popular materials. His design for the medal presented to the winner of the Modern Plastics Competition Award in 1934 highlighted in textured bas-relief the malleability of the product.[65] He himself won that award in 1939 for his work at RCA.[66]

Eventually, Vassos encountered failure, in the form of a streamlined beverage dispenser contracted by the behemoth Coca-Cola Company but never produced. Vassos first encountered Coca-Cola through his work developing the first drink-dispensing station at Nedick's hot dog stand in 1930.[67] He shrewdly realized that dispensers would become increasingly necessary as soda fountains grew in popularity across the country. In preparation for the project, Vassos patented his design for a dispenser.[68] He knew he had to work quickly to convince the company to hire him. Set to premiere at the 1933 Chicago World's Fair, the automatic fountain dispenser mixed caramelized syrup with carbonated water. It reduced bottling costs, enabled employees to serve drinks faster with the flick of a nozzle, and enabled restaurants to measure their beverage output.

Vassos started communicating with Ross Treseder, a vice president at Coca-Cola in 1932, who clarified the company's specific needs.[69] The dispenser unit had to be compact, to fit into limited counter space, and it had to be easy to clean, so that the sugary syrup would not cling to the surface. In addition, the exterior had to serve as a display and advertising device. As his design patent shows, Vassos addressed the issue of compactness by creating a tight, small base with a larger bucket bulging on top. The designer apparently drew inspiration from architecture, as the shape was similar to that of the water tanks on the roofs of many New York buildings at the time.[70] To make the colors stay bright, Vassos chose the material Bakelite. Although its colors were typically available only in dark tones, the Bakelite Corporation was experimenting with a new plastic formulation that would enable the malleable material to take on the vibrant red and green associated with Coca-Cola. The colors Vassos chose were essential to the visual appeal of the dispenser, which was intended to stimulate sales. The red and green bands were meant to give the sense of a guarded treasure. The chromium coils at the bottom of the little barrel that would sit on the soda fountain counter were meant to suggest coolness.[71] Vassos explained the benefits of the new material in a letter to Treseder:

> [It] would be very simple to make a die of the Coca-Cola trademark to be inlaid in the Bakelite itself, making it sanitary and easy to keep clean, permanent and of course very smart looking. My personal choice would be Bakelite if they can guarantee permanency and correct shade of color, however I will survey the field for any other suitable material.[72]

Vassos's decision to use the plastic eventually led to the project's undoing. A string of letters to Allan Brown at Bakelite revealed Vassos's frustration with the color issue. Brown acknowledged that fading was a problem, writing, "Lighter colors

John Vassos says...

...*"Design in industry has given added beauty and proven a strong selling factor"*

THEN HE ADDS—"Through the designer's use of synthetic materials such as Bakelite, the objects designed have achieved that most difficult thing—identity." An example of Mr. Vassos' skilful use of Bakelite Materials in his designs, is provided by the Coca Cola dispenser, the large surfaces of which are made of Bakelite Laminated in red and green, with inlaid metal lettering. The base and cover are of chromium plated metal.

Manufacturers in every field, from watches to locomotives, are discovering that the beauty added to utility through employing the talents of an artist designer, reaps a gratifying harvest in increased sales. It also is significant that these designers make extensive use of the beauty and economy of Bakelite Materials, both Molded and Laminated, in making products more attractive and desirable.

John Vassos has designed a wide variety of products including turnstiles and telephones, modern stores and radio cabinets, and his architectural interiors have received wide recognition. He is consultant designer for such well known companies as RCA-Victor Corp. and Wallace & Sons, silversmiths.

We would be glad to discuss with you the advantages of redesigning for increased sales as it applies to your own products. An appointment for this purpose involves not the slightest obligation. We also would be glad to send, upon request, copies of our booklets 26M, "Bakelite Molded" and 26L "Bakelite Laminated".

BAKELITE CORPORATION, 247 Park Avenue, New York, N.Y.....43 East Ohio Street, Chicago, Ill.
BAKELITE CORPORATION OF CANADA, LIMITED, 163 Dufferin Street, Toronto, Ontario, Canada

BAKELITE

REGISTERED U.S. Pat. Off.

"The registered trade marks shown above distinguish materials manufactured by Bakelite Corporation. Under the capital "B" is the numerical sign for infinity, or unlimited quantity. It symbolizes the infinite number of present and future uses of Bakelite Corporation's products"

THE MATERIAL OF A THOUSAND USES

AUGUST 15, 1934

[157]

will fade somewhat if subjected to the direct rays of the sun over a long period of time. Therefore, if it is absolutely necessary to retain the original color indefinitely, we cannot recommend the material for this particular application."[73] Treseder liked Vassos's modern design, with its elegant ringed base and its metallic touches. As he wrote, "Most everybody that's capable of understanding modern treatment in designs is greatly pleased with the unit. I know I am."[74] However, Coca-Cola was not pleased with the prospect of fading color, and Vassos lost the contract. More than a decade later, Raymond Loewy redesigned the dispenser, moving away from Vassos's streamlined shape to a curving, modern shape more suitable for the postwar period. Loewy's metal dispenser, in bright Coca-Cola red, was a popular addition for soda shops in postwar suburbia. More than thirty thousand Coca-Cola soda fountain dispensers were built using Loewy's design.[75]

Vassos, who had invested tremendous energy in acquiring the Coke account, rightfully took credit for the innovative design. On a few occasions, he sought to exhibit the model of his dispenser as an example of his work, such as at modern design exhibitions at the Art Center and at Radio City, but the Coca-Cola Company, careful of its image, refused to grant him permission to use the model at these events.[76] However, Vassos and his design were featured two years later, in 1934, in a full-page ad for Bakelite that appeared in *Sales Management* magazine, allowing Vassos to promote his affiliation with the soft drink giant, of which he was very proud.[77] This ad was one in a series that Bakelite produced highlighting the top ten industrial designers, who contributed designs that used Bakelite in significant ways.[78]

Ultimately, Vassos's most reliable contract would be with another major corporation, and he was thrilled to find a home base. By 1934, he found his niche at RCA, where he designed radios and the exteriors for other media technologies. He preferred working mostly for a single client and focusing on a range of products rather than dealing with one-off contracts as he had in the early 1930s. Although he continued to juggle other clients, his primary relationship was with RCA, where he worked on numerous projects and was able to create an impressive portfolio. He even experimented with Bakelite again.

OPPOSITE "John Vassos says . . ." Advertisement for Bakelite featuring John Vassos with his Coca-Cola soda dispenser. *Sales Management,* August 15, 1934. Courtesy of the Library of Congress.

3. MODERNIZING THE HOME THROUGH RADIO

The new technology of radio had no design precedent. The earliest designers of radio sets hid the machines in ornate wooden furniture. Like the automobile before it, radio challenged designers to think about new forms of visual identity for a product that had never been imagined before.[1] Radio design was a priority for manufacturers, who sought to beat their competitors in the growing receiver market. They knew that the radio had to be more than a collection of wires and tubes to escape the garage workshops of the amateur radio builders and be accepted into the home by consumers. Beer barrels and glass spheres were among the shapes that radio took while its form was being worked out. Design historian Adrian Forty argues that the difficult consensus for the design of the radio stemmed from the radio set's primary function as a receiver for broadcast media. In discussing British broadcasting, he identifies the problem with radio as its perceived potential for disruption of domestic life, which led manufacturers to take a conservative design approach and house the radio in a familiar furniture form. Thus, radios were concealed in large cabinets, in phonographs, and even in piano cases.[2] Forty identifies three phases of radio design, starting with the furniture cabinet, evolving to the plastic case, and then becoming a conspicuous modern object of technology.[3] As the public eventually became more comfortable with the device, radio became one of the first electrical appliances to use futuristic design.

After Vassos was hired by RCA in 1933, his first radio designs followed this trajectory. He was determined to bring modern design into the home, but he would have to wait until the furniture cabinet phase of radio was over before he could create the modern shapes that plastics like Bakelite allowed. For Vassos the transformation of the radio form meant rejecting the tall, domed, vertical wooden shape known as the cathedral (grounded in the architectural tradition of the church), or the "tombstone," as he liked to call this dying radio shape. As early as 1931, he had imagined creating a new form for the radio to replace the "monstrosities we now suffer from known as radio cabinets."[4] He preferred for the radio to be built into a wall during a home's construction, so that the provision of sound would be its only function. The architecturally planned interior was a recurring theme throughout his career, even as he grappled with the physical shape of the radio receiver as a stand-alone object.

The issue of radio's future was discussed at the "Radio Style Clinic," which took place on March 20, 1933, at the National Alliance of Art and Industry, where Vassos was an honored guest. The clinic brought together radio manufacturers and leading American designers, including Henry Dreyfuss, Walter Dorwin Teague, and George Ball, to exchange design ideas "so that a common direction might be given to the new styling trend" and to "increase radio-receiver sales through improved external design and artistic appearance." As the ad for the event emphasized, "The time to re-style radio sets is now!"[5]

The purpose of the meeting was not only to share design ideas but also to facilitate connections between manufacturers and designers. It gave the "radio men in attendance . . . an opportunity to contact the design people" and to convince them that the redesign and restyling of radios had indeed helped sales.[6] Vassos mentioned this clinic in a pitch letter to George Throckmorton, a vice president at RCA, in order to demonstrate his familiarity with issues in radio design: "I recently attended an important meeting sponsored by the National Alliance of Art and Industry between the leading designers and the radio manufacturers which clarified in my mind many of the issues involved." He explained to Throckmorton that the clinic's purpose was to address "the problem of increasing radio-receiver sales through improved external design and artistic appearance," and he offered his expertise to RCA, a company struggling in the increasingly competitive market of radio manufacturers.[7]

In case RCA did not hire him, Vassos also wrote to Isaac Levy, co-owner of radio station WCAU in Philadelphia, that same month, asking if he knew of any other manufacturers hiring designers. He told Levy, "I know I can design a line of radio cabinets that will give the radio personality, beauty and appeal without being too radical."[8] At this point, Vassos had not designed a radio, nor did he have any actual experience with electronics. His closest experience was likely working with engineers on the mechanical dolls in the windows of Kaufmann's department store in Pittsburgh. Vassos's participation in the design clinic, where he was a featured designer, his early experiments with plastic, and his interest in futuristic technology all contributed to his enthusiasm for the radio industry.

Radio purchases skyrocketed in the United States in the early 1930s. The number of American homes with a radio increased by 4.5 million over a three-year period. The radio was perhaps the most prominent and expensive piece of furniture in the home. Some 13.5 million more homes had radios than had telephones, and the number of radios in American homes exceeded the number of bathtubs by more than 5.8 million, according to statistics presented by the National Association of Broadcasters.[9] RCA's main competitor at the time was Philco, which sold less expensive radio models. RCA wanted to grow the Victor radio side of its business, as the company had lost money from 1929 to 1937.[10] The possibilities for synergy between the company's major growth areas were enormous, and RCA was poised to be the national leader in both radio broadcasting and radio manufacturing.

Manufacturers like RCA depended on designers to move their products in the newly opened radio market. Vassos realized that working for RCA would enable him to shape radio design for the emergent market and to establish himself as a major American designer. This was the ideal opportunity for him to compete against the other prominent industrial designers with whom he organized the first major conference on radio. Designers were competing for a role in this industry, with the major players fanning out to various radio manufacturers throughout the 1930s.

Walter Dorwin Teague contributed the embellished circular glass radio called the Nocturne, available in blue or rose glass from the Sparton Company. Norman Bel Geddes created the 1931 best-selling "lowboy" side chair radio for Philco and the plastic flag design Patriot radio for Emerson in 1939. Raymond Loewy created the New World radio for the Colonial Radio Company, with its base carrying a terrestrial globe covered by a map of the world. In England the radio was also being transformed, and the Ekco Company approached modern architect Serge Chermayeff to design a molded-plastic cabinet in 1933.[11] However, none of these designs took hold as a dominant radio style.

In his letter to Throckmorton, Vassos wrote, "The problems for radio design have been of constant interest to me since radios first entered the home, and I feel convinced I have a contribution to make."[12] Shortly after he had an interview with Throckmorton and during a period in which he observed RCA's operations, Vassos realized that RCA needed him for multiple reasons, beyond merely designing radio receivers.[13] In a follow-up letter to Throckmorton, he stated, "After two and one half days of intense activity . . . there is no doubt that there is a great need for a designer to shape up, guide, and hold together harmoniously your whole line of

"Spend Wisely." This 1933 advertisement shows the radio styles that Vassos wanted to modernize, including the arched cathedral style and the six-legged lowboy model. Private collection.

radio products, working along with your present design set-up, your sales promotion and engineering departments, as well as bringing in a fresh point of view."[14] On the strength of Vassos's letters and their meeting, Throckmorton offered Vassos the opportunity to prove himself.

Vassos's first assignment was to survey the field of radio display and sales through interviews with managers at selected retail locations.[15] He was asked to produce a report outlining problems with RCA's products and advise how to make them right. Immediately after he submitted his report, Vassos was placed on a retainer of twelve thousand dollars per year for two full days of work a week.[16] In a letter to Ross Treseder, he excitedly described his role at RCA, saying that, in addition to producing the survey, he was put "on a retainer fee to redesign their whole line, which was a job that all the designers in the country were after."[17]

His next effort for RCA was to go to the major department stores to evaluate how the radios were being marketed and to determine what was selling and what was not. As he wrote: "The next activity was to canvass the big furniture departments in three major cities: . . . at Altman's and A&S in Brooklyn, Wanamaker's, Gimbels, and Macy's," as well as Marshall Field's in Grand Rapids and Chicago.[18] He reported that better merchandise would enhance facility of use and improve appearance. In addition, Vassos found that an education program for both sales and engineering teams was desirable.[19] However, his first priority was to get rid of the popular cathedral arch shape, which he likened to a grave marker: "My first job with RCA was the elimination of the wooden tombstone radio."[20]

In various articles, Vassos expressed his ideas about what radio should look like. In 1931, prior to his hiring by RCA, he complained about having to tailor his work to the masses, but he recognized that "we are still far from arousing public enthusiasm" for modern design. He suggested that RCA develop "a fuller line of merchandise representing the major periods used in interior decoration in America. This is for the majority of people who still insist on traditional furniture."[21]

In an article titled "Radio Cabinet Design," published in *Electronics* magazine in 1934, Vassos continued to articulate his view of appropriate radio design. He maintained that radio should neither look like period furniture nor imitate modernism. "Both are affectations," he argued, "and neither is a true radio." He further elaborated that the designer's job is to "clean the surface and clear the radio of over-decoration while still retaining that so-necessary 'eye value' and preparing its form for the proper installation of the perfect speaker. The radio set has weathered the horrors of the modernistic, and I have no doubt but that it will muddle through neo-classicism, geometric modern, and romantic modern before it evolves into its true identity."[22] He ultimately believed that designers should "use the machine to create new materials, to evolve new forms, and to make possible new synthesis."[23] Finally, he anticipated "the realization of my idea that the radio must eventually derive its design and form from its function—which is sound."[24] He had articulated this ideal radio design, in which form follows function, in his first report to the company, where he proposed a "modern . . . and distinct device that breathes the spirit of to-day. . . . It is the importance of sound and its faithful reproduction that should be stressed, and it is these elements that will determine the design of the object."[25]

In Vassos's first styled radio receiver, he strove to define this modern radio form. The 1933 Model 210 was a wooden lowboy console with delicate art deco styling over the speaker and small round dials. Besides not fulfilling his dream of creating a functional modern radio, this receiver lacked automatic volume control and had a limited number of tubes, making it difficult to tune in weak stations, "which prevented its success in the rural districts."[26] In a letter to George Throckmorton written early in 1934, Vassos's tone was positive. He noted that RCA was making progress toward more modern radio styles. He also told Throckmorton about a project called "Vox Humana," which he was working on with Dr. Irving Wolff, a member of the research staff, to obtain better volume control and faithful sound reproduction.[27] No doubt he was concerned about his status at the company as well, given that RCA wanted to see quick results from its star consultant.

The company did retain him, offering a longer-term contract and a substantial raise in February 1934. Vassos became more involved in the styling department's organization and settled comfortably into his office at the Camden, New Jersey, facility.[28] He participated in a range of activities: advertising, planning the unification of building facilities, developing an educational program for engineers, managing sales staff, consolidating the design team, and streamlining work with the engineers. When he first arrived to work for RCA in Camden, three other designers were employed there: "Mr. Stevenson, Mr. Nicholas, and Mr. Vogel."[29] This team expanded to include two more.

Before Vassos joined the company, the usual procedure of a design plan involved the engineering department asking the styling team to help with a feature, such as a dial, to determine the size and graphic information, such as numbers and color, that would appear on the device. Vassos suggested reorganizing the procedure to involve the style team from the inception of a project. A series of tests with users made it clear that design issues went beyond superficial features to include the very processes through which the product was developed. Other information gathered on the product in the process of styling included length and type of use, which would affect the placement of dials; heat dissipation mechanisms; and other critical elements of functioning. This expanded notion of design encompassed the very creation of the product; design no longer served only as an adjunct to technological advancement. Vassos listed the major responsibilities of the styling department:

> Standardization of components, materials, and finishes; The Field in which they will be sold; Type of surroundings and location; Associated apparatus or auxiliaries; Location of visual units, dials, meters, etc.; Type and arrangement

of controls; Manufacturing methods and equipment; RCA family resemblance; Countries in which product will be sold; Selection of basic materials, plastics, metals, wood, synthetic materials, and colors; Number of hours or control manipulation; Whether one or more will be used side by side; Accessibility for servicing or dismantling; Heat dissipation allowance for tubes, transformers, and the like; Underwriters and local requirements; Finishes for components and unit; Trend; Safety; Method of shipping; etc.[30]

By the end of 1934, Vassos had made tremendous progress, simplifying the entire established lines of cabinets and creating a new line called the Neo-American, which led to reduced production costs and higher sales. His designs were popular among salespeople from the beginning. One department store representative praised his work: "Mr. Vassos has done more than 'style' a line of cabinets; he has helped rekindle enthusiasm and hope in many an anxious heart, and that is not art but psychology."[31]

Vassos explained his philosophy of radio design: "It was to be a simple statement expressing the medium. All extraneous features which were in contrast to this statement, such as the legs and over-ornamentation, were rejected."[32] The Model 6K10, a 1936 modernistic radio with "tubular metal" features, was among Vassos's first designs to express this "true radio" philosophy.[33] He essentially removed the radio receiver from its outer, furniture-like wooden casing and propped it on the floor with curving metal arches, doing away altogether with legs, which were Vassos's bête noire of radio design. The model marked a departure from the Gothic arches and ornate grilles of the "cathedral" or tombstone radio and created a vision of radio as a medium that should be associated with modern materials and shapes in a bold and dramatic way. The minimalist design of the radio, with sleek bends of tubular steel supporting the rectangular black receiver, was clearly influenced by the furniture style of Bauhaus designers such as Marcel Breuer, who incorporated industrial materials and geometric forms in his work. Two vertical metal pieces at the edges of the wooden radio speaker complemented the arches and drew attention to the radio's central feature—sound.

This design exemplified a stylistic pattern that defined Vassos's work for RCA, including the use of elemental lines, geometric shapes, and tonal colors. The radio had clearly marked tuning windows for easy navigation and a well-defined speaker section. Vassos pared the radio down to its function to provide sound while keeping in mind the user's requirement for utility and aesthetics. The audio aspect of the speaker, defined by its textured grille cloth, and the visual aspect—the knobs, dial, and cabinet—came together beautifully in this radio. The design must have been too severe for the company, however, since Vassos's ensuing designs for console radios were more traditional in form.

The following year, Vassos designed a new console radio. The Model 811K reflected the priority he placed on the console radio, with its legs that reached to the floor and

This Bauhaus-inspired floor model radio designed by John Vassos, Model 6K10, uses tubular metal to support the receiver, circa 1936. Photograph courtesy of Heritage Auctions (HA.com).

curved arms—stylistic features that he later brought to the 1939 television receiver. This elegant radio had a longer, lower chassis to blend in with a room's furnishings and vertical wooden slats over the speaker. The geometric profile of the console replaced the highboy and lowboy styles, with their thin, furniture-like legs. Clearly visible rectangular tuning windows, a boxy shape, and generously portioned knobs made the 811K and ensuing console radios different from what had come before. For example, the Bel Geddes–designed Philco consoles (1931) placed the radio receivers inside decorative cabinets with various-size legs, tiny tuning windows, and sliding doors.

By 1938, the reality of working for a major company had tempered Vassos's view toward radios. In an article titled "A Case for Radio Design," Vassos advocated that designers should cautiously experiment with radio design.[34] The radio he chose to illustrate modern design in this article stood safely within the margins of what would be acceptable to most consumers. It integrated both modern elements, such as streamlined curved edges and a console with no legs, and traditional elements, such as layered treatments of wood.

While wanting to bring modern design into the home, Vassos conceded that radios should come in a variety of decorative styles to make them acceptable to the American consumer. In a 1940 article for *Electrical Manufacturing*, he noted: "There is hardly a living room in America be it Georgian, French, provincial, Spanish or just home that does not have a radio, or phonograph, or both in it. And the reason for this is that the radio and phonograph companies adapted the styling of their product to fit the room in which it was going to be placed."[35] With profits in mind, Vassos suggested that RCA introduce period furniture along with the standard cabinetry, such as his curved Sheraton consoles with side-by-side radio and phonograph, making them quite wide. This American period line, which came in a range of wood colors and trims, enabled the radio to blend in with other living room furnishings. Vassos was pleased that these models "offer[ed] an opportunity for the use of a variety of fine wood finishes—maple, mahogany, oak, cedar, and some in pine."[36]

Regardless of the style, Vassos used visual approaches to differentiate the tuning and listening areas of the console radios. This was particularly true for the Model 811K and Model 813K four-band consoles, which offered remote control and came with attached armchairs. These radios featured the first commercially successful spread-band receiver for accurate tuning. Vassos also designed eighteenth-century-style radio cabinets that used various methods of hiding the components, such as the 1940 U-26, with a phonograph and radio tucked under the two-piece lid, and the U-45 model, with the phonograph and radio hidden behind the console doors.

Despite having to concede that console radios would not usher in the most modernistic designs, Vassos remained hopeful that plastic tabletop radios would. He wrote in his report to the company that "there still needs to be another line," one that would use the newest of synthetic materials for smaller radios. "You have missed an opportunity," he wrote, noting that "when wood is reduced to a small compass, it

This 1937 advertisement featuring NBC radio personalities W. C. Fields and "dummy" Charlie McCarthy with the Vassos-designed Model 811K wood console radio emphasizes the "thrill" of automatic push-button tuning, by hand or dummy or with armchair control *(inset)*. Private collection.

loses its rich significance and becomes cheap looking."[37] Vassos realized that Bakelite, which had been improved since he designed his Coca-Cola dispenser, could allow him to move away from the limitations of wood. Although many designers considered Bakelite to be the best material to interpret the modern form of radio, many consumers considered plastic dirty and were resistant to using it in their living rooms. In a letter to Throckmorton early in his tenure with RCA, Vassos emphasized the "absolute necessity of using synthetic compounds like Bakelite not only for trimming but for the whole radio."[38]

As early as 1933, his correspondence with the Bakelite Corporation revealed his hope that RCA would let him design that radio. Vassos wrote a detail-packed yet obscure letter to Allan Brown at Bakelite regarding the use of the material at RCA: "I cannot reveal the particulars of his recent tie up with one of the largest radio manufacturers but can say that of the many recommendations I am making and suggestions for radical changes, Bakelite comes in for good measure, for handles

A Case for Radio Design

Presented by John Vassos

"It has become almost a standard routine for industrial designers to take a fling at radio . . ."

The curved corners that were introduced by radio have been the inspiration for many new and pleasing motifs in furniture design.

IT HAS become almost standard routine for every industrial designer either to take a fling at radio design when commissioned by a manufacturer, or, if not so fortunate as to be commissioned, to take a fling at it anyway by writing an article telling what is wrong. This is not an article on radio design intended to end all such articles, but it does seek to set forth some conclusions made after a careful study over a period of five years, and of intensive and practical application to radio design.

I am much more interested in knowing why radios have gone through their various design stages and the psychological effect they have had upon the public than I am in why radios look the way they do. Socrates, who created the school of sophistry, always insisted at the beginning of a discussion on defining "what we are talking about," and I say, let's look into the function of radio and define what its purpose is. Radio is a device for the reproduction of sound in your home. Its mechanical aspect is incidental because its main function is to bring you sound clearly and correctly. Since when, therefore, has sound at any time had any definite pictorial identity or even form?

Since this publication reaches manufacturers and buyers primarily, we can discuss our problem with more frankness than if we were addressing the general public. Science has at last learned to reproduce sound effectively.

For the best tonal results engineers say we must provide a minimum baffle area for the loudspeaker, of six feet by six feet by two inches thick. The baffle area must be made of wood with speaker mounted in the center 18 inches away from the wall; or, a seven-foot multiple horn system that is now in use in moving picture theaters. So, it can be readily seen that the art of reproducing sound, limits us to such unruly forms that it is practically impossible to consider them as "home decoration." Just imagine this huge baffle board hanging in a living room, or a seven foot horn meandering through the parlor.

However, the limited baffle area that a radio cabinet now

"A Case for Radio Design," written by John Vassos for *Furniture Index*, March 1938. John Vassos Papers, Archives of American Art, Smithsonian Institution.

and surfaces as well as trimming particularly for the smaller cabinets."[39] Vassos also asked about the new Plaskon material, which he wanted to use in his radios. Brown wrote back immediately to say that the company was "extremely pleased to hear that you have recommended Bakelite to a large radio manufacturer, and when the job is done, will you send us a photograph?"[40] Jeffrey Meikle points out that Bakelite first gained widespread consumer acceptance with the "great radio do-it-yourself boom," when components made from phenolic resin or Bakelite entered American parlors and carved a niche in the domestic sphere for other plastics products.[41]

Vassos made it clear that RCA should invest in lightweight plastic receivers. As he wrote in his report, "It is in your smallest instruments that you have missed an opportunity to use synthetic materials like Bakelite, Formica, or some of the other lightweight compounds, where the introduction of metal could also be successfully brought in, and subtle harmonious color schemes could be worked out."[42] He re-iterated this complaint in a letter to Throckmorton: "As I see the potencies in our cabinetmaking set-up, we can build expensive cabinets cheaper than anyone else, but when it comes to the small stuff, outsiders have us licked."[43] He proposed table-top radios on which he could use a new speaker dial, which Walter R. G. Baker, vice president in charge of manufacturing and engineering, had asked him to design.[44]

Plastic radios were among Vassos's most successful designs. These included the Little Nipper line, the widely popular and affordable Model 15X, and the 96X series. In the designs, Vassos relied on streamlining, adding vertical or horizontal lines to the bodies of the radios. He used plastic molding to give the radios an aerodynamic appearance that was hard to achieve using wood. The 96X series radios released in 1939 were striking examples of the merging of geometric modern shapes with the rounded streamlined form. These radios, which featured curved speaker grilles, came in a range of neutral colors, including walnut, ivory, and black. Some models had contrasting knobs and speaker grilles to add visual impact. Push-button tuning was available, depending on the model. The tuning buttons were located cleverly near the dial window to differentiate them from the ridged knobs near the base. The unique setback design and the asymmetrical sweep of the grille make this one of the more distinguished American radio designs.[45]

The 1939 Little Nipper radios (the 9-SX series) stand out as some of the most elegant miniature plastic radios of the era. The crisp geometric shape of the square body blended with horizontal grooves and circles of contrasting, stacked large and small dials. The lack of a grille cloth and celluloid dial face gave the radio a clean look unlike anything else in the genre. Little Nippers came in eight lively colors and were marketed as low-cost radios for all the members of the family. With more than six different models, the Little Nippers constituted a long-lasting product line; they were marketed by RCA International in Canada well into the late 1950s.

Also designed by Vassos, the spare molded-plastic tabletop radios in the 9TX series, including 9TX-22 and 9TX-32, featured strong vertical lines, narrow louvres

Two views of the RCA Model 96X, which came in varying colors and with or without push buttons. The photographs show RCA Model 96X-11 ABOVE, which included push-button tuning, circa 1939, and RCA Model 96X-1 RIGHT, which was sold in a walnut finish. John Vassos Papers, Archives of American Art, Smithsonian Institution.

covering the speaker grille, and a square tuning window. The small grooved, round tuning knobs added contrast to the interplay of shapes and textures.

The best-selling 1941 15X Super Six plastic tabletop radio for RCA illustrates both the versatility of plastic and Vassos's modern style for a mass audience. The 15X was a splashy big radio with the characteristic neatly arranged buttons at the base. It had user-friendly features such as three different tuning arrangements, an edge-lighted dial, and a bull's-eye pointer. The automatic push-button tuning was cleverly placed on the upper surface of the radio, physically separating the different modes of tuning to avoid confusing the user.

Besides shaping the new material in unprecedented ways, Vassos explored different placements for grilles, knobs, and buttons. Bakelite was a good material to use: it was smooth and versatile, and it could conceal the inner workings of the machine.

The manufacturing process of compression molding led to even smoother, more streamlined shapes and fewer joints.[46] Other radio manufacturers had used Bakelite earlier, but they had retained the cathedral look, changing the material but not the established style. Vassos sought to create a small-format radio that expressed modernistic design, but in moderation. In a letter to Richard Bach of the Metropolitan Museum of Art, Vassos clarified his philosophy of radio design, saying that by using the term "progressive styling, I mean I advise against going into ventures too functional and of too pure design, Russell Wright's radio design for Lyric as an example."[47] He also did not push radio designs in a playful direction, as did Norman Bel Geddes, whose Patriot radio for Emerson, with its red, white, and blue color scheme, is now considered an icon of radio design. "Extraneous meaningless decoration has never helped any device," Vassos wrote.[48] In his letter to Bach, he

"Be Modern . . . with a Radio in Every Room!" A range of radios in the RCA 1940 catalog, including the molded-plastic 96X-1, the Little Nippers 9TX-31, 5X5-W, 40X-31, and the 5Q-55, all designed by Vassos. Private collection.

reiterated his functionalist association, specifically through his affiliation with Philip Johnson, the curator of MoMA's April 1934 *Machine Art* exhibition.

Vassos rejected extreme radio designs that "affect modernism by reason of their mechanical appearance, lack the essential quality of the true radio—that of freeing sound from the speaker."[49] He preferred to mix circles and squares in his designs, with clarified protruding knobs, and he used curved plastic to soften the edges. Soft, sweeping grilles over the speakers created long horizontal lines, tracing the tops of the radios to create elegant and asymmetrical receivers that were not harsh or "too radical."[50] His philosophy was to use modern design conservatively. As he explained,

EXTRA QUALITY **EXTRA PLEASURE** **EXTRA VALUE**

Get All 3 with an *RCA Victor* Radio

...at no extra cost!

MAKE your next radio an RCA Victor—and you'll be sure to get the extra quality and extra pleasure of the newest features of RCA Laboratories. These include RCA Victor Preferred Type Tubes ... stage of radio frequency amplification for better reception ... powerful Electrodynamic Speaker ... Built-in Magic Loop Antenna, and more than a score of others. All are yours in RCA Victor Super-Six Model illustrated at left. The low price of this and other RCA Victor models is proof of extra value!

FEWER, BUT FINER!

RCA Victor is cooperating to the full with National Defense Priority Requirements. Because of these requirements, shortages exist in certain raw materials needed for radios and phonograph-radios, and there will be a universal decrease in the number of instruments to be made. Hence RCA Victor products for the home will be *fewer*. But they will be *finer* than ever. For, as a result of defense work, of which, we, too, are doing our share, RCA Victor quality standards, always the highest, are now more exacting than ever.

A SERVICE OF THE RADIO CORPORATION OF AMERICA. In Canada, RCA Victor Co., Ltd., Montreal. Trademarks "Magic Brain", "RCA Victor" and "Victrola" Reg. U.S. Pat. Off. by RCA Mfg. Co., Inc. RCA Victor Radios and RCA Victrola Models may be purchased on C.I.T. Easy Payment Plan.

MODEL 28X5

TOP PERFORMANCE AT MODERATE COST...RCA Victor De Luxe *Super Eight* Model 28X5 has 9¼" Electeon Speaker providing super tone ... 8 RCA Victor Preferred Type Tubes for super performance ... Electric Tuning ... Overseas Dial with Spread-band Tuning ... American and Foreign reception, tremendous reserve power, AC-DC operation and many other splendid features.

RCA VICTOR 3-WAY ALL-PURPOSE PORTABLE ... "Pick-Me-Up" Model 25BP operates outdoors on batteries, indoors on either alternating or direct current. It has 5 RCA Victor Preferred Type Tubes...Permanent Magnet Dynamic Speaker ... Built-in Magic Loop Antenna ... Easy-reading, clock-type Dial ... Large knobs for easy tuning. Finished in durable two-tone tan simulated leather.

MODEL 25BP

Now...an amazing new way to play records!
The MAGIC BRAIN of RCA VICTROLA

Model V-215 also has 9-tube, push-button radio featuring new Teletube and new Audio System. Available in either walnut or mahogany for reasonable down payment.

MODEL V-215

1 NO LID TO LIFT ... NO ORNAMENTS TO MOVE ... Comfort level record loading with new Roll-Out Record Changer.

2 NO MORE OBJECTIONABLE MECHANICAL NOISES ... Exclusive Flexible Tone Bridge of new Magic Tone Cell ends objectionable "needle chatter."

3 REAL LIFE TO YOUR MUSIC...Jewel-Lite Scanner and Magic Tone Cell recreate each record with brilliant new fidelity of tone.

4 NO NEEDLES TO WORRY ABOUT ... Old-fashioned needles are entirely eliminated by tiny sapphire point of Jewel-Lite Scanner.

5 RECORDS LAST INDEFINITELY ... By exerting astoundingly light pressure on records Magic Tone Cell gives them extraordinarily long life.

6 RECORDS PLAY, STOP, CHANGE—AUTOMATICALLY ... Completely automatic Record Changer even shuts motor off when program is over. Your enjoyment is uninterrupted, complete.

"Get All 3 with an RCA Victor Radio!" Advertisement showing the popular appeal of the Super Six RCA radio designed by John Vassos, circa 1941. Private collection.

"A program of gradual change must be laid out and followed because any radical change, even if it be for the better, is dangerous for any standard product on the market. The public will not accept it."[51]

The "gleaming plastic" New Yorker radios that Vassos designed for RCA in 1939–40 marked a departure from the streamlined styling of the Bakelite models. Among tabletop radios, the New Yorkers were truly original in the size and centering of their speaker grilles. These radios were marketed primarily for their distinctive look, and with their array of features—including international shortwave band and big, edge-lighted dials—they were "designed for listening in the modern way." Although all the advertising copy for these radios used the terminology of modern design, the ad text for the Model 5QS emphatically described it as "a masterpiece of modernity created along simple but dynamic lines." Strikingly, the New Yorker models made visual reference to RCA's larger ambitions—the television. The prominent square speaker grilles in the centers of the radios set the stage for the radio's transformation into the television set. The Model 6Q8 clearly resembles the Model TT-5 television receiver.

Each New Yorker had a dark square embedded in a lighter body with an edged top. The 6Q8 and the 6Q7 were clean-looking boxes, devoid of "speed whiskers" or decorative horizontal lines. They were marketed both domestically and to the South American market. The radio's shortwave reception and its ability to withstand extreme heat made it suitable for South American climates. Selected as the best "1940 plastic expression of contemporary radio" by *Architectural Forum,* the 5Q6 sold more than 120,000 sets.[52] The 5Q6, with its checkered speaker grille and molded curves, featured streamlined detailing and dedicated knobs. This radio was a slimmed-down version of another model offered that year—the heavier molded-plastic 6Q1, which had wider knobs.[53] The 1940 6Q1, with its molded Bakelite colored to resemble wood, featured broadcast and two shortwave bands. Each of these radios featured a vertical crease at the top, drawing the eye to the speaker grille, and a wide, beveled tuning screen positioned for easy viewing.

Some of Vassos's most striking radios used a range of woods to create texture. These radios offered various placements for the tuning windows and knob apparatus, but continuity across them was achieved through Vassos's use of well-defined geometric shapes. This includes the clean-lined 7Q4 shortwave tabletop receiver with glossed wood and the handsome 1940 Q-33. The latter radio weighed more than thirty pounds, but the marbleized wood and wide, light-colored speaker grille lightened the appearance. The 1941 tabletop Q-14, with its striated bands of highly polished wood, achieved a luxurious effect. The boxy 1942 Q-31 featured a marbleized texture on its speaker grille to contrast with the layered wood. Promotional

OPPOSITE This advertisement features the 1940 RCA Victor New Yorker model radios, which "embody the genius of John Vassos, noted designer." Model 6Q7 is at top, followed by Model 6QU with chrome bands and a phonograph, Model 6Q8 (which resembles the Model TT-5 television), and the Model 5QS. John Vassos Papers, Archives of American Art, Smithsonian Institution.

DESIGNED FOR LISTENING IN THE MODERN WAY!

THE 1940 RCA Victor NEW YORKER MODELS

THE RADIOS OF TOMORROW . . . *TODAY!*

Glamorous as Broadway . . . modern in styling . . . marvels of radio engineering . . . "New Yorkers" match their name. Cabinets of gleaming plastic, in brown, ivory, maroon, and black, embody the genius of John Vassos, noted designer. They harmonize with their surroundings in the most artistic homes . . . supply an added note of beauty.

Short-wave and local programs are brought in with rare fidelity by these wonder radios—even when signals are faint. Two latest-type frequency-focusing Radiotrons keep the "New Yorker" tuned to the frequency of the station selected. A big edge-lighted dial makes tuning easy. New up-to-the-minute circuits bring in hard-to-get programs. Other features include extra-sensitive speaker, tropic-proofing throughout.

You must see and hear these new radios to appreciate their matchless tonal qualities and beauty. Come in for a "New Yorker" demonstration. It will be a pleasure for you and for us. No obligation, of course.

D E A L E R ' S   N A M E

"NEW YORKER" MODEL 6Q7: A 6-tube radio with the flow and sweep characteristic of modern thought and expression . . . yet sufficiently conservative to harmonize with any surroundings. Among its distinctive features are 6" Electrodynamic Loudspeaker, Magic Eye; Edge-lighted, Straight-line Dial; Continuously Variable Tone Control; New-type Tubes, Simplified Plug-in Victrola Connection; Improved Short-wave Reception. Tuning range: 540-1720, 2300-7000, 7000-22,000 kcs., including the international short-wave bands (49, 40, 31, 25, 19 and 16 meters).

"NEW YORKER" MODEL 6QU: An amazing performer in a combination radio-phonograph table model . . . The pride of the master craftsman; the joy of the music lover and radio enthusiast. Here is a 6-tube radio and 10" and 12" record-playing phonograph which has no counterpart today. Some of its features: Improved Short-wave Reception; Magic Eye; radically new and improved circuit design; Self-starting Phonograph Motor; Crystal Pickup; Special Tropic-treated Chassis and Cabinet. Tuning range same as 5Q5.

"NEW YORKER" MODEL 6Q8: The result of the inspired efforts of the modern stylist, engineer and master craftsman, this 6-tube table model meets the demands of the most discriminating buyer. Just review a few of its features: New-type Tubes; Magic Eye; Improved Short-wave Reception; Continuously Variable Tone Control; 6" Electrodynamic Loudspeaker, Edge-lighted, Straight-line Dial; Simplified Plug-in Victrola Connection. Tuning range: 145-405, 540-1720, 5800-18,000 kcs., including the international short-wave bands (49, 40, 31, 25, 19 and 16 meters) and the European long-wave band.

"NEW YORKER" MODEL 5Q5: A masterpiece of modernity created along simple but dynamic lines . . . Modern plastic cabinets in ivory, black, maroon or brown . . . Edge-lighted, Full-Vision Dial . . . Tuning range: 540-1700, 2300-7000, 7000-22,000 kcs., including the international short-wave bands (49, 40, 31, 25, 19 and 16 meters). MODEL 5Q6—Same as 5Q5, except for AC-DC, 220-volt operation only. MODEL 5Q8—Same as 5Q5, except for tuning range 145-405, 540-1720, 5800-18,000 kcs., which includes reception on the European long-wave band, and 110-220-volt AC-DC power supply, and chrome metal grille.

The Vassos-designed RCA Model 6Q1 radio, circa 1939. John Vassos Papers, Archives of American Art, Smithsonian Institution.

photos and advertisements featured Vassos with his rendering for the New Yorker series, his hand hovering over a knob.

A 1942 *Fortune* magazine ad for Durez plastics highlighted Vassos's New Yorker radio.[54] Historian Jeffrey Meikle notes that Durez ran a series of sophisticated advertisements featuring individual designers—including Henry Dreyfuss, Egmont Arens, and Donald Deskey—in order to convince manufacturers to use plastics as they shifted from military to consumer products after World War II.[55] Durez tapped Vassos in the late 1930s and featured his designs in the May 1939 issue of its company magazine. The magazine praised him for his "many contributions to functionalism" and noted that "his most recent accomplishments in the art of plastics in the field of radio have brought a new high to the medium."[56] The company hoped to strengthen its brand by tapping into postwar optimism and visually linking Durez with international economic success, such as the opening up of Pan-American trade. The Durez ad featuring Vassos used a map to convey the distance covered by this powerful radio's international shortwave.

Among Vassos's most iconic designs is not a radio but the RCA Victor Special model phonograph, which is widely held in museum decorative arts collections. This

Vassos in his office at RCA Camden with a rendering of a radio in the RCA New Yorker series, circa 1939. John Vassos Papers, Archives of American Art, Smithsonian Institution.

versatile suitcase phonograph could be used indoors or outdoors, as it was powered by a hand crank. The phonograph, which played 78 rpm records, featured Vassos's trademark minimalist knobs and the linear, streamlined needle that he incorporated in widely produced phonograph models. Inside the exterior's shiny aluminum streamlined shape, the interior was uncluttered and clean. The pronounced speaker grille gave height and added drama to the otherwise flattened interior. The Special was offered in different models, with red velvet detailing and without. The red velvet detailing, used on the back of the cover, the turntable, the interior speaker, and the tip of the crank, added visual interest and drew the user's attention to key elements. Another visual treat for users was that they could watch the records spin on the reflective sheet at the back of the phonograph. Vassos also gave thought to storage needs for the user on the go, adding folders with quick-grab tags, so that users could

JOHN VASSOS, *Industrial Designer*

HOW TO LOCATE NEW YORK, N. Y., on the map of South America!

Accustomed as we are to constantly improved design . . . what could be more commonplace to the average American citizen than a fine, streamlined table-model radio?

Yet wire that radio for short wave reception . . . distribute it throughout South America . . . tune it to *our* good-neighbor broadcasts—and you're helping to write the future history of Pan-American commercial relations . . bringing the broadcasting studios of New York as close to Rio as Copacabana beach!

But let John Vassos tell you about this "commonplace" table-radio . . .

"Collaborating with the RCA Manufacturing Company, Inc., I designed this radio set especially for use in Latin America. In experimenting with different materials for the housing, we finally selected a Durez plastic.

It met every design requirement; proved particularly economical on a mass-production basis; possessed the durability to withstand the rigors of deep-water transportation and the extreme differences in climate between points of manufacture and distribution. Not only were sales outstandingly successful, but also we were able to establish a definite Latin American preference for a U. S. radio over competitively priced foreign sets."

To business and industry . . . planning for greater Pan-American trade after the Victory . . . this radio points up Durez plastics afresh as the materials of "tomorrow." Their versatility and efficiency are understood in any language. Would you like to keep abreast of plastics developments? A request on your letterhead will bring *Durez Plastics News* to your desk every month.

DUREZ... *plastics that fit the job*

DUREZ PLASTICS & CHEMICALS, INC. **DUREZ** 1025 WALCK ROAD, N. TONAWANDA, N. Y.

"How to locate New York, N.Y., on the map of South America!" Advertisement for Durez Plastics featuring the designer and a New Yorker model radio. *Fortune*, May 1942. Private collection.

ON THE SALESROOM FLOOR

At RCA, Vassos maintained his commitment to defining the role of industrial designer not just as a stylist but also as a salesman. He realized that in order to sell the new designs he had created, he had to educate people about good design so that this information would be "followed through to the point of sale." Education was one of his favorite ways of getting people to appreciate modernistic design, and he found RCA receptive to this approach. In the fall of 1936 (and possibly at other times) he gave a series of lectures aimed at teaching managers and sales representatives the basic principles of design.[66] Like a minicourse in visual literacy, the lessons were intended to convey the value of design and to emphasize that the radio designs were works of art.

Vassos drew much of the material for his lectures on the history of art and design from his earlier talks on the modern art lecture circuit that followed the publication of his illustrated books. As an educator, he sought to give sales managers a vocabulary that would allow them to articulate new ideas about style. In one lecture, he explained the importance of language in educating the customer. He advised the sales staff to use specific words:

> Use correct conversational lingo [that] will make your speech sound authoritative. . . . Avoid the word "modernistic." This word has been misused to be euphemistic with "futuristic." Avoid the word "functionalism"—it is unhappily an anathema. Use such expressions as "simplified form, . . . well arranged, . . . beautiful woods, beautiful design, beautifully styled, of the modern age, . . . contemporary expression of artistry, . . . smart, . . . a functional chassis, . . . a functional speaker."[67]

This simplified vocabulary list would help salespeople describe the special qualities of the new design. Vassos's full list included many euphemisms for "modernistic," including "simplified form," "in good taste," "well arranged," "contemporary expression of artistry," "of the contemporary age," "horizontalism," "functionality," and "smart." He also suggested that salespeople use words that conveyed the dangers of the nonmodernistic and evoked mental distress, like "disturbing surfaces" and "badly thought out," to describe competitors' brands.[68]

On one occasion, at a meeting of sales managers, Vassos gave tips on more covert forms of psychological manipulation. He drew on his knowledge of psychoanalysis to describe the importance of involving the customer's body in the sale by having the customer move around the radio—a technique similar to that used by magicians to get an audience involved. In a letter to one manager, he wrote:

> I know the district managers are coming Monday. . . . Why don't you ask the star salesmen . . . to come down and go through the motions of the simplified method of selling Magic Voice, which I worked out in Philadelphia three

weeks ago? Since that time letters have come in from the stores applying it—Gimbel's, Litt's, and Strawbridge & Clothier's—proving that it actually works without a lot of paraphernalia or any cost. Because its psychological effect is this: the salesman, to prove his point, proceeds to command the prospective buyer to bend down, to stand up, to bend down to the other set; this sort of an approach is similar to a magician's in the theater. . . . After they have taken an actual part in this routine, their resistance is bound to be weakened, and they are far readier to say yes.[69]

While it may seem crass to manipulate customers' bodies to weaken their sales resistance, this approach reveals the extent to which Vassos saw himself as a technician of human behavior, a self-perception that motivated most of his styling decisions. He wanted to convince the customer to buy his radio, and he applied a variety of techniques to accomplish that, including being a persuasive and educational salesman. On each level, Vassos was involved in predicting and shaping the needs of the customer.

Writing *Phobia* gave Vassos the confidence of a psychologist, despite his not having any training beyond his association with Harry Stack Sullivan. Vassos did all he could to take advantage of his psychological knowledge, which, as a 1934 *Fortune* article about the nation's top industrial designers noted, distinguished him from other designers. According to Vassos's colleague Carroll Gantz:

> Though Vassos was not a tall man, he made up for this with his personality and leadership qualities, and dominated meetings with his dynamism. It was these qualities that landed him at RCA in 1933 to organize the design organization there and produce results, even as he continued his private practice.[70]

By 1937, RCA offered an expanding range of radios in modernist and traditional styles, as an advertising poster for that year's radio collection described. The offerings included "a complete choice of authentically designed cabinets for every type of home furnishing, including exquisite 18th century cabinets, ultra-modern console, and continental style models."[71] New radio forms consisted of "superb sets for unwired homes" and models like the 9K, with a "Magic Brain and Magic Eye." The 9K, named for its nine tubes, aired weather reports, domestic programs, practically all foreign programs, and calls of police, airplane pilots, and amateur radio operators.[72]

In his work for RCA, Vassos sought to bridge the gap between the simple yet harsh cubism advocated by the "pure" design movement and the bright colors and bulbous shapes of popular streamlined radios. A photograph from around 1939 shows Vassos proudly leaning against a display of RCA tabletop radios that reflect the visual coherence across the entire line. The radios all share Vassos's trademark

John Vassos (*front*) and RCA executives with a selection of RCA radios, including many of the export radios Vassos designed. Note the clean geometric designs, wide rectangular grilles, and evenly placed tuning buttons across the line, circa 1939. John Vassos Papers, Archives of American Art, Smithsonian Institution.

large dials and wide rectangular grille cloths. These radios, with their simple shape, could be flawlessly integrated into any living room scheme, and the spacious, screen-like areas of the speakers also seemed to anticipate David Sarnoff's dream to "add sight to radio sound" with television. Vassos saw himself as a member of a national design movement, not just a stylist pandering to mass taste. RCA boasted about its alliance with artists and even mentioned the styling of its radio knobs in marketing literature. As one promotional piece read, "RCA Victor master stylists and the famous consulting authorities retained by RCA Victor have evidenced their ability and art in the cabinet and dial styling of this year's model."[73]

In his radio designs Vassos used streamlined features, like curving edges, rounded knobs, and horizontal lines, but these designs looked nothing like the formulaic shapes of his streamlined bicycle or streamlined stove. At RCA Vassos used a range of methods to both "improve" and "simplify" the radio, terms he viewed as synonymous. Vassos was extremely imaginative and creative in his approach, which contributed to his success. He thought "outside the box," as it were, and occasionally

Vassos designed this handsome wooden tabletop radio with multiple shortwave bands, Model Q33, circa 1940. John Vassos Papers, Archives of American Art, Smithsonian Institution.

came up with outlandish suggestions along with iconic ones, such as horizontal tuning, remote control, and push buttons. Among his suggestions in an early report to RCA was to add a lock for radio buyers who suffered from "radiophobia" and those fussy people who do not want anyone to touch their radios. Above all, Vassos conceived of home electronics' smooth integration into a functional "entertainment system where ease of operation, acoustic qualities, and visibility will be the prime objectives, and meaningless decoration will play no part."[74] His ideal would be realized two years later in the Living Room of the Future, presented in the America at Home Pavilion at the 1939–40 New York World's Fair.

4. DESIGNED FOR ELECTRICITY
VASSOS'S ARCHITECTURAL INTERIORS

In the 1930s, the massive modernization of businesses kept designers like Vassos busy with architectural renovations. According to Jeffrey Meikle, a survey conducted by *Architectural Forum* revealed that from 1924 to 1938 three-quarters of the nation's commercial establishments conducted modernizing efforts.[1] Industrial designers' wide participation in this effort suggests that their services were still affordable for small businesses. With their understanding of consumer engineering, designers showcased their multiple talents by transforming physical spaces and creating total environments, where dominant themes coordinated all elements.[2] Vassos, like many modernist designers, was influenced by the concept of *Gesamtkunstwerk*, or the idea that all parts of an architectural scheme can be orchestrated as a seamless whole under the direction of a single inspired imagination.[3] This ideal, related to the integration of art forms, goes back to the nineteenth century and was adopted by a range of architects, including Charles Rennie Mackintosh in Scotland and Frank Lloyd Wright in the United States, who argued for an alliance of architecture and design. It informed Vassos's all-inclusive approach to interior design, from store display windows and hot dog stands to private apartments.

Like other artists who would become industrial designers, such as Raymond Loewy, Donald Deskey, and Norman Bel Geddes, who created dramatic window displays for Franklin Simon's department store in New York City, John Vassos sold his services to department stores that wanted modern displays to complement their art deco merchandise. The wide glass window, made possible by the greater availability of sheet glass, revolutionized the genre. Earlier shopwindow schemes were often unimaginative responses to scarcity, featuring artless piles of goods stacked high.

As cultural historian Neil Harris notes, the new art of commercial display that emerged in the late 1920s sought to portray luxury, fashion, and style through design. A far cry from the previous piles of merchandise, the new window displays told stories of the artistry of unique products and the consumers who bought them.[4] Influenced by the styles exhibited at the 1925 decorative arts exposition in Paris, department store owners brought art deco design and display into merchandising. Ruth Vassos, who was styling windows for Gimbels department store, was an early adopter. In 1925, she was clamoring to bring posters from the Paris show to the store's windows.[5] A 1926 exhibition at the Metropolitan Museum of Art included more than four hundred objects from the Paris event. The modern department store window began to be characterized by carefully lighted singular items rather than by a jumble of discount merchandise or elaborate scenery.

Vassos claimed to have created the first modern Christmas window display in the United States with his 1929 commission for Kaufmann's department store in Pittsburgh. His creation, in fifteen windows wrapped around the edge of the storefront, featured many toys, including animals in motion and boxed sets, arranged in a composition of contrasting geometric shapes.[6] A bi-level step decorated with stars created visual unity across the windows. The display was not particularly Christmassy, but it did enable the store to highlight individual toys as gift ideas. Vassos's work on the Kaufmann windows featured cubist shapes, multilayered spaces, and architectonic arrangements of toys with skyscraper motifs. Each toy was allotted its own frame or multiples were artfully stacked to emphasize the packaging design. Vassos took owner Edgar Kaufmann Sr.'s direction in creating the modernistic windows; as he later described his experience: "I was invited to Pittsburgh to do storefront windows. Edgar Kaufmann was a very elegant guy with a lot of imagination. He said the kids want a modern Christmas."[7] In addition to the display, Vassos produced an "animal circus" for children during the Christmas season, with the characters acted by store personnel.

He also designed the window display for the toy department, which delighted the eye with its many shapes and textures. In the left side of the window, stacked square boxes created skyscraper shapes and complemented the blocks at the base. Rectangular board game boxes were artfully placed in a circular cabinet in the background, while a silly stuffed cat with big eyes sat next to a tilted house in the front of the display.

With the slogans "Good design is good business" and "Modernism is design," Kaufmann's was among the first department stores to hire modernists. Edgar Kaufmann Sr. was an early champion of a distinctly modern aesthetic in display window and store design. He aggressively promoted the work of modern designers, including Frank Lloyd Wright, who received more than a dozen commissions from the Kaufmann family, including their famous home, Fallingwater.[8] According to historian William Leach, in 1929 Kaufmann also hired artist Boardman Robinson to create murals for his store.[9]

In his window designs for Kaufmann's, Vassos incorporated theatrical techniques, such as innovative lighting with spotlights and colorful backdrops.[10] His window

Vassos designed this store window display for the toy department at Kaufmann's department store, circa 1929. John Vassos Papers, Archives of American Art, Smithsonian Institution.

displays demonstrated the importance of proper lighting in creating a balanced presentation. As he explained in a letter to the editor of *Display* magazine: "Ninety-seven percent of the [store] windows in America are badly constructed and architecturally wrong. . . . It is erroneous to think that windows must always be lighted from the top."[11] Despite such innovation, modernistic windows did not always appeal to the public's taste. Many people found them too stark and angular, preferring window displays with richly decorated mannequins. Vassos more successfully applied his ideas of planned lighting and shaped environments to his designs for restaurants.

MAKING FAST FOOD ELEGANT: VASSOS'S RESTAURANT DESIGNS

Licensing requirements prevented industrial designers from treading on the turf of architects. Vassos and his peers turned to interior design, where they could shape physical space according to modernist and sales-driven principles.[12] Vassos first ventured into interior design with his application of his design philosophy to two New

York restaurants, Nedick's hot dog stand in 1930 and the Rismont Restaurant and Tearoom at 1410 Broadway in Manhattan in 1931. These restaurants' transformation reveals the extent to which modernistic decor became the norm in the early 1930s.

Following the publication of his book *Phobia,* Vassos was eager to apply the psychology of interior design, and the restaurant provided the perfect setting for him to use these ideas to stimulate sales. The concepts that he presented in *Phobia* influenced how he designed restaurant interiors and allowed him to justify his decisions later in trade publications. He was most interested in the psychology of urban dining and creating a setting that would encourage customers to buy more food but not linger too long, as table turnover meant more profits. He compared dining to theater. Drawing on his work in *Phobia,* he wrote:

> Should the artist for instance be called upon to design a restaurant, the achievement of beauty is not his only objective. He must bear in mind that a great number of people suffer from topophobia—stage fright—and his aisles and seating and lighting arrangements must be conceived with this in mind, if the place is to be successful.[13]

In 1930, Vassos redesigned Nedick's at Broadway and 47th Street using the idea of restaurant eating as theater-in-the-round. Unlike most "fast-food" stands, Nedick's had an integrated interior; customers had to walk inside to buy their food, as they did at the wildly successful Nathan's Famous Brooklyn hot dog eatery. Vassos's redesign took density and traffic into account and aimed to increase sales through a standardized eating experience. To suggest speed, Vassos added a curvilinear counter and one of the first freestanding counters for soda service.

This concept was impressive enough to lead the Coca-Cola Corporation to tap Vassos. Besides hiring him to design a beverage container, the company employed him to convince Nedick's management to sell "something other than orangeade."[14] Vassos anticipated that the restaurant would be a new kind of bar for soda and eventually for beer, once Prohibition was repealed. He imagined the possibilities in a letter to Ross Treseder of the Coca-Cola Corporation: "I feel that a dignified modern and freshly conceived place, keeping the good features of the Nedick stands plus what the Nedick stands lack, would be sure fire. It couldn't help but be a paying proposition providing it sells the best Coca-Cola drink on Broadway . . . and a good sized glass of beer."[15] He even went so far as to build in a polished keg with a black Formica background and base decorated with white metal trim, for "near beer or possibly real beer."[16] Vassos was prescient in realizing the importance of soft drinks in the growing consumer culture, although sales of the drinks did not really take off until the postwar rise of the fast-food chain. At Nedick's, Vassos hoped his design would become part of a standardized restaurant chain, but it never did.

Nedick's refreshment bar, with paneling, ceiling and bar of Bakelite Laminated. The colors used are black, green, orange and cream. John Vassos, designer.

John Vassos says . . .

. . ."Out of the union of art and industry one thing has been born— beauty of design. It is beginning to be accepted as a practical necessity in industry"

John Vassos, New Canaan, Conn., is a designer of repute in many fields. He has added sales compelling beauty to such commonplace products as stoves and turnstiles, and also has created designs of conspicuous artistic merit for furniture, windows, floor coverings, and containers.

★

Don't miss the Bakelite Exhibit when you visit the Century of Progress Exposition.

WITH THE PUBLIC there is a conscious or sub-conscious preference for the beautiful. The weighing scale, gasoline pump, or refreshment bar of unusual beauty of design always entices coins from more pockets. People place more confidence in goods that are pridefully offered for sale.

The artist-designer adds to the most utilitarian products, a form and color that appeals to the eye, and makes them stand apart from those of competitors as something superior. He also realizes that beauty of form must be expressed in appropriate materials. Like Mr. Vassos who used Bakelite Laminated in Nedick's refreshment bar, many designers have found in this and other Bakelite Materials practical mediums for the economical interpretation of their ideas.

Bakelite Materials of laminated and plastic types are strong, durable, resist wear, moisture, and most chemicals. They are obtainable in black, brown, and many colors, and have a rich finish. Their use often leads to production economies. Regardless of what your product may be, you will be interested in the story told in Booklets 26L and 26M, "Bakelite Laminated" and "Bakelite Molded". A line from you will bring copies.

BAKELITE CORPORATION, 247 Park Ave., New York • 43 East Ohio St., Chicago
BAKELITE CORPORATION OF CANADA, LTD., 163 Dufferin Street, Toronto, Ontario

BAKELITE

THE MATERIAL OF A THOUSAND USES

"John Vassos says . . ." Advertisement for Bakelite featuring John Vassos, who, as the text explains, used Bakelite Laminated in the paneling, ceiling, and bar of Nedick's concession bar in black, green, orange, and cream. *Sales Management,* July 15, 1933. Courtesy of the Library of Congress.

Vassos's design for Nedick's heralded a new age of dining centered on the counter and with the strong use of color as an enticement. At the restaurant's orange-and-cream Formica platform, two employees dispensed food and drinks. Without the burden of having to walk to and from tables, the employees were able to serve thousands of customers. Besides speeding up dining, Vassos's design took into account the factors of time and distance required to serve the customers. As he explained, the workers' hands moved faster in an enclosed space.[17] In addition to improving speed of service, Vassos created a packaged experience by designing all the restaurant's details, including employee uniforms, which were made out of a light-green washable material that matched the color of the company's logo. To add to the elfin "employee at your service" look, the pants legs were cropped above the knees, and the pants were belted with black patent leather. The matching hat, made of straw for use in the summer, had a band of black patent leather.[18]

As Vassos explained, the beauty of the restaurant would help sales: "With the public there is a conscious or sub-conscious preference for the beautiful. The weighing scale, gasoline pump, or refreshment bar of unusual beauty of design always entices coins from more pockets. People place more confidence in goods that are pridefully offered for sale."[19] Specifically, Vassos used architectural features such as lighting, color, and furniture to shape the dining experience, making the restaurant more inviting and the display of food and drink more appealing. Proper lighting in a restaurant could shift the customer's mood. Vassos explained, "The idea was to light up the stand and create the feeling of excitement, color and light and brightness."[20] While the service counter was brightly lit, the rest of the restaurant was not. Vassos felt strongly that the customer should be enveloped in a soothing environment. "When one is in a hurry and wants to cool his throat . . . he wants to be disassociated from the unpleasant things of his daily life—he does not want be reminded of the white tiles of the subway."[21] Vassos also considered the relationship of the restaurant to the people passing by on the street. He found that he was able to create the most pleasant and least intrusive atmosphere when "the light [was] directly focused into the interior and on the counter rather than thrown out into the street or on the people who were eating. This is most important."[22] As Vassos said, customers do not like being "in the limelight."[23] This was an improvement over the old eating space, where "the food looks as though it were spread on a table on the sidewalk" because of the interaction between the people and the light inside and outside the restaurant.[24] As these quotes reveal, Vassos clearly analyzed the impact of the space's whole visual range on the eating experience.

The restaurant's central, curving counter was made out of a seamless surface of Bakelite laminate. Bakelite's colorful synthetic resin was perfectly suited for creating an exciting as well as clean effect. The slippery surface could be quickly and easily wiped, making it increasingly popular as an interior architectural material. Vassos used Bakelite plastic generously in the restaurant's paneling, ceiling, and bar. The material's bright-orange colors created visual harmony and drew attention to the restaurant's iconic sweet orange drink.[25] In addition, the counter was edged with chrome trim, and its black "kick plate" visually emphasized horizontality while adding a serious edge to the playful design. Nedick's thrived on the East Coast until the 1970s, and today it is remembered nostalgically by New Yorkers as much for its interior design, bright lights, and sparkling orange counter as it is for its fruity citrus drink.[26]

For the Rismont Tearoom, at Broadway and 38th Street, the Garis brothers, Greek restaurateurs, asked Vassos to create a unique, modern restaurant in a heavily trafficked area where many restaurants were located. To accommodate their request, Vassos gutted the former restaurant on the site and created a tightly organized space with dramatic lighting featuring fixtures by the Egli Company. The restaurant departed from the usual tearoom style of quaint Spanish, Italian, or English motifs, with an entire decorative scheme based on the importance of light. Specifically, the Rismont was one of the first restaurants in the country to use indirect lighting inserted into the architectural structure, including the beams and along ledges.[27] Magazines such as *Pencil Points* and *Lighting* praised Vassos's innovative use of lighting.[28]

As with Nedick's, Vassos approached designing the Rismont dining experience from the perspective of the customer and drew on his theories of consumer psychology to shape the space. To attract customers from the street, he spread out the letters of the restaurant's name on the exterior in wide neon lights, using big, modernistic, sans serif forms at an angle reminiscent of contemporary motion picture credits. These curving lights hugging the edge of the restaurant created a sense of motion and excitement. Inside, a specially designed drop gallery was installed over the fifty-foot eating counter to act as a light conductor as well as an air ventilator and air conditioner.[29] Vassos illuminated this drop gallery with sweeping, dramatic lighting, which became the motif of the restaurant and its primary unifying feature. To diversify the floor plan, he partitioned the room into three distinctly lit sections. Ranges of light highlighted each section, appearing in such unexpected places as behind the bar, in the walls, and above the tables. Vassos was not the only designer to use lighting to shape the modern restaurant during this period. As Arthur Pulos points out, the desire to control and manipulate light had a profound impact on the architecture of public spaces in the 1930s.[30]

Vassos used new materials and decorative flourishes to unify the restaurant's diverse elements. He covered the seats in rose-colored Fabrikoid and replaced rectangular wooden display cases and ornately molded baseboards with a single glass display counter featuring brass fittings.[31] The counter was made of black Carrara Glass. This material, originally used for utilitarian purposes such as refrigerator linings, became popular among architects and designers in the 1920s for its slick, shiny appearance.[32] For solitary diners, Vassos added a counter that spanned the width of the room to maximize the number of people the restaurant could accommodate. The dramatic counter swept the tearoom's length and ended in a full curve. Delectable lighting fixtures shimmered above the counter. Despite the beautiful

A Small Modern Restaurant

By John Vassos

Space for a new soda fountain and tea room restaurant had been contracted for at 1410 Broadway, Manhattan. Conservative plans had been drawn up for the interior, and at this point I, as a designer, was called in to make recommendations. The competition is very keen in this section, and it was necessary to do a restaurant that was different if business was to be lured away from established places. It has always been my contention that a so-called modern interior does not necessarily belong to any particular stratum of life or of business—it is as good on Broadway as on Park Avenue, and vice versa. So without hesitation, I immediately recommended a complete change of plans to an interior of the modern type.

The shape of the room was ugly and difficult—funnel-shaped, wide in front and narrowing greatly in the back. Interest had to be created, as the room itself held none. I proceeded to divide the room in three definite light sections, treating the soda fountain and counter as a separate unit. I created an architectural light beam that runs almost the entire length of the counter, giving a feeling of interest and intimacy to the counter at the same time lighting it completely with no shadows, the lights being behind opaque glass. (The upper part of this beam holds the air-cooling system and the air circulates constantly through this, purifying the entire room and keeping it cool.)

The room held four structural columns, clumsily placed as one usually finds them in buildings today. These presented a problem, but I accepted them as part of my decorative scheme rather than trying to hide them. Their solidity I killed by lighting them with perpendicular troughs of light and the solid mass of plaster and steel became a shaft of light. From these columns I started my divisions of the ceiling. A trough eighteen inches in depth, closely wired with bulbs giving an almost perfectly even light radius, stretched semi-circularly until the light thrown from this trough faded and the light from the next similarly constructed trough began (this can be more easily understood by looking at the photograph on page 890). The installation of the lighting and the troughs and beams presented several problems, one of which was very amusing. The ironworkers claimed the job was theirs, the plasterers claimed it was in their

EXTERIOR VIEW AT NIGHT—RISMONT RESTAURANT, BROADWAY, NEW YORK
DESIGNED BY JOHN VASSOS—LAURENCE AND JOHN SCACCHETTI, ARCHITECTS

[889]

surroundings, the restaurant owners needed high-volume sales to maximize their profits, so Vassos intentionally made the seats slightly uncomfortable to ward off any temptation a customer might have to lounge or smoke another cigarette after the meal was finished.[33]

Finally, Vassos sought to unify the space by designing a singular visual cue throughout the interior. On the exterior signage, the lighting amplified the modern architecture of the building in the crisp font of the name and in the glowing center beam separating the doors. As Vassos explained, "Even the lettering for the restaurant name and the cards for the windows were especially designed and lettered to be in conformity with the whole."[34] He called out the visual motif of long, thin vertical lines in the letters of the restaurant's name, in the chrome piping, in the lines created

A SMALL MODERN RESTAURANT

SODA FOUNTAIN AND LUNCH COUNTER—NOTE METHOD OF LIGHTING FROM ABOVE

A DETAIL OF THE FOUNTAIN AND ONE OF THE BENCH UNITS
RISMONT RESTAURANT AND TEA ROOM, NEW YORK—DESIGNED BY JOHN VASSOS
Laurence and John Scacchetti, Architects

[891]

The triangular seats and banquettes at the Rismont Tearoom were deliberately made uncomfortable. Soda and lunch counter *(above)*; the fountain and a bench *(below)*. *Pencil Points,* December 1931. Private collection.

by the chairs at the counter, and in the movement of light across the ceiling. Vassos would later extend this idea in his interior designs for the RCA Company's offices and studios.

In addition to his modernist interiors, Vassos was fluent in "Old World style." For the design of a Manhattan bar, he created a Bavarian effect with heavy antique tables and chairs cut from thick oak planks, stained oak ceiling beams and wainscoting, and chandeliers made of cart wheels hung from chains.[35] These few projects marked the end of his interior design for restaurants; after 1935 he devoted his attention to shaping media viewing spaces at RCA, and after World War II he designed modernized movie theater interiors for United Artists.

Alongside his interior designs for commercial establishments, Vassos worked on designs for private homes, starting with his own Upper West Side penthouse apartment, where he and Ruth lived before moving to the Silvermine area of Norwalk, Connecticut, around 1932. More completely than in other areas of his work, Vassos's apartment designs explored the principle of modularity, an idea that he would express more fully in his plan for the Living Room of the Future at the 1939–40 New York World's Fair.[36] His main idea was to make furniture as functional as the people who used it.

Vassos was an early public advocate of modernism in interior design. Giving talks on interior design at hotels, social clubs, and cultural institutions, he promoted "his theory as to what a truly modern interior should be. [It] is most arresting," as an E. P. Dutton brochure claimed.[37] In his lectures, Vassos argued on behalf of the American modern design movement by telling the story of modern art movements and how they related to industrial design as a method of styling mass-produced goods, which he then related to his own interior designs. He traced the movement of modern design from Europe to the United States, revealing the interaction between art and architecture. He wrote, "There could be no more definite tie up than that between the supremacists who eliminated all beauty and expression to a black square and the white box-like houses on the landscape in Le Corbusier's architecture."[38]

Presenting slides of examples from both art and industry, Vassos illustrated the influence of machines on art and architecture. His slide collection ranged from paintings by Cézanne, Picasso, and de Chirico to photographs of machines by Margaret Bourke-White. It included images of American vernacular architecture such as the grain silo, which European modernists like Le Corbusier hailed as exemplary.[39] Vassos also presented other reflections of modern design that showed the relationships among "industry, in architecture, in advertising, in décor—and in our daily lives."[40] He sought to provide a visual vernacular through which his audience could understand modern design and its larger context. This period marked a turning point in the cultural recognition of the importance of modern design in the United States.[41]

Design, Vassos argued, could take the technological advances of the workplace and, through careful planning and prefabrication, incorporate them literally into the fabric of the home. This relationship between home and work was originally explored by Le Corbusier. According to urban theorist Henri Lefebvre, Le Corbusier tried to unify the elements of home and work, nature, and urban planning:

> The homogeneity of an architectural ensemble conceived of as a "machine for living in," and as the appropriate habitat for a man-machine, corresponds to a disordering of elements wrenched from each other in such a way that the urban fabric itself—the street, the city—is also torn apart. Le Corbusier ideologizes as he rationalizes—unless perhaps it is the other way round. An ideological discourse upon nature, sunshine and greenery successfully

concealed from everyone at this time—and in particular from Le Corbusier—the true meaning.[42]

Vassos was intrigued by this notion of the home as a machine for living. I would argue, however, that his ideas presented an alternative version of modernist design that sought to separate the home from workplace rationality while still using elements of the machine. For Vassos, despite his affinity to modernism, the home remained a refuge, a "haven in a heartless world" filled with light and people, rather than a rational cave. He expressed this notion clearly in a letter responding to a fan who had received a copy of *Phobia* from Mr. Richard Bach at the Metropolitan Museum of Art.[43] The fan wrote to Vassos and inquired if he had any ideas for using the book *Phobia* in a lecture on modern art. Vassos responded directly: "I cannot see how you will link *Phobia* with modern art. But I can easily see a true marriage between [phobias] and modern living, which perhaps is the out spring of any contemporary expression."[44] Design could provide emotional and physical scaffolding for the agitated soul. Modern design was not only an aesthetic, but it had a hygienic and mentally calming effect as well.

Vassos received acclaim for his application of modern design to his own apartment. It was among the first modern apartment interiors featured by the architectural magazine *Pencil Points.* Following the Wall Street crash of 1929, Vassos's plan for his "small modern apartment" was both elegant and economical, a skyscraper abode appropriate to the scaled-down expectations of the Great Depression. Vassos sharply defined his priorities in terms of the pared-down era, writing that "the true modernist" eliminates "all unnecessary detail in attaining a practical—and by reason of its intense practicability, a beautiful—result."[45] Walter Storey, writing for the *New York Times,* also applauded Vassos's apartment design, particularly his merging of simplicity and comfort: "There is not an air of stiffness in the room. This effect is no doubt due to the variation in size and form in the furnishings and the studied lack of formal balance of masses true of the traditional style."[46]

In addition to spare decor, Vassos valued flexibility that would allow a home's inhabitants to shift furniture to suit their needs. To this end, he featured movable units and built-in furniture to create different areas without constructing walls. His apartment design alternately allowed for sociability and isolation within a single room by using variations in lighting sources, such as lamps of differing heights and light that differed in quality. A chair in a corner was lit separately from the corner couch area. His low-lying, built-in bookshelves created privacy barriers between occupants and provided useful storage space. In addition, Vassos separated spaces for different experiences, such as reading and listening to the radio. This represented a new way of coordinating the various media forms within the home.[47]

Modularity was not new in furniture design. Designers at the Bauhaus added new storage features for the home that borrowed from office aesthetics. For example,

A SMALL MODERN APARTMENT

DESIGNED BY THE ARTIST FOR HIS OWN USE

By John Vassos

EDITOR'S NOTE:—*We present here what we believe to be an example of a sane, logical, modern interior. Comfortable city life for a young couple is admirably provided for in these rooms where everything is worked out in an orderly restful way. As the author and designer of the apartment suggests, there seems no reason why adequate and practical furniture, such as is shown here, cannot be designed and built when the apartment is erected.*

SINCE IT IS our privilege to be the most efficient people who have inhabited the earth to date, it is this motivation that causes the true modernist to eliminate all unnecessary detail in attaining a practical — and by reason of its intense practicability, a beautiful — result. Floor space is expensive in large cities and the luxury of apartments or houses with eight or ten large rooms is not for many. Therefore we put our inventive minds to work to create interiors comfortable, livable, and spacious in effect, with only a limited floor space. My living room has a floor space 15′ x 23′. In this room at one end is my dining table and small bar, another wall has a working study with a large desk, there is a sun lounge—and there

DESK UNIT WITH DOORWAY TO TERRACE
IN THE BACKGROUND
(See detail on page 792)

are over 500 books in the room. All this with no effect of crowding, in fact an actual feeling of space. This is accomplished, first—because the furniture is architecturally planned and appears as part of the walls, and second—because the color tones are neutral, though warm, beiges. The floor is carpeted in plain deep beige chenille, the walls are a flat, almost dead, white. The north end of the room with the river view has a four-inch platform built across it, giving the effect of a separate room. The flat top surfaces of the architectural furniture are used for sculpture, bronzes, etc., all forming a part of the whole general design, while low tables are used for articles of use, such as cigarettes, ash trays, magazines, etc.

To avoid chaos in my architecture, I am an apostle of verticalism; I have used squares and parallel verti-

cal lines following the lines of the room itself everywhere, with the exception of the dining chairs, which are curved. This is because the curved chairs made a better design with the oblong table. One might think that the use of neutral beige color tones would give a colorless effect, with the beiges and natural wood tones of the furniture, but the result is surprisingly warm and creates a flattering background for people who are in the room—they supply the color. For handles on the various doors and openings I have used Monel metal, which adds greatly to the interest of the room by the changes in its silvery surface as the light strikes it. The baseboard is cork, in its natural shade of dark brown, and where wood has been used it has been left natural and the beautiful grain of maple and walnut forms a design in the room. The radiator covers act as seats beneath the windows. Their top is of natural wood and the front and sides are rounded bars of Monel. The hangings are of monk's cloth (a burlap-like material) which is a natural linen color and the window shades are pale, water-green Venetian blinds. To achieve an efficient but not too prominent light over the dining table, I installed an extra beam in the ceiling. In this beam is an opening covered with opaque glass, through which light is cast directly on the table.

In the bedroom, the problem was perforce a little different. It was one of individualism in close quarters. There I created two entirely separate and distinct units. One for Mrs. Vassos consisting of dressing

[789]

during the early years of the Bauhaus, Marcel Breuer applied a modular system to an apartment. At the same time, modular furniture was becoming popular in Germany and England. It first appeared in the United States in 1929–30 in designs by Donald Deskey and Gilbert Rohde. Rohde's designs were shown in the Design for Living House of 1933 at the Chicago World's Fair. However, the unit idea did not become popular in the United States until after 1938.[48] Functionalist modern interiors eventually became icons of expediency and frugality among the elite who could afford them. They were seen as being neither trendy nor wasteful, and they allowed the merging of various styles, which was an economic necessity. Consumers could buy single pieces whenever they were needed and integrate them into their existing furnishings.

Vassos remained wedded to the modular style in interior design and in his corporate work for RCA. At his home on Comstock Hill, on ten lush acres in the Silvermine area of Norwalk, Connecticut, Vassos installed black lacquer built-in cabinetry with streamlined edges and ample shelving to separate the dining room and living room. The geometric dining table with tubular steel legs and a matching sideboard, which he designed and built, matched the cubist room divider. The rounded hardware of unadorned, smooth metal on the doors and drawers of this cabinetry broke the darkness of the lacquer with a muted silver flourish.[49]

In clarifying the space of the home by removing excess ornament and emphasizing functionality, modernists articulated a notion of selfhood that viewed an individual's personality as reflected and shaped by his or her surroundings. Vassos expressed this notion in *Phobia* through his portrayal of nervous urbanites oppressed by gloomy surroundings. According to the philosophy of the modern self, an individual should be unfettered by the accumulation of historical junk or personal clutter. Home, no longer a center of production, offered a reflection of the inner life of the inhabitants. As art historian Hal Foster explains, this philosophy of the emergent self was part of the reason that modernists fought against the overstuffed clutter and engulfing femininity of traditional home design. The modern home, in their view, should be a setting for the expression of the self and not a space laden with the historical residue of others.[50] The simple modernistic plan, with its emphasis on bare spaces, clean lines, and hidden objects, was seen as an ideal setting for the private lives of rational modern people.

When Vassos described his color choices for his penthouse apartment's living room, he was obviously attuned to the idea of the home as theater for the self. He chose neutral beige, combined with the wood tones of the furniture, to create "a flattering background for people who are in the room [as it is] they [who] supply the color."[51] This neutrality represented a shift from the purely feminine home of the Victorian era, which historian Beverly Gordon argues was meant to mirror the deeper self of the woman who decorated it. The conflation of the home and the woman's body reflected the ideology of the home as the woman's sphere.[52] Vassos's androgynous design style blended the tufted sofa with decorative cushions with the cubed table and the stone bust on the top of the bookshelf. Kristina Wilson notes that interior designers "employed a variety of rhetorical and design strategies to ensure that their work was perceived as neither too feminine nor too masculine," taking into account myriad details and significant markers such as paint color.[53]

Following the 1920s, the novel concept of the living room suggested an increasingly unisex home, where men began to inhabit what was once the women's domain of the parlor. Historians Mary Ann Clawson and Mark Carnes argue that Victorian men, in contrast to modern men, spent many of their evenings at meetings of fraternal organizations, which, like their jobs, kept them away from the perceived female world of the house. These meetings allowed men to break away, psychologically, from the inhibiting bonds that tied them to their mothers. This image of the father as a stranger under his own roof was consistent with the movement of work from within the home to outside it: men's worlds of both work and leisure lay beyond the white picket fence.[54] For Vassos, who at times both lived and worked at home, the functionality of modern design provided a solution to the domesticity-as-feminine problem. It was not always easy for him to introduce new furniture forms into the home he shared with Ruth. He noted that he finally convinced his wife to get rid of her "Adam desk and colonial dresser, and fine spool bed" at their penthouse, and that she eventually came to prefer her husband's taste.[55]

Vassos applied the modernist principles he used in his own home to the Chrysler Building studio of his friend and photographer of the machine age Margaret Bourke-White.[56] She was a fitting first client on which to experiment with the values of the machine age in interior design, and both Vassos and Bourke-White recognized the publicity value of the two modern artists working together.[57] Vassos hoped that "the prestige of the combination of John Vassos designed and Margaret Bourke-White working in that interior would influence . . . London editors" to publish stories on the apartment. He was specifically referring to coverage by *The Studio,* a prestigious British decorative art and interiors magazine. The photographer, whose images of industrialization had been widely published, was also concerned with clarity, form, and the impact of machinery on perception. In her new studio housed in one of the city's most important new skyscrapers, Bourke-White wanted an interior to match her growing reputation as a major photographer of the industrial age. Her biographer, Vicki Goldberg, describes the space as intensely modern:

> The studio announced that Margaret Bourke-White was poised on the edge of tomorrow. It was a streamlined, art moderne environment; all built-in curves and decorative angles, with an aquarium for tropical fish at eye level on the wall, Venetian blinds of corrugated aluminum and light fixtures of aluminum and frosted glass. She moved to another penthouse studio, larger but less expensive, in 1933 to 521 Fifth Avenue. Once again, John Vassos designed the interior.[58]

STUDIO OF MARGARET BOURKE-WHITE
DESIGNED BY JOHN VASSOS

"Studio of Margaret Bourke-White Designed by John Vassos." Detail of the brochure *John Vassos: Famous Illustrator and Modernist,* circa 1930. John Vassos Papers, Archives of American Art, Smithsonian Institution.

Vassos used new materials, modular furniture, and targeted lighting. As he recalled, Bourke-White's own clientele inspired the use of the new materials:

> In 1929, she approached me and asked me to design her studio. This is the year of Art Deco. I said, Margaret you work for Pittsburgh Plate Glass, you work for Armstrong Cork and Alcoa and DuPont products. I am going to surround you with all the things you do for your friends. And she loved that desk.[59]

Vassos also made the studio comfortable in other ways by surrounding Bourke-White with her photographs and books. He created boundaries between spaces by using innovations such as an L-shaped nook where books made a natural shelf. He used books as a decorating device, adding lighted columns to prop up the bookshelves and create a sculptural, architectural form.[60] This semi-indirect lighting system, which featured frosted glass held by aluminum strips, was designed to furnish "cakes of light" where concentration was most desirable. Vassos also blended comfort and technology when he placed multiple throw pillows on a daybed surrounded by geometric lights.

Vassos often incorporated books into his modular units because he believed that they expressed the owner's taste and helped organize the living space. Bookshelves were archives with an architectural character, emphasizing horizontal and vertical stretches that added depth and visual interest.[61] In Bourke-White's studio he built a shelf above the reading corner on top of which a photograph was displayed. In his own apartment, he used bookshelves to divide space and reflect his own reading practices. As an author intimately involved in the growing book market, he also had a personal interest in making books important in interior design. Books would continue to play a role in his interior designs, especially in the Musicorner, where old and new forms of media could coexist.

THE MUSICORNER: THE MEDIA-CENTERED LIVING ROOM OF THE FUTURE

Vassos faced a new challenge with the introduction of electronic media devices into the home. His interiors had to move beyond the display of books to incorporate these new forms of audio and visual entertainment. Not surprisingly, he relied on modular solutions, similar to those in his modern apartments, that integrated the various electronic appliances inside boxy housings with expanded storage space. He found that modular cabinetry served as the perfect solution for new media forms and, more broadly, expressed what he thought would be a significant entryway through which modern design and "functionalism" could enter the home. Vassos was aware that many Americans rebelled at the idea of giving up their period furnishings, but he hoped that the multimedia-centered living room would be an ideal space to convince them finally to accept functional twentieth-century modernism. His own home embodied this ideal with large built-in furniture pieces and even walls that seamlessly stored electronic equipment.[62] The Musicorner, a display room in the America at Home Pavilion at the New York World's Fair in 1940, was the fullest expression of Vassos's plans for an integrated entertainment area.

This display—which was referred to variously as the Musicorner, the Living Room of the Future, the Entertainment Corner by John Vassos, and the Living Room of To-morrow. It represented an opportunity for Vassos to express a central theme in his interior design philosophy: that the home should be made as functional and as integrated as possible. In an article for *Electrical Manufacturing*, Vassos argued that, given the rise of new broadcast media machines in the home, "electrically energized units can now be accepted as functionally and dynamically related units creating and complementing an ensemble that will definitely reflect our age."[63]

The special pavilion housing the America at Home exhibit was added to the New York World's Fair for its second season in 1940, as the fair's focus became less

John Vassos's Musicorner at the America at Home Pavilion, 1940, 1939–40 New York World's Fair. Photograph by Richard Averill Smith. John Vassos Papers, Archives of American Art, Smithsonian Institution.

international and more entertainment oriented. Representing the future of domestic design, the exhibition drew from the most talented industrial designers, some of whom had been invited to design the fair itself. America at Home consisted of twelve interiors by well-known architects, designers, and decorators from across the country. According to the exhibit organizers' pitch letter to designers, it was "a program planned to dramatize the development of design in manufactured articles and consequent improvement of taste in everyday living."[64] The organizers invited prominent manufacturers and design curators to serve as jurors to choose the spaces; among them were Richard F. Bach of the Metropolitan Museum of Art; architectural historian, curator, and critic Edgar Kaufmann jr.; architect Edward Stone; Francis Taylor, director of the Worcester Museum; John McAndrew, who was associated with MoMA; and Carl Feiss of Columbia University School of Architecture. The goal of the exhibition was to present an elite, yet exciting, vision of America's home of the future—or rather homes of the future—with rooms that were to be compact yet elegant.[65] The jury members acted as a planning body, and the copious minutes of their meetings recorded their process of planning the rooms and awarding prizes to top designers and their products. The official records of the fair, housed in the New York Public Library's World's Fair collection, include information on the production of the Musicorner, although scant scholarly attention has been paid to the exhibit.

The America at Home Pavilion was an impressive building with large columns, surrounded by Greek sculptures. Located at Rainbow Avenue, near the gas exhibition, the pavilion comprised twelve rooms or "living concepts," each created by a top designer or team.[66] Participating architects included John Yeon, who designed a room titled North Pacific Slope, and William Muschenheim, who created the Parent's Retreat. Industrial designers Russel Wright and Gilbert Rohde contributed the Winter Hideout in the Adirondacks and the Unit for Living, respectively.[67] Other contributors included Virginia Conner and Theodor Carl Muller. Shepard Vogelgesang laid out the complex plan, with rooms distributed along a system of curving ramps.[68] The project raised awareness about both regional and national trends in modern design and gave media attention to the participating manufacturers. The series of showroom exhibits did not sell merchandise, since the rooms, with the exception of Rohde's Unit for Living, were made of products not immediately available on the market. The pavilion was popular, with roughly 18 percent or more of all fairgoers visiting the curvilinear space.[69]

As revealed by the jury's correspondence and meeting minutes, Vassos did not join the project until February 26, 1940, after ten to twenty other major designers were invited to participate.[70] His room design was formally dubbed the Musicorner, for the familiar radio and phonograph components it incorporated. Vassos had already been part of the fair through his involvement in the RCA Pavilion, for which he designed the TRK-12 television. He responded graciously to the offer to produce a living room for the fair, writing to Louise Bonney Leicester, the director of the America at Home Pavilion:

> I have read with interest the brochure of the Fair that you sent me, also your letter. My clients have their own pavilion, which we are now planning to enlarge and improve over last year. However your project "America at Home" appeals to me and I am taking the matter up with the powers that be to see if we cannot participate and have something designed especially for this exhibit.[71]

Vassos viewed the invitation as a good opportunity to express his new ideas about radio in the home. As noted in chapter 3, he felt that the appliance should be liberated from ornate cabinetry and modernized to suit contemporary society. As he told Leicester, "To date most manufacturers as you know are reluctant about developing uncompromising well-designed sets that may be the best designers can create yet are far from commercially sound. This is particularly so with the radio industry.

However the magnitude of your project and my own persuasion may induce them to be included in this particular case."[72] Always a collaborator, Vassos suggested that his colleagues at the American Designers' Institute might be interested in participating, although it is unclear whether anything resulted from this suggestion.

Despite his early interest, Vassos required approval from RCA to do the project. The negotiations that ensued reveal the complexity of his role as both an independent contractor and an affiliate of RCA. It was agreed that the room would be identified as a "Musicorner by John Vassos" and that RCA would be given full credit for all products.[73] Vassos, acting as the company's intermediary, requested that RCA be the pavilion's exclusive radio provider in return for paying a fee of one thousand dollars and setting up the room. However, Leicester could not promise this. She wrote:

> If any other radio account comes in we shall be obliged to submit it to the jury. However, I can assure you that we are not taking any steps to get other accounts. We have stopped all aggressive selling of industrial participation in order to concentrate on the exhibit of rooms and assume the completion of the exhibit.[74]

Vassos would not sign the deal without an exclusivity clause. His curt letter in reply blamed Leicester for being unclear from the start and expressed his deep disappointment over his impending withdrawal from the project. He had already done most of the work, as he explained:

> I had already lined up my electric units, lamps etc. also some comfortable and functional furniture. However, my plans and sketches have not been completely in vain as one of the big furniture manufacturers has asked to do a room along these lines for his company.[75]

After more haggling, the "Entertainment Corner by John Vassos" was confirmed. The letter laid out the contract's terms, including the freedom that Vassos would have in designing the space:

> Mr. Vassos and RCA will be responsible for the furnishing of this room and the Fair will build the envelope. It will be 10 feet by 14 feet. If Mr. Vassos uses outside sources for chairs or lamps they must definitely be custom made products by cabinetmakers that do not have showrooms.[76]

The wording suggests an exclusive agreement without ever really saying that one existed. In addition to the Musicorner, a separate display was set up outside the sealed room, featuring an RCA television cabinet (the TRK-12) and three small radios, including a black-and-white model of RCA's new Bakelite radio.[77] The creation of the Musicorner did not run entirely smoothly. The head of the exhibition crew wrote angrily, "What happened to the TV cabinet, the stand for installation has been complete for nearly a month!"[78] Despite this delay, the production of the space went smoothly. The only major change to the room's plan was the omission of a large RCA fax machine depicted in an early rendering as an adjunct device to the television that would provide hard copies of breaking news stories.[79]

At sixteen feet by fifteen feet, a little larger than originally planned, the richly decorated room contained a range of media formats, including a 16 mm sound film projector, a radio, a phonograph, and a television receiver, housed in a curving built-in modular unit with a shiny chromium base. Vassos was characteristically attentive to the color scheme. The official description of the room noted the "television colors," with a "television-blue wall above music cabinets" to enhance the image and the "effect of light transmission."[80] A white wall served as a screen for the motion picture projector. The consolidated unit's cabinets were constructed of bleached mahogany, and a warm beige carpet and gray wall created a smooth blend of neutral colors. The furniture, which included a Plexiglas table with an aluminum base, used gleaming, modern materials that suggested a futuristic style. Four special Vassos-designed chromium-and-aluminum lamps with adjustable shades were manufactured for the room by the Egli Company. These lamps, with both fluorescent and incandescent bulbs, were expressly designed for the varied lighting conditions of television viewing.[81] Streamlined bar accessories from the Manning-Bowman Company sat on the coffee table, including six highball glasses on a metal tray, six cocktail glasses and a metal shaker on a mirror, two metal ashtrays, and an ice tray and tongs.[82] Sixty-eight books donated by Vassos's publisher, the E. P. Dutton Company, were squeezed into the built-in bookshelves. A desk was also incongruously included in the modular unit. Flowers in the "plant solarium" soaked in light from the curtained window and added visual texture.[83] In the soundproofed room, the sofa and chairs, upholstered in blue textured cotton, could seat eight or nine people, although that seems like it would have been quite a squeeze. In promotional photographs, the television showed a close-up of a baseball game, solidifying the masculine focus of the room, which was no stuffy Victorian parlor.

In addition to the television, Vassos prioritized the phonograph and radio among the many media forms displayed; indeed, the room's name was the Musicorner. RCA's marketing staff invited prominent musicians from the company's record label to curate music selections for discrete times of day. Arthur Fiedler, conductor of the Boston Pops Orchestra, chose the luncheon records, popular bandleader Tommy Dorsey picked those to be played in the the afternoons, and Serge Koussevitzky, "rightly ranked with the greatest living conductors since the Boston symphony as developed under his direction is accounted among the finest the world has ever heard," made evening selections.[84] A total of 129 phonograph records were included in the display.[85]

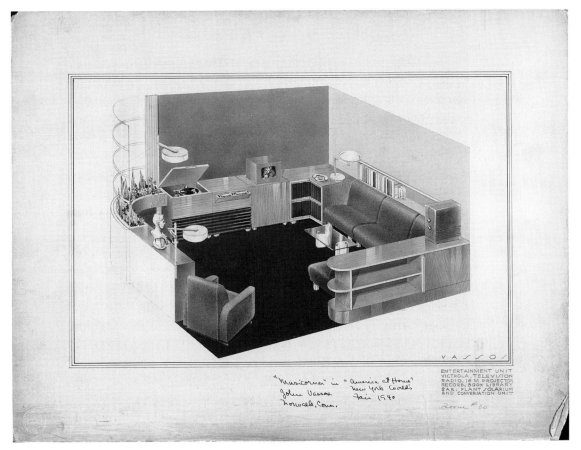

This rendering of the Musicorner's modular cabinetry allows each format its own space, although the cabinet is visually harmonious. The television seems to stand apart from the radio, but in reality the sound from the television was heard through the radio. One of the special television lamps is in the foreground. John Vassos Papers, Archives of American Art, Smithsonian Institution.

As an assemblage of movable sectional cabinets, with the fluid, rational arrangement of mechanical devices, the space represented a culmination of Vassos's key ideas for modern living. Vassos downplayed the television set, drawing attention away from its transformative qualities and presenting it as just another piece of the entertainment unit, along with the audio components. When not in use, all the media cabinets—or, as the literature called them, "music cabinets"—could be closed to create a uniform and unbroken horizontal line. This space was intended to represent an easily mass-produced unit for a home or apartment, one that could be built into the suburban tract homes of the future.[86] "I am convinced that the day will come when homes will have living rooms and bedrooms as completely furnished when one moves into them as are the bathrooms and kitchens now."[87] Vassos described the Musicorner as "clean, simple and honest."[88]

Not surprisingly, the promotional literature focused on the unit concept's easy reproducibility and mobile modern design in relation to Gilbert Rohde's contribution to the exhibit. For example, in a pitch letter to Roman Slobdin of the then bimonthly graphic arts magazine *PM,* Leicester sent a photo of one of Rohde's housing units along with a picture of the Musicorner. Another publicity letter described the room as "a 20th-century music room [with] cabinets specially designed as separate movable units—radio-phonograph, record library, movie projector, and television sets. The units are adaptable to a number of other arrangements."[89] Like Rohde's designs, Vassos's prefabricated modular electric units were a departure from the fair's dominant streamlined aesthetic. These spaces, in their easy reproducibility and disregard for craftsmanship in furniture design, anticipated the prefabricated housing market.

The Musicorner, despite being a place for recreation, was not particularly cozy. The overload of electronic elements kept the space from feeling warm and inviting and gave it an assembly-line feel. Journalist George Howe was not concerned by this. He was impressed by the effort to include television and radio in the home, as "provision for the complex mechanisms of sound and sight reproduction seems indispensable in a modern house." He praised Vassos's composition, writing that it showed "skill and taste . . . with interesting forms and colors." Howe did wonder, however, how the rapid obsolescence of mechanical appliances would affect the design of the room.[90]

Despite the fair's central theme of the future, judging from the other spaces included in the America at Home Pavilion, television would play only a small role in the home of the future. Only a few other rooms had radios, among them Wright's Winter Hideout in the Adirondacks, which was outfitted with a Crosley radio, and Rohde's Unit for Living, which included an Emerson plastic radio.[91] Other electronics in the America at Home Pavilion, aside from radio and television, included General Electric's air-conditioning units, a refrigerator, a garbage disposal unit for the kitchen, and Westinghouse's sunlamp for the "all American budget nursery."[92]

Vassos's Musicorner departed from previous product displays of the 1930s, which sought to evoke radio equipment's style and status through Victorian settings. The Philco radio company's 1934 exhibition at Radio City Music Hall featured its radio in a nineteenth-century aristocratic parlor. In this "Radio Music Room," the architectural firm of Stair and Andrew showcased a collection of antiquities, including paneling from 1760, an old mahogany work table, four black and gilt Sheraton armchairs with loose cushions of ribbed green silk, and an antique harp of black and gold lacquer. The room, which was intended to "give radio a setting worthy of its importance as the center of family life and as a cultural instrument of great value," could not have been further from Vassos's modernist version.[93]

Vassos was critical of the Philco exhibition, complaining that, although the rooms were inventive and provocative, the show did not "go far enough [toward] looking to the horizon."[94] His comment suggests the failure of other exhibits to present the unification of standardized home appliances. As the radio and the lamp were clearly becoming integral parts of the home, Vassos sought to integrate their electrical features under the cover of singular sheets of plastic material. In planning and predicting the consumption of Americans, the furniture designer would reign supreme in the home of tomorrow. Vassos insisted that the home "will be designed and built from the inside out; and by that I mean that these units will be preconceived and placed before the house or apartment is completed to give maximum enjoyment and comfort for the man of to-morrow, and that is really something for the furniture manufactures to worry about."[95] He most fully expressed these ideas for coordination among builders, furniture makers, and electrical appliance companies in his 1940 article "Why Not All-Electric Living-Units in the Home?" In this piece, Vassos used photos from the Musicorner to illustrate his argument for integrated "electrically energized units." He also claimed that his exhibit room "ranks as number one in public interest out of an entire exhibit."[96]

The designer suggested merging electrical components inside singular modular structures and centralizing the electrified areas. He argued for the integration of nearly all of a room's electrical devices into a single unit. He explained the benefits this way:

> These units [would be] electrically energized to supply any such definite function as light for instance for the dresser, desk or headboard of the bed.
>
> Today with the advent of television, with the 16 mm. film project no longer a novelty but a commonplace in many homes, with the radio and phonograph so permanently established that they have become the focal point of the room, electrically energized units can now be accepted as functionally and dynamically related units creating and complementing an ensemble that will definitely reflect our age, not as separate items unrelated to the interior as a whole.[97]

According to Vassos, the electric unit would increase residents' comfort because it would unify disparate elements of furniture in their homes. He wanted to "create an interior which is not only pictorially and dynamically interesting, but which expresses a directness and restfulness achieved through the comfort and convenience of electrical invention."[98] The plastic laminate of the electric unit, however, was yet to be accepted in the living room.

For the "entertainment unit deluxe," Vassos presented another version of his "electric living unit" that unified "the wide range of activity in the living room today."[99] By combining the living room activities associated with drinking and listening, this semibiomorphic form evoked both the Rismont Tearoom's counter and the "skyscraper feel" of Vassos's designs for Kaufmann's department store windows. The cabinet's horizontal unit combined the utility of a bar, liquor storage cabinet, and buffet with a table for games such as backgammon, chess, and roulette. In addition, it had considerable storage space for phonograph records, television, radio receiver, and phonograph.[100] With its doors closed, the unit blended into the wall, its unobtrusive shape maintaining the lines of the room while providing valuable storage space and integrating units of activity.

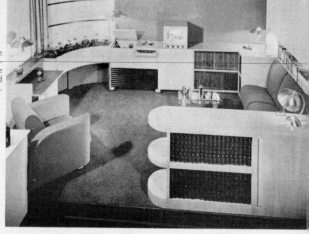

ENTERTAINMENT room in exhibit, America at Home, at the New York World's Fair. Here Mr. Vassos has given expression to his contention that electrical goods and furniture are but one in the mind of the home furnisher of tomorrow. Integrated are light, radio, television, home movies, phonograph, etc.

Why Not All-Electric Living-Units

WHEN one observes the home furnishings business of America (an industry that ranks fifth in the country and involves more than a billion dollars, it becomes a point worthy of serious consideration that in the furniture group itself no more than 7 to 9 per cent of the manufacturers actually made a profit in 1939, and this in spite of the fact that production in the manufacture of furniture is by no means sluggish and is in fact, markedly active. Nevertheless, busy or not, this group has not found it possible to arrive at a paying basis of operation.

This definitely discloses the fact that at some point a weakness exists, because makers of electrically energized products for the home such as refrigerators, ranges, washing machines, radios, air conditioning units, ventilating fans and the smaller portable units such

BY JOHN VASSOS
INDUSTRIAL DESIGNER

as radios, toasters, food mixers, sun lamps and the like—constituted one of the outstanding profit-making industrial activities in that same year. Also, in the case of electrical things, though the field has been established for some time, there still remains room for the introduction of new methods, for instance the comparatively recent and revolutionary Bendix washer as well as a wealth of greatly improved air-conditioners, drink mixers, etc., etc., that come into the marketing without disturbing its very foundations.

In this very situation may lie the key, it seems to me, to the solution of the problem of the furniture manufacturers. A solution of mutual interest to all concerned with home furnishing and appliances whether electrical or non-electrical. But many difficulties may lie in the path before a co-operative solution can be reached.

Let us go back a little. There was determined opposition once on the part of well-to-do-people with 18th Century living rooms when the radio first made its appearance. Why should they have an object in their room which was out of key with the scheme of decoration? Today, however, there is hardly a living room in America be it Georgian, French provincial, Spanish or just home that does not have a radio, or phonograph, or both in it. And the reason for this is that the radio and phonograph companies adapted the styling of their product to fit the room in which it was going to be placed.

Functionalism actually manifested itself in America long before Europe began on a large scale to present to the world architectural concepts of the functional dwelling. Sullivan and Frank Lloyd Wright were the advocators here of such construction before Le Corbusier built his white boxes. However, Europe did begin to relate the interior to the exterior before we did, although we had accepted certain units in the house, such as our bathrooms and sections of the kitchen, strictly from the functional angle.

The perfection of our electrically-energized kitchen has reached its highest degree in the past five years;

"Why Not All-Electric Living-Units in the Home?" Article from *Electrical Manufacturing,* October 1940, which explains John Vassos's ideas about integrating electrical appliances to create visual harmony and make the home more functional. John Vassos Papers, Archives of American Art, Smithsonian Institution.

5. VASSOS AND RCA
MONEY, MEDIA, AND MODERNISM

I n 1932, John Vassos was hired to create three murals at WCAU, the newly constructed flagship station of the Columbia Broadcasting System (CBS) in Philadelphia. This appointment led to his hiring at RCA, where he stayed for the next thirty-eight years as a leading consultant designer. Meant to be "a modern monument to the art of broadcasting," the extravagant CBS building at 1622 Chestnut Street towered over the city's skyline and was topped at night by a 150-foot beam of light that could be seen for twenty-five miles.[1] The first building in the United States specifically designed for the purpose of radio broadcasting, it was a towering homage to the medium, with the most modern broadcasting studios in the world, according to the press materials. The building had taken four years to complete and was a broadcast powerhouse, eventually reaching a 50,000-watt clear-channel status. It was managed by Leon Levy, a charismatic dentist who was the brother-in-law of William Paley. In 1927, Leon Levy and William Paley, together with Sam Paley, Ike Levy, and other investors, had formed CBS, which would go on to become a major producer of radio and television programming. The WCAU building was a significant architectural symbol of the company's emergent strength.

Having gained entry into the radio industry through his mural work, Vassos wrote a persuasive letter to George Throckmorton, RCA's new vice president, expressing his interest in "the problem of radio design" and his desire to work as a consultant with the company. Throckmorton wrote back immediately, inviting Vassos to meet with him.[2] The early 1930s was a crucial period for RCA, which was massively expanding its radio receiver business. Vassos was certain that he could help the company. Following an encouraging meeting with Throckmorton, he was confident that he could offer the company "a fresh point of view, creating that new path which the radio industry is so badly in need of."[3]

At RCA, Vassos applied his stylistic influence in three major areas: the design of radio receivers, the design of in-house studio equipment, and the architecture of

Vassos *(center)* and his staff at work in the new studios of the radio station WCAU in Philadelphia, circa 1932. *Broadcast News,* February 1934. Courtesy of the Hagley Museum and Library.

buildings housing radio transmitters (which send radio frequency signals). He was committed to bringing the company into the new machine age through design and education. Working out of his stylish office at RCA's Camden, New Jersey, manufacturing plant, he forged his role as a key company stylist by creating everything from murals to advertising campaigns. In the 1930s, with Vassos as its guide to the new style, RCA incorporated modern design into many aspects of its corporate identity. Vassos spoke exuberantly about radio's vast cultural and corporate influence, noting: "Radio is advanced—a modern art. People in radio business must be modern to the core. Best procedure is to think modern, talk modern, be modern."[4] He believed it was imperative for RCA to pay attention to the smallest visual details because these affected the experiences of visitors and employees. More important, the right details could solidify the image of the company as modern.[5]

Vassos styled a range of machinery at RCA, including cameras, speech equipment, sound amplification machines, portable recording mixers, and other equipment that RCA distributed to its affiliates. He also worked on top-secret projects, such as the seminal electron microscope designed in 1940 by Canadian scientist James Hillier under the guidance of Vladimir Zworykin. This work was in addition to Vassos's other role as designer for consumer equipment, design educator, and representative to the sales team.[6] He designed modern architecture and interiors for studios nationwide, including transmission towers and studio layouts.[7] Vassos's role in shaping RCA's identity across products is well documented through internal memos, letters, lecture notes, sales meeting notes, and in-house journal articles, all of which had been confidential before Vassos's archives became available.[8] The company, as a conglomerate with many parts, needed greater product cohesion between its entertainment and equipment divisions. RCA wanted radios and phonographs that would mirror the high quality of the company's musical recording division, that would "do justice to the Toscaninis, the Stokowskis, the Koussevitzkys, the Tibbetts, the Flagstads, and the other great artists in the Victor and NBC repertoires," as David Sarnoff wrote in a brochure introducing the 1938 line of listening equipment.[9]

The aesthetic history of RCA in the twentieth century has yet to be told, mainly because media studies have emphasized content or regulatory issues over aesthetics in broadcast history. However, there is growing scholarly awareness of design's value as a lens through which to view the priorities and shifts in broadcasting's corporate strategy. Television historian Lynn Spigel has examined the institutional practices at CBS around modern art.[10] Design historian Dennis Doordan has examined the influence of William Lescaze, an architect and industrial designer who designed CBS radio studios during the 1930s. Doordan tracks Lescaze's earliest work for CBS in 1934, converting an existing Broadway theater into a radio production facility.[11] This study provides an important early case study of studio design history, revealing the value of live audiences to broadcasters in the early years. Lescaze's work for CBS was very similar to Vassos's at RCA studios, as he too was infusing theater with radio's modernism by changing the studio from a live experience to a broadcast arena.

In the 1930s, the advent of widespread broadcasting changed the institution, apparatus, and experience of radio. Networks improved technology and consolidated radio broadcasters with increased power and capital. The institution had to overhaul its image as a rough military technology, a transition that was ripe for a designer's repackaging efforts. In its newest phase, radio's movement from the battlefield and garage to the living room was described in class terms, as a social status that needed to "stop wearing work clothes" and start "dress[ing] up for visitors."[12] This shift was expressed in terms of content, sound quality, and production, as well as through the visual metaphor of streamlining.[13] Manufacturers hired designers to help dissociate their products from the raw, early radios of the 1920s, which provoked images of tangled wires in back rooms and transmitters spitting blue sparks accompanied by an earsplitting din.[14] Radio listening was no longer limited to men wearing headphones and searching for stray voices in the ether.[15] The audience was now a nation of listeners united by the technology. This newly captive audience held seemingly endless potential for advantageous public relations and ever-increasing advertising revenue. The era when the devices leaked battery acid onto living room floors was over, and radio comfortably entered the home.[16]

Styling radio meant retooling the public's image of the machine by associating it with Hollywood glamour and prestige. Beyond the listener's experience, which Vassos's elegant designs made more pleasant (as discussed in chapter 3), RCA recognized the power of remaking the corporate image through the architecture of its studios and production units. Here, the company promoted an aesthetic of corporate elitism, imbuing the once-amateur medium with the symbolism of luxury and class, first through art deco design and later through streamlining. Radio's sophistication was best represented at Radio City Music Hall, RCA's spectacular theatrical outpost and the site of company's most important studio.[17] Even in spaces where there was no live audience, radio studios featured sumptuous surroundings designed by the nation's top art deco interior designers. Vassos renovated transmitter stations in rural as well as urban locations nationwide to match the modern RCA corporate style that he helped forge.

Through sophisticated imagery and stylish radio receivers, RCA successfully dissociated itself from vaudeville's stagecraft while salvaging some of its formatting.[18] RCA's owners, poised to sell their programs to millions, were hopeful that the future of radio would be as streamlined and unidirectional as their studios. The restyling of RCA was a marketing effort in the visual vernacular of the 1930s, a style that would soon be out of step with the postwar pace of technological achievement. Radio would be a new, free form of media that was shared by the public but controlled by the corporation. As radio historian Susan Douglas has observed, the invention of radio "from its first public unveiling and through the next twenty-five years . . . evoked a range of prophecies—some realistic, some fantastic, and nearly all idealistic—of a world improved through radio."[19]

RADIO MURALS AT WCAU

Vassos's murals at WCAU created a striking backdrop for the emergent industry. Large-scale murals constituted a popular political art form in the 1930s, and corporations commissioned (and co-opted) top artists to create such murals to awe and impress visitors at their headquarters buildings. As business historian Roland Marchand notes, companies employed ornate decor and architectural innovation to project their place in history right on their walls.[20] In hiring Vassos, the Levys were contracting a top illustrator with an iconic style. Vassos's murals complemented the lofty ambition of the building. *The Spirit of Radio* in Studio D, *Radio Tempo* or *The Merging of Industry with Art in the Form of Music* in Studio J, and *Great God Radio* in Studio C reflected the theme of a world improved by radio. In addition to the fact that the murals conveyed lofty themes of a world improved by radio, the commissioning of a successful artist like Vassos conferred status on the station's owners, who were instrumental in the formation of CBS.

The revamped WCAU studio was a big improvement over the previous makeshift facilities in old garage-type buildings. "No longer is the broadcast studio of the progressive radio organization a makeshift arrangement" at Studio J, exclaimed the RCA in-house trade magazine *Broadcast News.* The studio's modern backdrop featured deep blue, black, and chromium colors; indirect lighting; and triple plate-glass windows along with Vassos's dramatic black-and-white mural with rich tones of gray, which echoed his book illustrations.[21] Performers were said to benefit from being surrounded by the richly decorative decor, which evoked a "peculiar stimulating effect." As one *Broadcast News* article noted, "Artists who have performed amid these pleasant and unusually beautiful surroundings agreed that here they feel inspired to put forth their finest efforts."[22]

CARLOTTA DALE, CHARMING SOPRANO, WHO REGULARLY ENTERTAINS THE AUDIENCES OF WCAU AND W3XAU FROM THEIR MODERN STUDIOS IN PHILADELPHIA

Soprano Carlotta Dale sits in front of the mural *Great God Radio* at WCAU in Philadelphia. *Broadcast News,* May 1934. Courtesy of the Hagley Museum and Library.

The flagship studio building's new features included talkback microphones (which were used to communicate with various studios during transmission), improved acoustics, graphic-patterned carpeting, and modern time clocks. Every studio's interior design expressed "radio modern," such as the "client's audition room" with its cubist sofa and chairs. On the exterior, the company installed "condenser plates . . . silent, motionless but nevertheless hurling far and wide the voice of this new radio giant."[23] The building's lavish technological sophistication was well matched by the glamour of Vassos's modernistic art. Vassos's murals used visual metaphors and the methods of crosscutting and montage to tell the story of radio.[24] As large-scale narratives, the murals evoked ecclesiastical art, creating a vertical triptych for the new radio "cathedral."[25] Historian Emily Thompson notes that the new technologies of sound control were also celebrated in the exterior decoration of the RCA Building at Rockefeller Center, where "the architects celebrated the center's new role as the epitome of modern aural culture by decorating their buildings with ornamentation representing all the sounds being created within."[26]

In her discussion of the 1930s "boomlet" in murals, historian Karal Ann Marling notes that while artists increasingly found work as muralists in new urban buildings, they had to temper their private views. The destruction of Diego Rivera's Rockefeller

A Visitor Tours WCAU

By KENNETH W. STOWMAN, In Charge of Public Relations, WCAU

AS A casual passer-by walks along the busy and fashionable Chestnut Street in Philadelphia, he sees a handsome blue building on the south side between 16th and 17th Streets. This new structure stands as a symbolic monument to the radio industry and is noted for its striking beauty. The front of the new home of WCAU is trimmed with stainless steel in designs created by the architect to express impressions of radio.

After sundown the large glass tower atop the building, illuminated from within by mercury vapor lamps, casts a blue light throughout the center of the city and can be seen twenty-five miles away.

A visitor entering the portals of WCAU for the first time is greeted at the entrance with beautiful stainless steel doors and overhead are architectural designs depicting Drama, Music, Literature and Comedy.

The interior of the entrance lobby is of Italian marble with indirect lighting overhead casting a silver glow. As we await the arrival of the elevator to the studio reception room on the seventh floor, we notice a

A PERFORMANCE IN PROGRESS IN STUDIO J. ARTISTS WHO HAVE PERFORMED AMID THESE PLEASANT AND UNUSUALLY BEAUTIFUL SURROUNDINGS AGREE THAT HERE THEY FEEL INSPIRED TO PUT FORTH THEIR FINEST EFFORTS AND THAT SUITABLE ENVIRONMENT IS OF GREAT IMPORTANCE IN ENABLING THEM TO ACHIEVE THE BEST RESULTS.

STUDIO B, LOOKING TOWARD THE "DEAD END." CONSIDERING THE BRILLIANT COLORS AND THE CHROMIUM METALLIC TRIM EMPLOYED IN THE DECORATION SCHEME OF THIS STUDIO, THE ABOVE VIEW IN BLACK AND WHITE HARDLY DOES JUSTICE TO THE SUBJECT.

copper cut plate on the outer doors of the elevator. Here the architect has created a masterpiece in the figure of a man holding a WCAU microphone with radio waves emanating from the transmitting station.

As we step into the elevator we are impressed with the unusual interior decoration of the car itself and we imagine that we have been transferred into a new world of modern and artistic conception. The

John Vassos's *Radio Tempo* mural is featured in an article about the striking modern decor of the new radio station building for WCAU. *Broadcast News,* April 1933. Courtesy of the Hagley Museum and Library.

soft harmonizing color scheme of silver and blue has been carried out in these elevators.

Stepping off at the seventh floor reception room, we are greeted by the welcoming hand of the receptionist. This room has been finished in a striking alliance of chinese red, and black putty color, with furniture finished in light tan leather. As we leave the reception room we walk into the first observation gallery from which point we are afforded a view of studio "B" which is two stories high and is furnished in gray, blue and chromium plated metal. On the other side of the gallery we see studio "F," one of the smaller broadcasting rooms, decorated in salmon, gray and black.

Pausing for a moment in the visitors' observation gallery, we observe through the double thickness plate glass windows on the right a program in progress in Studio B, and through the medium of the concealed loudspeakers in this gallery, we hear perfectly all that is in progress in this studio just as though we were in there with the artists. However, we may converse and comment upon the program from this vantage point without in

MURAL DECORATION IN STUDIO J, AT WCAU

ELECTRICAL TRANSCRIPTION EQUIPMENT IN STUDIO H. THIS STUDIO IS A SPECIALLY AIR CONDITIONED CHAMBER DESIGNED TO PREVENT WARPING OF THE RECORDS IN THE METALLIC FILES AND TO INSURE UNIFORM PERFORMANCE DURING ALL ELECTRICAL TRANSCRIPTION PROGRAMS. THE AVERAGE PERSON DOES NOT REALIZE THAT FOUR PERSONS ARE REQUIRED TO HANDLE PROGRAMS OF THIS TYPE—ONE PRODUCTION MAN, ONE ENGINEER, ONE ANNOUNCER, AND A TESTING AND TIMING SUPERVISOR.

"RADIO TEMPO"
By John Vassos

Here is an actual union between art and industry—art in the form of music serving industry.

In this decoration is shown the activity which takes place behind the scenes—and reaches ends of the earth.

In the lower left are the architects and designer planning this radio building and above a glimpse of Philadelphia's new rising skyline the female figure is a symbol of voice coming into the rhythmic modulations of the new radio organ with the organist, above are current events—politics, conflicts of nations, personalities of rulers, etc.

At the lower right are the factories and above industrial wonders of man—railways, bridges, dams, tunnels, airplanes, Zeppelins, motors, ships—all typifying industry served by radio with "big business" in the form of the rising skyscraper.

any way interfering with the program, or without danger of having our voices picked up by the sensitive microphones in the studio.

Shifting our gaze to the left, we observe through another large double plate glass window that a rehearsal is being held in Studio F, and as our attention is attracted to this new scene, our guide touches a switch

Center mural featuring Vladimir Lenin in 1932 demonstrated what could happen if they refused.[27] To associate a company with the modern, urban art of the period, artists' preferred style was cubist rather than representational, which also allowed them to scale objects in an imaginative way. This scaling is evident in *Radio Tempo*, where layers of images representing different possible news subjects float up the vertical plane, although curiously not the public who would be listening to the radio.

Vassos described his mural images in detail, using transportation as the dominant metaphor for radio. For example, about *Radio Tempo* he wrote:

> In this decoration is shown the activity which takes place behind the scenes— and reaches ends of the earth.
>
> In the lower left are the architects and designer planning this radio building and above a glimpse of Philadelphia's new rising skyline, the female figure is a symbol of voice coming into the rhythmic modulations of the new

radio organ with the organist, above are current events—politics, conflicts of nations, personalities of rulers, etc.

At the lower right are the factories and above industrial wonders of man—railways, bridges, dams, tunnels, airplanes, Zeppelins, motors, ships— all typifying industry served by radio with "big business" in the form of the rising skyscraper.[28]

Although Vassos tailored the mural to WCAU's Philadelphia context, his depiction of dynamic modernity would have been familiar to visitors. *Radio Tempo* actually borrowed scenes from Vassos's advertising illustrations to express the dynamic modernity of radio. The tall skyscraper on the top right side resembles the building in an advertisement for the Sherry-Netherland hotel. The boat confronting a waterfall is the same as that in an advertisement for Artcote papers.

For Studio C's mural, Vassos repurposed the *Contempo* illustration "Radio" but renamed the image *Great God Radio*.[29] As discussed in chapter 1, *Contempo*'s text expressed ambivalence toward this new medium, which had the power to save human lives but also sold banal "bunk": "Something to be advertised, something to be sold. The triumph of the commonplace. STAND BY, the program continues."[30] This reuse of the book illustration suggests that the artist's ideology was flexible enough for him to use *Contempo*'s socially critical image to decorate the corporate offices of radio executives. The WCAU studio represented an advanced vision of radio as a stylish and modern medium, which Vassos would replicate in his radio designs for RCA. He wanted broadcast studios and radio sets to be aesthetically pleasing, to have "eye value as well as ear value," as one major scientist put it.[31] Vassos also loved this image, as it connected two vital parts of his career: book illustration and industrial design. He hung a print of *Great God Radio* in his office at RCA, and the image later became embedded at RCA Laboratories as the illustration on its library bookplate.

MODERN COMPANY–MODERN ARTIST

RCA's sprawling operations began in 1919, when the stations formerly owned by American Marconi were turned over to RCA, giving it control over "radio telegraphy in the United States."[32] The 1926 creation of a new company with General Electric and Westinghouse, named the National Broadcasting Company, or NBC, gave RCA, the world's largest distributor of radios, the greatest stake in programming. An antitrust suit in 1930 broke up the radio patent monopoly of GE, Westinghouse, AT&T, and the United Fruit Company.[33] This case forced RCA into becoming an independent company. The Radio Act of 1927 and the Communications Act of 1934 facilitated the rise of privately owned radio stations through deregulation and allowance for commercial programming. The 1934 Communications Act accepted the equipment "trust" and the network system of chain broadcasting.[34] Emerging victorious in the battle over privatizing the airwaves, RCA expanded rapidly.

The company had gained a new, aggressive leader in 1931 when David Sarnoff became the head of RCA. His reign (until 1967) largely overlapped Vassos's career with the company and marked RCA's emergence as a broadcast and media production giant. Over a period of five years, RCA grew exponentially, including gaining ownership of NBC operations, moving its operations to the seventy-story RCA Building in "Radio City," and growing its affiliate stations in major cities.[35] RCA also acquired the research and development department of the former GE vacuum tube plant in Harrison, New Jersey, and that of the Victor Talking Machine Company in Camden, giving the company rights to musical reproduction technology. It was an exciting time for the company.

Not only did RCA have a new president, but also NBC had begun experimental television broadcasts from New York's Empire State Building in 1932. Indeed, some were hopeful that RCA would release its commercial television sets in the following year.[36] In addition, the rapid modernization of acoustical equipment improved sound quality, transmission, and speed of delivery. Reverberation equations, sound meters, microphones, and acoustical tiles were increasingly used in places as varied as Boston's Symphony Hall, New York's office skyscrapers, and the soundstages of Hollywood, all helping to cause a cultural shift in the consideration of sound.[37] When Vassos came on board in 1933, RCA was reeling from these recent dramatic changes.

The company heartily welcomed its new consultant in a lengthy *Broadcast News* article announcing his hiring. The montage layout of the article's illustrations positioned Vassos's head at the center of his design projects, promoting his artistic range from Nedick's in the upper left-hand corner to *Phobia* on the lower right, but without prioritizing one project over another. This arrangement visually united the disparate parts of his career and signaled the acceptance of the industrial designer's multidimensional achievements. The comprehensive article also listed Vassos's theater productions and his radio designs among his many accomplishments:

> As an indication of his versatility, we might add that he has designed the ballet costumes and scenic sets for two recent theatrical productions—one being the "Sixth Sense" presented at the Theater Guild and the other "Phobia" at the Barbizon Plaza. Such magazines as *House and Garden* are already beginning to use the new RCA Victor radio sets, bearing the Vassos influence in external appearance . . . befitting the up-to-date artistic home, and it can be safely said that the Vassos influence in the radio industry is only at its beginning.[38]

Vassos worked quickly to cordon off design activities from the engineering department. In 1934, he recommended that the company establish a "design styling

Making America Easier to Look At

John Vassos, RCA's newly hired designer, is featured in an article welcoming him to RCA. He is surrounded by his illustrations, products, and interior designs. *Broadcast News*, February 1934. Courtesy of the Hagley Museum and Library.

John Vassos's office and seating area at RCA in Camden, New Jersey. John Vassos Papers, Archives of American Art, Smithsonian Institution.

section for engineering products."[39] This team would have sustained involvement in the design process with greater access to the engineers at the earliest stages of new product development than was previously granted. As the "styling" center of the corporation, the team would also be responsible for coordinating RCA's image across its product lines and through its departments. These tasks ranged from "designs [of] broadcast stations, studios and control rooms, mobile units, exhibits, theaters and special installations of customer equipment, [to] interior decoration."[40] RCA approved the formation of the team, which consisted of Vassos; Lynn Brodton, a full-time RCA in-house designer; and W. B. Stevenson, also a designer.[41] The results were immediate and included the creation of coordinated components and eye-level meters for broadcast engineers, later copied by GE, Westinghouse, and DuMont. Vassos quickly settled into his office at the Camden plant. He designed it himself, and it featured art deco styling such as a desk chair with slender tubular steel arms and legs and a modular corner seating unit. As noted above, a print of *Great God Radio* was displayed on the wall.

Beyond their design responsibilities, the members of the styling team tried to prove to the largely technology-driven company that artists were an important and an intrinsic part of the production process. They accomplished this objective through a series of lectures that educated managers and sales staff about style and promoted sales techniques. As one of Vassos's departmental colleagues pointed out to an undoubtedly incredulous engineering audience, "Artists are not crack pots."[42] By 1938, the company's marketing materials highlighted the design team with photographs of William Stevenson, head of the styling department, who "is never satisfied unless his product is fit for the finest home," and John Vassos, "internationally famous artist, author and designer who contributes substantially to the authentic beauty of RCA Victor Radios."[43] At the same time the company was promoting its stylish, modern-shaped radios, it was paradoxically emphasizing the traditional values of handmade craftsmanship. RCA literature highlighted the cabinets built by "skilled woodworkers" who "have built Victor and RCA Victor cabinets through three generations." It emphasized the "beautiful, heavy woods, carefully selected and matched for strength and musical quality," and the workers who "pridefully and by hand" rubbed the surfaces of radios to a glistening luster.[44]

EQUIPMENT DESIGN AND IMPROVEMENT: FORM FOLLOWS FUNCTION

Vassos helped redesign RCA's major in-house technology, including AM transmitters, the electron microscope, television cameras, speech equipment, and the RCA streamlined truck.[45] Streamlining RCA's in-house equipment saved space, reduced production costs, eased pressures on personnel caused by stressful machines, and enhanced the look of the production facility. Improvements, which were both decorative and functional, included the removal of ornate or protruding design elements and the integration of speakers into machinery or the folding of the elements into a single, integrated shell. Vassos layered materials to create elegant and understandable tools for broadcasters. For example, the chromium-plated brass head on his polydirectional microphone, with its swiveling arm and black enameled metal lower portion, showed users where they should and should not touch the microphone while using it, lest they interfere with the recording.[46] Vassos's design for the one-sided microphone for outdoor concerts and motion pictures similarly used visual markings to establish clearly which side the speaker should use.[47] Perhaps most important, planned obsolescence generated revenue for RCA, as affiliates "discard[ed] usable equipment" in favor of the restyled machines.[48]

To achieve his plans for renovating RCA's in-house machinery, Vassos required the support of his superiors, and Throckmorton provided that through his promotion of the design team within the company. Vassos thanked him for "imbuing the existing staff with this consciousness of appearance."[49] Vassos noted in a report that he had updated David Sarnoff, the company's president, on his extensive activities, telling him "that I had a hand in designing our more rugged merchandise, such as transmitters, microphones, centralized sound, and other equipment."[50] Apparently, Sarnoff was both pleased and "rather surprised at the all-comprising way the new regime was tackling the situation in Camden."[51] Vassos also reported that L. M. Clement, vice president in charge of engineering and research at RCA, had asked him to discuss the styling of a chassis. The styling team eventually gained acceptance in the engineering-driven company, helped, no doubt, by the good publicity generated by RCA's in-house magazine.

Vassos approached each project from the psychology of how people interact with things, and he understood that a successful design is one that enables the user to know what to do by looking and feeling. Writer and usability engineer Donald A. Norman uses the term *affordance* to refer to the perceived and actual properties of a thing that determine just how it could be used.[52] Vassos was sharply attuned to affordances, using things like knobs and the visibility of tuning mechanisms to give clues about how to operate complex machinery. He unified disparate elements to simplify operations. For the 50-kilowatt 50-D transmitter, he centralized three large chunky units, integrating the machine with the surrounding room and converting a space previously filled with random, discordant equipment, knobs, and devices into a harmonious facility. Not only was the machinery more appealing visually, but it was also more cost-effective, saving 30 percent of the previous units' budget.[53] This fit with the goals of the engineering styling department: to both modernize RCA products and save money for the company.

Vassos incorporated this principle as well as ergonomics and field tests to guide the redesign of RCA machines, including the 50-D transmitter and control desk. This desk combined controls for the transmitter and for audio channels. The design later became standard in the field because it allowed, as an advertisement noted, "every major function to be at the engineer's finger tips or within easy viewing distance."[54] Indeed, Vassos was thinking of the engineer who would operate the transmitter when he put all control knobs and buttons at hand level, taking into account the arm movements of the user. He recalled the difficulties that engineers had prior to the redesign.

> Then all transmitting equipment was installed on "racks" with meters sometimes on the floor. To operate these devices, one had to be an octopus. I designed the first unified transmitter where all control knobs and buttons were at hand level and all meters at eye level. . . . Westinghouse and G.E. immediately copied [the] new approach. Later, all industry followed.[55]

He also explained his process in terms of sexual attraction, offering advice to young designers: "You are artists. Don't start with logic and fight off intuition. Intuition first and logic after. That's the way you react to a girl, no question about it."[56]

A sketch of the Vassos-designed transmitter control room. The renderings of the Hohner accordion and the New Yorker radio at the top of the illustration create an unusual tableau and show the continuity of Vassos's style across products. Durez Molder brochure, May 1939. John Vassos Papers, Archives of American Art, Smithsonian Institution.

JOHN VASSOS

John Vassos is accepted as one of the most versatile of the younger American artist - designers. As an industrial designer he is internationally known for his many contributions to functionalism; creator of the multi-unit furniture; muralist, painter and stage designer. The American public at large knows him perhaps best for his illustrative work, he having achieved the reputation of being the first artist to create a new school of illustrative art since Aubrey Beardsley.

He is at present consultant designer and stylist for all of the products of RCA Victor. He has de-signed a wide range of products for various industries, from perfume bottles to giant transmitter stations.

His most recent accomplishment in the art of plastics in the radio field has brought a new high to that medium. Author—his work on human phobias was a valuable contribution to the field of practical psychology and lecturer.

His most recent work is the designing of the spectacular RCA pavilion at the San Francisco Fair and the Room of To-Morrow at the World's Fair.

He heads the American Designers Institute; and in the past has designed for Coca Cola, Bromo Seltzer, Remington, DuPont, Savage Arms, American Tel. and Tel., Wallace Silver, Hohner Accordions, Waterman Fountain Pen and many other industries.

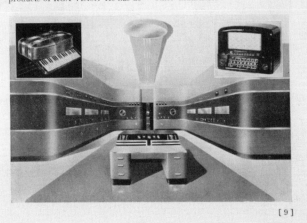

[9]

This U-shaped RCA 50-D transmitter and control desk gave the operator full view and "fingertip control of the working environment."[57] The integrated components were set into the wall, creating an undisturbed continuity. A dark band of color running the entire length of the transmitter, above the desk, enhanced the unity of the components. A series of control panels located at waist height along the transmitter were concealed by doors, which swung downward and became miniature individual desks for each control panel. Lumaline lamps illuminated the panels and desks when they were open for operation.[58] Prior models of transmitters (starting with the A in 1927) were bulky, confusing, meter-dotted towers.

Vassos viewed his job as that of an artist who unveiled both the beauty of a machine and its functionality.[59] Lynn Brodton, who worked with Vassos on the transmitter, wrote that the RCA 50-D transmitter was a pinnacle of modern design because of

John Vassos in his office at RCA with colleague Lynn Brodton, going over the plans for the 50-D transmitter building design. *Broadcast News*, June 1937. Courtesy of the Hagley Museum and Library.

its allegiance to the principle of a machine aesthetic. According to Brodton, it was an "outstanding example of form follows function since the panels are arranged to present a focal point at the control console from which all instruments are visible and controls accessible via the shortest distance from the operator."[60] At the 1939–40 New York World's Fair, the RCA Pavilion featured this transmitter on a large sign, highlighting it as one of the company's achievements in broadcasting. The accompanying text boasted, "RCA designs and builds radio transmitters from five to 500,000 watts. Over 60 percent of the power on the air is broadcasted by RCA equipment."[61]

Vassos streamlined studio equipment as well, such as the RCA speech input monitoring equipment used by technicians during radio broadcasts and recordings. This included the components associated with broadcast technology sent up to a radio or TV station's transmitter, such as the broadcast "consolette" mixer and the OP-7 mixer-preamplifier.[62] Prior to redesign, the portable recording mixer was a complicated machine with multiple layers of dials. Vassos improved the machine by encasing the legs with metal and simplifying the placement of the dials. He moved the meters from the awkward frontal positional and put them on the upper control tray. The illuminated meters, streamlined knobs, and fin-like air-conditioning louvers added to the modern style.[63] The redesign was meant to embrace the formal attributes of the machinery. In particular, the illuminated meters, streamlined knobs, and silver

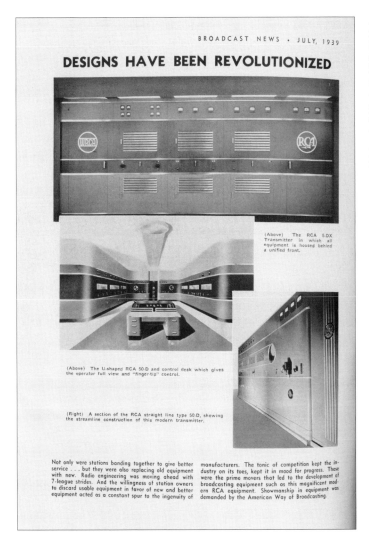

An article featuring "revolutionized" broadcast equipment, including the unified RCA 5-DX transmitter *(above)*, the U-shaped 50-D control desk *(center)*, and the streamlined 50-D transmitter. *Broadcast News*, July 1939. Courtesy of the Hagley Museum and Library.

louvers were meant to construct the form rather than "maintain it"—that is, to create a coherent machine whose parts were recognizable and also integrated into the larger machine. Vassos understood that the engineer's comfort and ability to maneuver amplifier dials and read meters were crucial. In the old mixer, these elements were awkwardly located, causing the engineer to have to glance downward. Vassos moved the dials to a centralized area on a single visible plane. A sleek case with decorative chrome detail replaced the boxy stand with little legroom. The mixer's gray steel exterior created visual harmony with other equipment in the RCA family, and the standardization of its components saved the company 66 percent per unit.

According to Vassos, the body of the operator should be considered in all aspects of equipment design, with components adjusted so they fit the needs of a human figure.[64] The knob was a critical aspect of the user's interaction and haptic experience with the machine. Vassos reworked the knob to make it easier to handle on a range of equipment. As part of his research, he examined the effect of pressure on the hand and created a putty model based on the proportions of an average engineer's hand.[65] From this model, he discovered that some operators developed calluses and infections from the metal pointers on the old knobs. His improved knob had no sharp protrusions and was more comfortable to hold for any length of time. Large and easy to grip, the enunciated pointer enabled the user to feel the knob without looking. The military later adapted the design, as it was especially useful for operators who had to run controls in the dark. This attention to detail proved pragmatically valuable, as it contributed to the user's control of the machine. Vassos understood the significance of the knob as it contributed to the object's core functioning. He explained that the knob was the physical manifestation of an idea about functionality: "It's only a knob. Only a little knob. But the effort and research and the intellectual approach to it was just as if you were designing a skyscraper."[66] This idea is clear in Vassos's humorous drawing showing a domineering knob controlling an engineer. Vassos understood design as a social practice, a way of communicating how the machine works, and approached the design of the knob with gravitas.

Taking the perspective of the user offered a new way of thinking about machine design. Industrial designer Henry Dreyfuss also applied ergonomics to his styling of machinery. His design work included measurements of every conceivable part of intended users' bodies—heads, thighs, forearms, shoulders—to create more efficient and comfortable machines. In his aptly titled book *Designing for People,* he wrote:

> We must know how far buttons and levers can be placed away from the central controls of a machine; size of earphones, telephone operators headsets, helmets for the armed services, binoculars—all are determined by our information on head sizes. From these facts we arrived at this maxim—the most efficient machine is the one that is built around a person.[67]

Vassos made the seminal electron microscope more functional by focusing again on the needs of the user.[68] This device, which was created by James Hillier, working with Vladimir Zworykin, director of RCA's Electronic Research Laboratory and inventor of the iconoscope, marked the second major phase in RCA's movement toward television.[69] This machine, which enabled magnification at an unprecedented level, was originally constructed only for use by physicists and not the commercial market. It was difficult to operate and extremely sensitive to vibration and changes in supply voltage, and it required a roomful of equipment in order to function. Vassos approached the design from the perspective of the user, mindful that the operator should sit in a normal posture and be able to observe the magnified image while working the controls. He created a tabletop for the microscope in blue linoleum that did not reflect light and could hold notebooks. For the operator's

STREAMLINED CONVENIENCE

A Minor Detail Becomes Important

By JOHN VASSOS

Gee! Are my hands heavy after a session with these old knobs.

SOMETIMES an apparently insignificant object is given a great deal of attention and one wonders whether the mountain brings forth a mouse or vice versa.

And this was the dilemma with which we were faced when it came to the problem of redesigning and standardizing the knobs for our various types of speech input equipment. At the first glance, the problem seemed to present a rather easy solution, which was, to smooth and clean the surface of the old-fashioned knobs, but, as the analysis proceeded, certain other pertinent facts were exposed. On active equipment, the control engineer spends hours manipulating these knobs without interruption, and also the fact was brought out that oftentimes the control engineer is in a sitting posture when working, changing the angle of the forearm to an entirely different plane and leverage of action as compared to the operation when standing. So, as the importance of this lowly object began to achieve gigantic proportions in its solution, a survey was taken to determine even further factors in trying to arrive at, and cover

practically all conditions under which the knob would be used.

Broadcasting stations and radio centers were approached for vital information. First it was necessary to arrive at the general proportions of the hand of the average radio engineer, assuming that, due to his particular type of work the hand development would be different than the average person. Then a plastic, soft putty similar to that used by sculptors was constantly molded and remolded until its overall form was of such size and proportions to suit this average hand, with the result that the most favorable proportions and dimensions were determined: It has no sharp or angular protrusions but soft indentations that act as a sure grip.

Another fact was disclosed. Seventy-five percent of the control engineers rested their hands on the knob by hooking the middle and index fingers over the knob and in a manner suspending and resting their entire arm thereon, and at the same time manipulating the knob. This meant in a short period of time the complete disfiguring of the panel proper and the rubbing out of the calibrated numerals. Often calluses and infections developed on the hands of the operator from the metal pointer that existed on these old knobs. Conse-

So you didn't realize how important I was?

quently, a flange was added at the bottom of the knob to prevent marring of the numerals of calibration and an integral fin was provided to act as the pointer, starting from the bottom of this protective flange and, in a streamlined fashion, blending into the top of the knob, the pointer portion extending from the center of the knob. This resulted in a beautiful and efficient form which had no sharp or angular protrusions foreign to the contours of the human hand, and assured protection for the instrument panel proper by the above mentioned flange.

(Continued on Page 24)

The Winnah! So say seven out of ten engineers.

"Streamlined Convenience: A Minor Detail Becomes Important." John Vassos's article and drawings describe the redesign of a knob. In the illustration at lower right, three engineers are pelted by the older, rounded knob. *Broadcast News*, November 1937. Courtesy of the Hagley Museum and Library.

"Radio Eyes for Microbe Hunters." Advertisement featuring Vladimir Zworykin *(standing)* and James Hillier at the Vassos-designed Model B electron microscope, 1940. Private collection.

comfort, he also improved its ergonomics, changing the height of the seat to create additional knee room.

Historian Nicolas Rasmussen argues that RCA's huge investment in the scientifically prestigious microscope may have been part of an effort to bolster the company's image after its failed launch of broadcast television.[70] The microscope enabled scientists to magnify otherwise invisible particles up to 100,000 diameters.[71] Vassos

reduced the enormous machine to a compact unit that was easy to transport and store.[72] This unit, in an attractive blue-and-chrome color scheme, won the Electrical Manufacturing Award for the finest design achievement in electronics of that year.[73] The electron microscope was a crucial technology for RCA's advancement in the field and proved to be profitable, as the company built and sold more than two thousand of the machines from 1940 to 1968.[74] Vassos was extremely proud of his styling work for this heavy-duty electronic device, particularly the unification of components into a console that made the complex machinery easier to handle.[75]

RADIO ARCHITECTURE AND INTERIOR DESIGN

While the improvement of in-house machinery was important for RCA, the company's most intense modernization efforts were focused on the places where it interacted with the public—its studios and architecture. As RCA franchises spread across the country, enormous resources were pumped into modernizing studios and transmitter buildings throughout North America. Starting around 1932, the company transformed a string of stations in rural areas as well as cities, in some cases from wire-strewn shacks to elegant offices. The company magazine announced these changes with exclamations like "WBRE at Wilkes Barre is modernized."[76]

Vassos created a fictional prototype, WRCA, as a standard design and modeled many transmitter buildings nationwide on it.[77] He wanted each building to "express the tempo and spirit of the most modern invention of the age—the radio."[78] He accomplished this objective through the building's shape and the use of materials such as steel, cement, glass, and aluminum. The building's form resembled a radio tube, with the smooth, rounded curves that characterized most RCA equipment and streamlining in general.[79] With decorative horizontal and vertical lines and external steel tubing in the banisters, the building took its strongest visual cue from the heat-releasing "louvers," which provided the vertical motif that Vassos later emphasized in his television design for the TRK-12. The slits also symbolized the speakers where sound was released from the machine, further mirroring, and perhaps helping to create, a communications aesthetic for radio.

The building's architecture expressed its function. Vassos's design integrated the transmitter by encasing it in Pyrex glass brick at the back of the building. Interior light created a "desired electrical effect, especially at night, since the glass is non-transparent but luminous."[80] Vassos's innovative use of glass bricks echoed RCA's Rockefeller Center headquarters, where a large Pyrex sculpture by Lee Lawrie dramatically marked the building's entrance.[81] Vassos also designed a glass archway above the main door, which provided strong light for the reception hall in daytime and a dramatic effect at night. The technology of the transmitter shaped the building in a harmonious fusion of light and electricity, merging the natural and the artificial. Transmitter houses that followed this model of modernization included locations

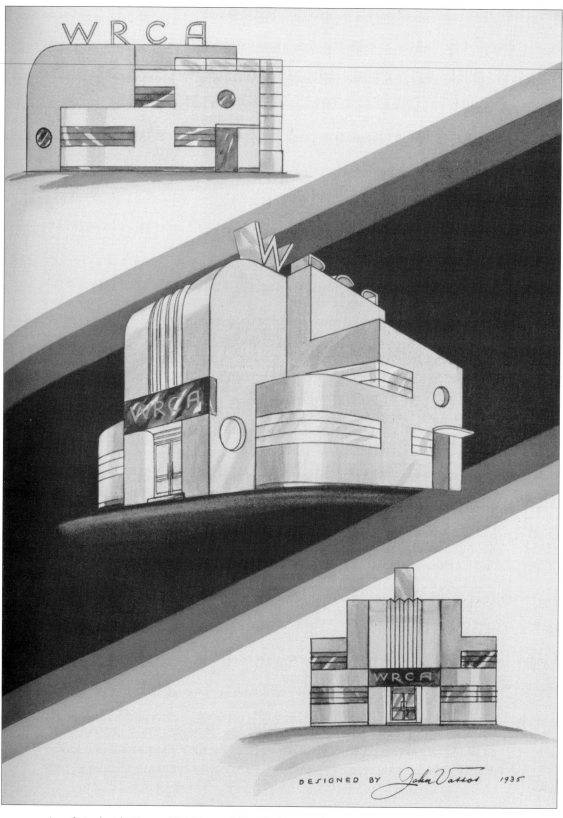

A rendering by John Vassos of WRCA, a model for a high-powered transmitter building. *Broadcast News*, December 1935. Courtesy of the Hagley Museum and Library.

Rendering by John Vassos of a 5-kilowatt transmitter building for station KROW, 1938. John Vassos Papers, Archives of American Art, Smithsonian Institution.

at Radio City in Hollywood; KFJZ in Fort Worth, Texas; KFAM in St. Cloud, Minnesota; WHBL in Sheboygan, Wisconsin; WWL in lower Mississippi; and WFMJ in Youngstown, Ohio. Stations in Canada were also modernized, such as CKCK in Saskatchewan.[82] Vassos submitted drawings of a streamlined 5-kilowatt transmitter building for station KROW in California. An article in *Broadcast News* gushed about KFAM: "The transmitter building . . . combines the utmost in efficiency and utility, reliability and permanence, together with modern architectural beauty. . . . The structure is of monolithic concrete with strips of dark finished granite and glass brick adding a modern tone."[83]

The interior of Vassos's studio prototype included a huge mural depicting the Spirit of Radio, "representing the union between Art and Industry," which was similar to the work he created for WCAU.[84] In *Broadcast News* articles, Vassos even laid out the prototypical modern transmitter building office, describing each element down to the "minute clock set obliquely in the corner" of the transmitter control

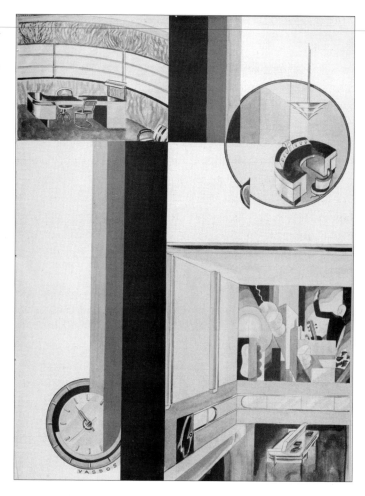

desk.[85] He explained the clock in exquisite detail, expressing the importance of time in radio transmission. The executive room's futuristic clock would be sunk into the wall, Vassos wrote, illuminated in a "manner showing the minute's progress" by a beam of light around the face of the dial.[86] The surface of the desk in this functional room would hold only utilitarian objects, leaving a clear space for the full horizontal effect of modernism's clean lines and open spaces.

By the 1940s, RCA was offering a blueprint of a modern transmitter house to broadcasters worldwide. Vassos detailed these plans in an article cowritten by Stewart Pike, then manager of RCA's functional design department. The authors explained, "For the first time, RCA is offering their experience and thinking in the layout of typical transmitter stations in a complete line of buildings covering all the various types and sizes of transmitting equipment."[87]

MAGIC BRAIN

As Vassos was involved in many different design and marketing strategies for RCA, he helped create the iconic logo for a major advertising campaign evoking the "Magic Brain" and "Magic Eye" of new radios. The Magic Eye was the green glowing cathode-ray tube located above the dial, which visually indicated for users the ideal tuning point, so they did not have to rely on their ears alone. Vassos recalled how he came up with the successful RCA Magic Brain campaign while walking around the engineering labs of the company. "On one of my trips through Building 7, I noticed an engineer working on a chassis with a hole in it. It looked like a 'magic brain' and a 'magic eye.'"[88] Proper tuning was a major issue, and listeners actually had to be taught how to tune in an efficient way to receive radio signals that were "clear and without distortion." Advertisements and other publications trained listeners how to use their radios. For instance, the RCA publication *Radio Travel-Log* featured an article titled "We Want You to Enjoy Your Radio," which addressed the barriers to clear listening, such as the three radio noises—natural static, "man-made" static, and internal set or tube noise—and fading.[89] The Magic Brain campaign was most closely associated with radios with motorized tuning and overseas dials, such as the 1938 models 811K and the 813K. Vassos not only created the Magic Brain advertising and in-store promotion campaign—"the sensational sales force that is going to bring people into your store," one advertisement promised—but he also designed push-button tuning.[90]

Vassos thought the Magic Brain slogan was particularly fitting since the hole in the chassis was an original feature that used filters to control sound quality. Company leadership eventually embraced this idea and used it in all of RCA's advertising campaigns and literature for more than forty years. The RCA Magic Eye and Magic Brain mobile advertising vehicles, with the "Magic" imagery emblazoned on their sides, toured the United States in 1935. The logo, featuring a large robot head with radio tubes for a brain, cleverly drew attention to RCA's technological wizardry, humanizing mysterious electronic processes by adding the bodily actions of seeing and thinking alongside the company's name. The Magic brand stamp became part of the company's visual identity and was added to the other dominant logos on its letterhead, alongside the rounded RCA logo (referred to in-house as the "meatball") and the RCA Victor dog, Nipper. Sarnoff preferred the traditional "His Master's Voice" logo, depicting Edison's faithful dog responding to the sound of the inventor's recorded voice. However, Vassos's symbol was given a five-year test run from 1935 to 1940 with the release of the Magic Brain radios. During those years, the corporation moved from fifth to first position among American electronics firms.

The Magic Brain icon had multiple meanings. It tapped into an old idea about the power of machinery to transcend and add to human capabilities. According to Siegfried Zielinski, the earliest ideas about television framed the "tele-vision," or kino eye, as an extension of the human body.[91] The radio receiver, a kind of magic box, went right into the brain, overcoming distances of time and space. Vassos was

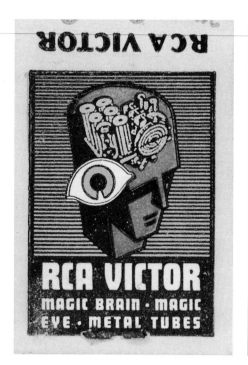

A matchbook cover featuring the Magic Brain logo, created and designed by John Vassos, circa 1939. Private collection.

"New 'Magic Brain' makes World-Radio doubly exciting!" Advertisement, circa 1935. RCA's round logo and the RCA Victor Nipper logo are in the lower left corner; the Vassos-designed Magic Brain icon is in the center. Private collection.

aware of the power of technology as an adjunct to the body. He expressed this idea in the *Phobia* image "Mechanophobia," which depicted a man overwhelmed by industrial machinery. The Magic Brain icon also resonated with the marketing of RCA's changing research team, which promoted the recruitment of geniuses like Russian scientist Vladimir Zworykin.

The merging of vision and cognition appealed to the customer as television began to become a reality, and RCA sought to associate itself with the awesome power of this new "magic eye." According to cultural theorist Andrew Ross, the visual expression of fear and fantasy merged in the radio age, when corporations extolled the powers of technology to expand knowledge and coordinate society. Today, a floating eye icon might evoke fears of Big Brother, but in the 1930s it suggested competent, assured leadership, similar to the corporate benevolence RCA expressed through its murals and its control of the airwaves.

Vassos was enamored of his logo and even imagined it would replace the iconic stylized lightning bolt. He described the Magic Brain concept:

> When I conceived the idea of the Magic Brain, its implication is so forceful and pictorial and so challenging that it soon began to supersede the RCA

trademark, which had no romantic or magical associations. The reason for this is, first that man believes that because he is fashioned in God's image that any machinery capable of functioning in a human manner must be good. Witness the success of "knee action," a mechanical spring principle that imitates the smooth and effortless activity of the human body.[92]

Evoking once again the importance of the human body in advertising and sales campaigns, Vassos believed the trademark gave the consumer "an emotional pictorial relationship where immediately a visual descriptive association is created."[93] As with the increasingly popular medium of comic books in the 1930s, the connection between the word and the image was essential to engage viewers' participation and elicit an emotional response.

The Magic Brain was a far cry from RCA Victor's long-lasting trademark showing a dog listening to "his master's voice."[94] It was also a departure from the company's other major logo, the letters *RCA* encased in a circle with a lightning bolt (the "meatball"). As Jeffrey Meikle argues, the 1920s and 1930s were the age of the logo; explicit signs of the machine age replaced stylized art nouveau motifs such as "stylized lightning bolts (electricity), gears, and radio waves, or abstract constructions whose impersonality, precision, regularity, and metallic look suggested by implication the machine."[95]

From the time he was hired at RCA, Vassos invested significant time and offered numerous suggestions toward improving the company's logo. In an early report, he criticized the company's confusing use of multiple icons:

> I do not feel that a successful result has been reached as regards your trademark since the merger of the two companies. You have retained the emblem of each . . . you are taxing the public's ability to memorize by giving them two ideas. And pictorially it is unsound, as the two designs are so radically unlike in composition that they not only are confusing but actually clash.[96]

Vassos suggested updating the Nipper logo by pairing the dog with a radio instead of a phonograph. The company rejected both this suggestion and his idea of "incorporat[ing] the RCA initials around the phonograph with the horn emerging from the letter C," as from a bull's-eye circle.[97] Vassos's critical engagement with the company's image continued until his retirement in 1970. For example, when RCA's "acucolor" television appeared on the market, he wrote an angry letter to Tucker Madawick, a collegue at RCA, complaining that the set's name in French would be interpreted as "asshole" television:

> Does anybody in the advertising department both in the agency and your own know? I ask you how can anybody be so lacking in the universality of

communications and not to check first. . . . What really happens when one begins to incorporate a little bit from here and a little bit from there . . . you end up in "acucolor."[98]

The styling for industrial radio equipment marked a new era in the production of "back-end" machinery, as RCA realized that its name had market value beyond its studios. In-house magazines like *Broadcast News* promoted this alliance of art and industry, showcasing RCA's resident stylists as a sign of the company's commitment to modernism and progressive design. Publicity photographs promoted the partnership between engineer and designer as a company strength. One posed shot showed Vassos and his colleagues at the production line, gathered around a mass-produced receiver and coming up with solutions. Although a visual depiction of this process would be rare today, RCA's emphasis on innovation and style in the 1930s inspired this photograph, which literally shows the unity of artist and engineer. As RCA entered the television age, company officials needed to prove that the cutting-edge design department behind the Magic Brain was not so magical after all, but rather the product of hard work and technological expertise.

In many ways, this image captured the RCA philosophy, depicting the full range of technical experts, acoustical consultants, structural engineers, electricians, and designers needed to construct the company's mass-produced machines. The Vassos shown in the photo, wearing a suit and working among engineers, was very different from the artist RCA hired in 1933. He was now responsible for a variety of technical, commercial, public relations, and artistic concerns. His design solutions reflected the corporate virtues of economy, efficiency, adaptability, and unity with other RCA products. The modern radio corporation subsumed Vassos's artistic ego into the company's plan, a deal Vassos was willing to make. In the RCA corporate culture, he was given authority and an outlet to explain his design decisions, share his opinions, and shape the design of the company's major products. In the postwar period, he worked for three distinct divisions of the company: engineering, RCA International, and RCA Victor Ltd. He also was a key consultant for RCA Laboratories, which opened in 1942 and was the epicenter for research on electron tubes, color television, transistors, high-power lasers, microwave technology, superconductor magnets, and more radical experimental projects, such as an electronically controlled highway.[99] Vassos's evolution from an independent artist to a corporate stylist at the heart of RCA's operations suggests a transformation in what constituted art in the age of mass production.[100]

In using streamlining and airplane imagery, Vassos created a design that embraced both the future and the past. It was associated with the progressive new technology of the airplane, but it looked back to the radio with nostalgia. Indeed, airplane design directly inspired Vassos's decisions to outline the body of the unit with bands of dark wood, as the edging crossed the body of the receiver like the wings of a plane. Undoubtedly, television's relationship to the airplane was not a great stretch, as both technologies offered mobility across time and space. Advertisements for television asserted its link to travel, in that it allowed viewers to see the world without leaving their living rooms. "You can be in two places at once with RCA Victor television," announced one 1939 advertisement for the TRK-12.

The TRK-12 receiver. Courtesy of the Early Television Museum.

Promotional materials also emphasized the link, using an airplane to announce "television's first year." The TRK-12 was even installed on a plane for a promotional event. For this flight, a program transmitted by NBC New York was picked up in a plane twenty thousand feet above Washington, D.C., two hundred miles away.[11] Vassos was happy with the TRK-12's overall simplicity. He felt that the receiver had been freed from the "shackles of over-decoration and meaningless form so associated with radio styling," which were inappropriate for the "new art of television."[12] The TRK-12 is now considered a classic in streamlined design. As design historian Lisa Phillips writes, "The craze for streamlining continued throughout the thirties . . . [in] larger objects such as a desk by Paul Frankl and the first commercially available television console by John Vassos, RCA's TRK-12 of 1938–1939."[13]

By the time of the 1939–40 New York World's Fair, at the inauguration of regular public telecasting by NBC, Vassos had designed four iconic televisions for RCA. These highly polished wood cabinets were, in order of size, the TT-5 tabletop television, the TRK-5, the TRK-9, and the TRK-12. Beyond streamlining, all of his prewar RCA televisions were very consistent in their balanced proportions and approach to design. The curves at the tops combined with the squared edges and stylized feet at the bottoms of the cabinets were distinctly Vassos. Other television manufacturers marketing their receivers by April 1939 included American Television, DuMont, the Andrea Radio Corporation, and GE. These sets varied considerably in size, image, design, and price, according to television historian Joseph Udelson.[14]

"You can be in two places at once with RCA Victor Television." Advertisement in the *New Yorker* featuring the TRK-12 television, 1939. Courtesy of the Hagley Museum and Library.

BELOW This photograph, taken in an airplane flying four miles above Washington, D.C., shows a group looking at television images on a TRK-12 receiver. The images were broadcast from New York City, two hundred miles to the north. The demonstration (the first successful one of its kind) was arranged by RCA with the cooperation of United Air Lines to mark RCA's twentieth anniversary, October 17, 1939. Courtesy of the Hagley Library and Museum.

TELEVISION RECEIVERS ARE HERE

(Left) The RCA Victor Television Attachment is designed to bring the wonders of modern Television to radio owners at a minimum cost. Sound is heard over your present radio; pictures are viewed on the RCA Victor Television Attachment.

(Below) The RCA Victor Television Console Model TRK-5 provides complete picture and sound reception of Television programs, plus all the entertainment of an 8-tube, 3-band RCA Victor Radio.

(Below) The RCA Victor Television Console Model TRK-12 is designed for those who demand the best in television.

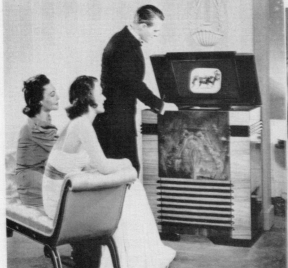

(Above) For those who want an excellent Television receiver plus the finest in radio, the RCA Victor Model TRK-9 will be found to be the logical choice. It is housed in an attractive modern-type console-type cabinet.

One has but to compare the first RCA Victor Television Receivers with the first radio receivers to appreciate what RCA's 7-year, $2,000,000 field test means to the consumer. No one can now forsee the future of television . . . but, with such a beginning, it seems safe to predict television will go hand in hand with radio as one of the nation's greatest public servants. Its services will be common tomorrow.

This article introduces Vassos-designed receivers. From top, clockwise: Models TT-5, TRK-5, TRK-9, and TRK-12. *Broadcast News*, July 1939. Courtesy of the Hagley Museum and Library.

David Sarnoff's dedication of the RCA Pavilion at the New York World's Fair on April 20, 1939, was a milestone in the television industry. Although RCA had conducted field tests of television transmission, the company celebrated the public debut of the new medium at the fair. Sarnoff proudly linked television to RCA's other blockbuster technology, radio, which had become an essential part of daily life. It was a marker of the company's success in its content, technology, and design. In his dedication speech, Sarnoff extolled television's potential social benefit, saying that it would "shine like a torch of hope in a troubled world. It is a creative force which we must learn to utilize for the benefit of all mankind."[15]

Ten days later at the fair, RCA started regularly scheduled broadcasting in the United States with a speech by President Franklin Delano Roosevelt. The ceremony was aired on W2XBS, RCA's first broadcasting station with a transmitter on the Empire State Building.[16] Visitors saw for the "first time how moving images are projected through space and splashed on the home screen by the electronic system of television."[17] The RCA Pavilion, echoing the fair's theme "Building the World of Tomorrow," sought to express hopefulness, albeit administered by big business. The country had endured a decade of economic depression and was on the verge of joining a war already under way in Europe. President Roosevelt succinctly expressed these hopes and fears when he declared, "The eyes of the United States are fixed on the future."[18] Roosevelt retained a part of this future as a TRK-12 television receiver was taken to the "Snuggery," the cozy room in his Hudson River home where it remains today.

At the ceremony, Sarnoff announced, rather prematurely, that regular programming would begin on the W2XBS experimental station.[19] Ten hours of programming, including shows from the NBC studio in Radio City, were played on the multiple receivers housed in the RCA Pavilion, located in the Communications Zone in the fair's Land of Tomorrow. After the fair ended, NBC sporadically broadcast sporting events like baseball and football games and a prizefight at Madison Square Garden. However, the development of regular programming would not occur until the early 1940s.

RCA displayed television technologies at its pavilion, and throughout the fair, to drive home the idea that television was the future. The displays, which featured the Vassos-designed TRK-12, had to be eye-catching to compete with the other futuristic promotions at the fair. The RCA Pavilion, designed by the modernist architectural firm of Skidmore & Owings to look like a radio tube, drew thousands of fair visitors daily. Prominent modernist painter Stuart Davis created sprawling murals for the pavilion's backdrop. The pavilion was a significant display of strength and power for RCA, and, as television historian Lynn Spigel notes, its display of television was "the most elaborate—and certainly most remembered—of all these early exhibits [that] took place in 1939 at the New York World's Fair."[20] RCA was not the only exhibitor of television at the fair. General Electric and Westinghouse also featured television studios where visitors were interviewed on camera.[21]

At the Hall of Television, on the ground floor of the RCA Pavilion, 150 people at a time could watch programming on model television receivers as well as on the larger projection-type television still in development. In the television laboratory, also on the pavilion's ground floor, visitors could observe research scientists at work on actual television technologies. At the Vassos-designed Musicorner in the America at Home Pavilion, visitors encountered the different technologies of television, facsimile machine, radio, and a phonograph all embedded in a single modern furniture cabinet. The Radio Living Room of Today was decorated in period furniture with separate cabinets for the reception of television, facsimile, and radio. A roving "Telemobile" unit moved around the fair with a television camera that enabled people to view themselves on-screen.[22] RCA had tested some of these display ideas a month earlier at the Golden Gate International Exposition, a world's fair held in San Francisco. For this event, Vassos designed the spectacular 5,000-square-foot pavilion where the first public showing of "high-definition" electronic television on the West Coast took place. Visitors had the opportunity to be filmed and shown on the demonstration television receivers. RCA also displayed such products as the radio facsimile, which printed news bulletins, pictures, and other text in the home.

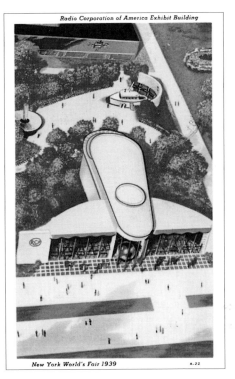

Postcard from the 1939–40 New York World's Fair showing RCA's exhibit building. Private collection.

Upon entering the RCA Pavilion at the New York World's Fair, visitors encountered a spectacular futuristic vision: the Phantom TRK-12 receiver, a large crystalline version of RCA's new television. Completely transparent, it enabled inspection of its inner workings from all sides. Almost every journalist at the event reported that the cabinet was made of glass, but RCA's publicity department had promulgated this belief—it was actually made of DuPont's newly renamed Lucite plastic. Journalist Orrin E. Dunlap Jr., writing in the *New York Times*, understood that the cabinet's transparency proved that the televised image visitors were seeing was real:

> By inspecting a special television set built in a glass cabinet, visitors at Flushing have the opportunity to observe the complexity of the radio-sight chassis

and [understand] why the . . . machines are priced from $200 to $1,000. To see this gleaming glass-encased instrument is to realize what a trick it is ahead to swing such an intricate outfit into mass production. It is evidence that the manufacturer as well as the showman has been tossed a challenge by the research experts who now anxiously watch to see what artistry can do with the new giant long-range eyes.[23]

The Phantom extended RCA's association of technology with powerful, scientific genius. It retained all of the streamlined design features of the actual receiver, but it was as if the color had been drained out of the television's casing. This display trick delighted visitors by its uncanny resemblance to the living room consoles they would see moments later in the exhibition hall—and which would soon be available for purchase. Throughout the pavilion there were reminders of television's relationship to radio, as well as reminders of the differences between the two, most fully expressed in the Lucite television. The use of Lucite, a transparent, pliable acrylic manufactured by DuPont and new to the commercial market, literally made it clear that television was real and not magic.[24] In doing so, the "spectacular" box inverted the receiver's typical function of hiding the machine's interior workings.

Thousands of people at the fair and at department stores within a fifty-mile radius watched and listened to President Roosevelt's address. During "television's coming-out party," as one writer called the opening events, stores struggled to contain the crowds. At Sachs Quality Furniture, more than seven thousand people arrived at the store between noon and 4:00 p.m. during the president's address, and fifteen hundred people had to be turned away. Sidewalks were jammed outside Bloomingdale's, which had placed three receivers in its windows.[25] Exposure to live television was not limited to New York audiences, however. Special jeep units brought demonstrations of television to more than eighty department stores from California to Maine after the fair closed.[26]

During the fair, RCA released the receivers for sale at major department stores like Macy's, Bloomingdale's, and Wanamaker's in the New York metropolitan area that could receive the broadcast signal, accompanied by advertising campaigns in major magazines and newspapers.[27] The ads for the TRK-12 flaunted its incorporation of RCA's top-of-the-line radio, a high-fidelity three-band broadcast radio receiver, with all-wave FM radio and nine electric push buttons for tuning.[28] Other sets available were the TT-5 tabletop model, with a 5-inch screen; the TRK-9, a direct-view console with video and audio; and the TRK-5.[29] The lowest-price television, the TT-5, at two hundred dollars, was out of reach for most Americans.[30] The top-of-the-line TRK-12 was six hundred dollars.

Despite RCA's best efforts, the initial press coverage of television technology was lukewarm. Journalists complained about the difficulty of seeing flickering images on tiny screens. *New York Times* reporter Orrin Dunlap was irked by the lack of

Visitors encircle RCA's "phantom television," a Model TRK-12 television with a clear cabinet, exhibited in the RCA Pavilion at the 1939–40 New York World's Fair. Courtesy of the Hagley Museum and Library.

variation of camera shots. It was not enough to show the president for fifteen minutes, he wrote: "For television to be interesting, on a small screen, it is vital that close-up shots be snapped. Otherwise the head is too small; facial expressions are lost and it is not easy to identify the people within the range of the optic's electrical vision."[31] Beyond that, the 9-by-12-inch screen was too small to make viewing pleasurable. Historian James R. Walker suggests that the ambivalent press reaction to television may have stemmed from journalists' anxiety that television news would supplant print journalism. David Sarnoff eagerly assured the press that this would not be the case and that television would be very similar to radio.[32]

Indeed, television was viewed as the natural extension of radio for a number of reasons. Historian Jennifer Burton Bannister argues that television's similarity to radio was the result of choices, assumptions, and negotiations among engineers, corporate radio executives, and the public.[33] The structure of the television industry was inherited from radio. Stylistically, the radio was literally absorbed into the television receiver, helping make the new device more palatable to consumers. RCA

An article shows curious spectators surrounding TRK-12 televisions at various locations in the New York City region. *Broadcast News,* July 1939. Courtesy of the Hagley Museum and Library.

also needed to gain approval for commercialization from the Federal Communications Commission (FCC).[34] The company hoped that associating the two types of media would allay any fears about television, so it highlighted the connection at every opportunity. Sarnoff described the birth of the company's newest medium in terms of its older one:

> Television again bids fair to follow in its youthful parent's footsteps and to inherit its vigor and initiative. When it does, it will become an important factor in American economic life. Also, as an entertainment adjunct, television will supplement sound broadcasting by bringing into the home the visual images of scenes and events which up to now have come there as mind pictures conjured up by the human voice.[35]

The radio tube shape of RCA's world's fair pavilion, where broadcast television was introduced, was consistent with this vision of television as radio's spawn.[36]

MARKETING TELEVISION

There was some confusion about what would actually be on television in the 1930s. One RCA publicity brochure for the TRK-12 showed an elegantly dressed woman gently fondling the dial. On the last page of the brochure, the same woman appeared on the television screen. In a Valentine's Day card featuring the TRK-12, a young couple appeared twice, once in the illustration's foreground and then also embracing on the television screen. The caption expressed the longing to be on television: "I'd love to-vision you for my valentine." This ambiguous relationship between the public and television was also evident at the New York World's Fair, where visitors were filmed and shown on-screen and then given certificates confirming that they had been televised. It is clear that marketing people were unsure how to present the receiver to the public.

The print ads for the RCA receivers imagined elegantly dressed viewers watching programs in their homes. The formality of these early visualizations suggest an awareness of the tiny audience of "early adopters" affluent enough to afford the expensive sets.[37] Television was at times ancillary in these early publicity photos. In one advertisement, for example, beautifully dressed women were shown glancing over their shoulders at the television rather than being absorbed by it. Vassos's sumptuously marbled machine, with its high price tag and depiction as a toy of the wealthy, was clearly not intended for the masses. Sarnoff himself imagined that television would become "the most glamorous of industry's children preparing to deliver its programs with the speed of light into the center of every home."[38]

Cultural anthropologist Orvar Löfgren argues that both radio and television, when they first entered the home, were accompanied by a sense of reverence until they became more familiar:

> Both the introduction of radio and television at first meant a period of happy experimentation and a multitude of utopian schemes. As the new commodities reached the homes, they were surrounded by a sacred and formal aura, which was also evident in the marketing. People remember the solemn atmosphere and the intense concentration in early radio listening, or the ways in which you dressed up for television evenings, hushing both grandma and the kids. Both the radio and the TV set were given a prominent position in the best room, rather like home altars. Gradually the media became routine, people learned how to listen with half an ear or having the television on as background screen for conversation. The radio moved into the kitchen and the bedroom. . . .
>
> Commodities like these may pass through a life cycle of sacralization to routinization or trivialization and then on to a process of cultural ageing which is often more rapid than the actual physical wear and tear.[39]

"I'd love to-vision you for my valentine." This valentine features the TRK-12 receiver, circa 1939. Courtesy of the Early Television Museum.

Löfgren's insight enables us to look beyond the limited notion that the radio and television appeared fancy merely because they were expensive or looked elegant. They were treated with reverence, as shown in the advertisements, because they were new.

Beyond the domestic setting, RCA anticipated that television would be used to show events to large audiences, as it was in Europe, where viewers collectively watched the Berlin Olympic Games in the summer of 1936.[40] Historian John Hartley notes the irony that the medium, which become known for its private and even isolating qualities, would be introduced to massive, jostling crowds eager for a peek at this modern marvel of technology.[41] Many factors, including the delay in the availability of broadcast programs, together led to the failure of RCA's first mass-marketed televisions to captivate the public. When programs aired, the viewing experience was fraught with technological problems that interfered with the audience's enjoyment. Television signals were subject to interference from cars, tall buildings, hills, and, in the early days of broadcasting, even the walls of viewers' homes.

Between 1929 and 1939, RCA had invested at least ten million dollars in television, yet the company would have to wait a few more years to reap the benefits.[42] In large part because of World War II, television did not take off as a commercial medium until later. Disappointing television sales led RCA to find new ways of disposing of excess inventory, such as by donating receivers to veterans' hospitals in the New York area.[43] The company sharply reduced prices in 1940. By the end of the war,

Formally dressed women glance at the tabletop RCA Model TT-5 television in this publicity image, circa 1939. This model would be plugged into the loudspeaker of a radio. Courtesy of the Early Television Museum.

This publicity photograph from RCA emphasizes the wealth and prestige of the first television viewers posed in front of the TRK-12 RCA receiver. Courtesy of the Hagley Museum and Library.

RCA and other manufacturers had recalled all their television sets for a complete realignment to conform to revised FCC specifications.[44]

Vassos's television on display in the Musicorner in the America at Home Pavilion was described as "one of the most unusual television exhibits of all."[45] This small television with its mobile screen was seamlessly sewn into the built-in living room furniture. It fit more closely with Vassos's idea of television's place in the home than the large, stand-alone receivers he designed for mass production. Vassos was clear in his opinion that electronics in the home should be integrated and centered on a single piece of furniture. However, the TRK-12's design significantly contributed to the visualization of a machine that had no prior form. Its cubist shape and almost anthropomorphized structure, with the screen as the head, were clever ways to diffuse fears about the power of this new technology. By encasing the machine's body

Viewers watch the June 1, 1939, television broadcast of the prizefight between Max Baer and Lou Nova on an RCA TRK-12 at the New Amsterdam Theater in New York City. Private collection.

with rich natural materials and letting the screen stand as the singular technological element, Vassos drew viewers' attention to the most important part of the machine, the screen. By hiding the controls inside the box, he created a sealed container that, when closed, gave no indication of the power and importance of the machinery inside. When opened, the receiver declared its function clearly—to show a screen. Vassos followed his stylistic philosophy in letting the machine's function dictate its design. In this case, the screen, and no other mechanical parts, constituted the centerpiece of the television set.

In later writings concerning television's domestic installation, Vassos advocated the idea of an integrated electronics suite, preferring to consider the design of the whole space rather than that of a singular appliance. He hoped that RCA would take a multiunit approach to entertainment, as he demonstrated in the Musicorner at the

New York World's Fair.[46] Besides the modular concept, Vassos had other ideas for receivers that would do away with bulky furniture, and even for designs that would totally discard the receiver and enable the screen to hang on the wall. "We must conceive of this new set in a totally different approach from the old-fashioned cumbersome box," he wrote in 1958 to Wally Watts, vice president in charge of engineering products at RCA, in his submission of a concept for a new television set with a narrow tube, remote control, and servicing from the front to eliminate cabinetry.[47] Vassos was right, of course, in foreseeing the supremacy of the flat screen over the wooden box, the size and importance of which diminished over time as consumers grew accustomed to the glassy presence of television in their homes.

7. JOHN VASSOS IN POSTWAR AMERICA

Artists had many opportunities to play important roles in World War II, especially with the proliferation of new visual techniques in warfare such as propaganda leaflets and camouflage. Vassos's hatred of fascism fueled his commitment to join the war effort, and he sought to find a high-ranking military position as an artist, specifically in camouflage design. He studied the art of camouflage at the American Design Institute, graduating with a certificate in July 1942. He asked his old Greenwich Village friend Harry Hopkins, now a top adviser to President Roosevelt, to help find a placement for him in the U.S. Air Force's camouflage division.[1] Hopkins believed that Vassos, at forty-three, was too old for the military, but he complied begrudgingly, soliciting a recommendation letter from high-ranking General Henry Arnold on Vassos's behalf.

In 1943, the designer was sent to Fort Belvoir in Virginia, where he was granted the advanced rank of captain in charge of camouflage in the Corps of Engineers. Next, he was transferred to the headquarters of the Third Air Force at Franklin Field in Tampa, Florida. While in Tampa awaiting assignment, Vassos practiced his skills in camouflage, creating multicolor installations with sniper suit demonstrations, decoys, and dummies.[2] Vassos also published educational booklets for soldiers featuring a character named Booby the Bear, which used humor to show the dangers of not employing camouflage properly.[3]

Camouflage's affinity to modernism, through its bare simplicity, lack of ornamentation, and decorative form, appealed to Vassos. Advancements in flight and aerial photography enabled both sides in the war to pinpoint hidden enemy operations from the air. Camouflage was used to disguise whole operations, especially munitions plants and storage facilities, so that enemy planes on bombing runs would miss their targets. By 1944, the U.S. Air Force's camouflage battalions had expanded to nearly six hundred from almost none the previous year.[4] Other industrial designers

Colonel Vassos featured in an OSS brochure titled *Schools and Training Middle East,* circa 1944. John Vassos Papers, Archives of American Art, Smithsonian Institution.

who worked with camouflage included Jay Doblin, director of the Chicago Institute of Design, and the industrial designer Norman Bel Geddes.

After nine months, the Office of Strategic Services requested that Vassos be transferred to lead its radio spy training camps at secret locations in the Middle East theater of operations and the Balkans. The OSS, a new branch of the military and the predecessor of the Central Intelligence Agency, focused on espionage and other secret and experimental techniques to gain intelligence on the enemy and disrupt enemy activities. Vassos was appointed head of the training school for the secret intelligence section of the OSS, which taught new methods of infiltrating enemy lines, and was also recruited as a spy himself. While with the OSS, he parachuted into Greece twice. The five-month beginning spy course that Vassos oversaw included parachute training, Morse code, sabotage, methods of escape, and annihilation.[5] In addition to overseeing the course, he created educational materials, including publications and films.

In his work for the camouflage unit and the OSS, he relied heavily on his skills as a graphic artist and educator. Vassos's brochures and film strips, which bore his unique illustrative style, featured OSS techniques for infiltrating enemy soil and spying on enemy activities. Other prominent designers and architects who worked for the OSS included architect Eero Saarinen, who oversaw visual communication; CBS

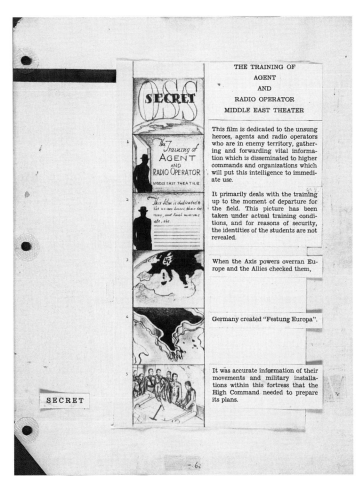

Vassos created this storyboard for an OSS training film, circa 1944. John Vassos Papers, Archives of American Art, Smithsonian Institution.

graphic art director George Olden; and Lawrence Lowman, vice president in charge of operations at CBS, who became chief of the OSS communications branch.[6]

Vassos revealed his discomfort with wartime duty through hundreds of descriptive letters to his wife, Ruth, during the war. After receiving a wound to his eye, he wrote despairingly, "I have to pretend it doesn't hurt or bother me at all, the price for setting the example and being called a Major. Nuts!"[7] In January 1944, Vassos contracted meningitis, a rare and sometimes deadly disease that caused him to be hospitalized for months. He made it through this difficult time by seeking solace in thoughts about his family and his dogs, and also in his design skills. While bed-ridden, he came up with new products, like a set of Lucite pens with a new filling device and two-tone effects; after the war, the pens were produced by the Waterman Company. "Lucite is the best material for two tone effects," he wrote to Ruth.[8] He explained losing himself in his art: "Creative people go off—something inside of them does and they disobey all orders of doctors and forget practically everything and everybody."[9] This work mode might explain his tireless drive and incredible productivity throughout his career. While convalescing from meningitis, he also wrote humorous, sometimes bawdy, lists, such as one describing twenty different types of men one found at the urinal, such as the "clever man" who uses "no hands" and the "sociable man" who joins a friend for a "piss whether he has to or not."[10]

When off duty, Vassos traveled to gain perspective and to remain in contact with dispersed friends, spending time with RCA head David Sarnoff, who was headquartered at Claridge's hotel in London, having been summoned by the War Department, and with Harry Hopkins.[11] These trips "gave him a respite from the monotony of the desert," he wrote to Ruth.[12] He also developed an appreciation for the modern design of Middle Eastern cities, writing, "Cities here are very modern, good examples of functional design."[13] Because of his illness he requested an early release from service, which was granted in January 1945; he left the OSS with the rank of lieutenant colonel.

DESIGNING FOR THE LEISURE MARKET

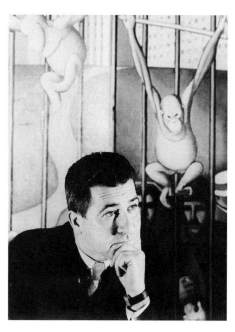

A pensive John Vassos at the Monkey Bar in the Hotel Elysée in New York City, early 1950s. Courtesy of Jayne Johnes.

During World War II the future of the United States changed dramatically. Only a few years earlier, the New York World's Fair had promised a future where new technologies would improve citizenship and national strength. The war years caused a shift. Private reward became more important than public gain as the war's end ushered in an era of suburban consumerism. Expanded automobility, rising incomes, and growing families, among other factors, supported this trend in the postwar era. As federal housing loans gave young families the incentive to move out of the cities to the newly developed suburbs, the cultural focus shifted from urban to suburban. Growing automobile ownership led to new consumer experiences in malls and on highways. Family discretionary income rose steadily, increasing nearly sevenfold from 1941 to 1958.

Amid this prosperity, couples who had postponed starting families during the Depression and war years gave birth at an unprecedented rate, producing the postwar baby boom. This burgeoning economy, with its shift of priorities from urban growth to suburban consumerism, forced industrial designers to change their practices and focus on designs for new markets. Additionally, the triumphs of American technology that had helped win the war were now being applied to consumer products and housing materials.

In the postwar era, industrial designers changed their practice. They moved away from civic issues of planning and reform that had been a feature of the New York World's Fair and turned their attention more to the suburban home market. Vassos's postwar career centered on design for suburban homes and new leisure markets. He still designed products and venues for media consumption, including movie theaters, radios, phonographs, and televisions, but his target audience was the suburban middle class instead of urban modernists. He focused his design activism, which previously had been expressed through wide public appearances and debates about urban growth, into the industrial designers' professional association and the Silvermine Guild. He worked mostly for RCA and also for a few other clients involved in creating leisure products and environments.

Vassos worried about the aesthetics of the new era and reaffirmed his commitment to modern design. In 1945, he penned his "Credo for Industry," which listed in vivid detail the outdated styles that threatened to defile American design:

> Are we again going to make jalopy radios and borax furniture? Fake streamline autos splattered with chrome? And Cape Cod cottages . . . Elizabethan bungalows, colonial mansions with Sheraton, Heppelwhite, Adam and Chippendale interiors, all created for people more than two hundred years ago. . . . When are we going to stop this nonsense and leave the chintzes, tester beds, the cobbler's benches and the Adam desks for the museums? When is this sickness that gnaws at the very vitals of our creative force going to be stamped out?[14]

Prominent industrial designers opened large agencies, like Donald Deskey Associates, hired employees, and took on international accounts. Demand for industrial design was booming, particularly in consumer packaging, suburban leisure-time markets, and the automobile industry. Recognizing the importance of design, corporations created in-house design teams to avoid having to hire expensive consultants like Vassos. These so-called captive in-house designers were paid salaries, which made them more cost-effective and more reliable than consultants who charged high fees. They were also more obedient than famously high-maintenance consultant designers such as Henry Dreyfuss and Raymond Loewy. Large corporations hired consultant designers only for special projects and large-scale architectural planning.

Upon returning from the war in 1945, Vassos knew he did not want to be a captive designer and soon opened John Vassos Associates in prestigious midtown Manhattan. While his office was a long commute from his home in Norwalk, Connecticut, it was accessible by train, and the location was essential to establishing his presence with the consultant design industry. The "associates" in the name made the agency sound bigger than it was. It was relatively easy to start up: Vassos hired an assistant, bought some modernist Herman Miller Canaletta-style chairs, and created a logo. "John Vassos Associates, Industrial Design, Product Development, Consultation" announced the new letterhead, with a capitalized emphasis on his now-famous last name.

NEW ROLE-GENERATING IDEAS FOR RCA

One of Vassos's first engagements with RCA following his break for military service began in 1944, even before he returned from war, when the company asked him to consult on the packaging for an important new album format that would revolutionize the music industry. Demand for recorded music had increased as consumers gained access to unprecedented amounts of new music via radio.[15] RCA and CBS, the major companies in the recording industry, were seeking to overcome the limitations of the 78 rpm record, the industry standard. The shellac 78 rpm was fragile, had low fidelity, and was limited to ten minutes of playing time on each side. Peter Goldmark of CBS solved these problems by inventing a twelve-inch microgroove plastic record that moved at the speed of 33⅓ rpm and produced high-fidelity sound. The long-playing album, or LP, was revolutionary in that it allowed a listener to hear twenty minutes of uninterrupted music on each side. RCA had been working since 1939 on the 45 rpm record. This seven-inch disc produced even better fidelity than the LP and was paired with a complementary record player.[16] Although the 45 rpm played only one song per side, the record player allowed the user to stack multiple discs for extensive listening. RCA released the 45 rpm in 1949, one day after CBS released its new LP format, leading Columbia Records to declare RCA's move a provocation of "war" in the fight for the more than sixteen million record player owners in the United States. Frank Folsom, president of RCA, denied this charge, but it is hard to deny that the timing of this release was intended to take some of the wind out of CBS's sails (and sales).[17]

In the immediate postwar period, Vassos played a role in the development of the new 45 rpm products, including packaging and portable record players, manufactured by the RCA Victor Division.[18] The Vassos-designed 45-J phonograph was the first model with an automatic record changer. Sold as "the modern way to play records," it allowed the user to stack up to ten records on a wide spindle so that they could be played one after the other for more than forty minutes of music, eliminating the need for the user to keep changing records. It was easy to use. Needing just two fingers to drop the stacked records onto the spindle, a listener could use the phonograph "even blindfolded," as the advertising text emphasized. The design of the elegant square phonograph, with its deep-maroon plastic turntable, gold-toned spindle, and elegant arm, drew attention to key elements. Without a built-in amplifier, the phonograph played through a radio or television set and could blend easily with any receiver style.[19]

Vassos was asked to devise a way listeners could know what record was next in the stack and that would also serve as a packaging feature. To start his research, he

John Vassos designed this 9-JY model 45 rpm record player for RCA. *Life Magazine,* 1950. Private collection.

gathered together a board of four practicing artists, a merchandise manager, a chemical engineer, and a music director. He then directed a meeting of the group that led to a plan for the unique color coding of the vinyl of 45 rpm records. The group chose differentiating colors for seven kinds of music: green for country and western, black for popular music, yellow for children's entertainment, cerise for rhythm and blues, sky blue for international, red for Red Seal or classical music, and midnight blue for

popular classics.[20] When the first color-coded 45 rpm records were released in 1949, the color choices intrigued psychologists at Johns Hopkins University. Having read about the color coding in *Newsweek* magazine, the Hopkins scientists contacted RCA Victor to find out about the thinking behind the color selections.[21]

Although the tinted records received much positive publicity, they were difficult to manufacture. The pressing plant was having nightmarish problems changing over from the production of one color to another. In late 1950 RCA Victor mostly stopped producing color-coded vinyl, retaining only the yellow for children's records until 1952 and red for classical records until 1953. The labels on the discs remained color coded until 1954, when the RCA dog, Nipper, was placed in color at the top center of the label.[22] For Vassos's contribution to the 45 rpm, RCA Victor paid him a generous $2,000 yearly retainer from 1944 to 1949, when the dedicated 45 rpm phonographs and records went on the market, in addition to his regular retainer.[23]

Despite his involvement in the launch of the 45 rpm record, Vassos had returned to RCA in Camden in 1946 with trepidation. "Sarnoff is cleaning Throckmorton's regime. What about us when we return?" he wrote in a letter to Tom Joyce, manager for radio, phonograph, and television at RCA.[24] There had been changes in staff. Skeet Rundle, who preferred building in-house staff over hiring outside consultants, was running the styling department for consumer products. Norman Bel Geddes had been brought on board as a temporary consultant for the postwar transition, which angered Vassos, who naturally wished that he had been available to do this job. Vassos felt that Bel Geddes was a poor choice, since "often a lofty idea falls way down below on the desk of a secondary designer, and that is why in the record of Mr. Geddes, we have some extremely costly adventures at the expense of the manufacturer."[25]

RCA moved Vassos to the engineering department, where he worked for vice president Wally Watts, who had replaced Throckmorton as the head of consumer products. The company was unsure about where Vassos would fit in, a discrepancy reflected in his 1945 retainer of $10,000, less than his 1939 salary of $12,000. His pay quickly increased as his value to the company rose—to $12,500 by the next year and to $13,500 in 1949.[26] To mitigate any fears his new boss might have about his role as a consultant designer, Vassos wrote a detailed letter clarifying his relationship to the company:

> It is apropos at this time for me to restate my relationship to the company and to your office. I shall continue to keep an outside and fresh point of view and only to take direct action when the design objectives deviate from a healthy pattern. I shall continue to give counsel and recommendations to our design department, to advertising when my services are required and in general to be of value.[27]

Vassos gave a clean design and portability to the first RCA television camera, the TK-30, in 1946. This camera was used in the field and in the studio. *Broadcast News,* October 1946. Courtesy of Hagley Museum and Library.

RCA was branching out in new directions in the postwar period, expanding into color television, home appliances such as air conditioners, and computers. Among his first jobs after the war, Vassos designed RCA's first television cameras for studio and mobile broadcast use. Here again he took accessibility, ventilation, and ease of operation into consideration, making the hulking cameras, which weighed more than three hundred pounds and were five feet long, look more compact. He redesigned the control panels to provide quick access to the operator.

Vassos worked on other studio equipment as well. His "Magic Lock" Boom Stand K5-4A was easy to operate with one hand and easy to assemble. Vassos listed fourteen key features for this model stand, including "universal one arm action." He continued to seek ways to reduce the size of bulky transmitters and used modular principles in designing consoles for broadcast studios. Expanding into home appliances, RCA turned to Vassos to help with the company's first electronic air-conditioning unit, to be produced in collaboration with Fedders. The artist came up with an air-flow type of grille design to replace a huge, light-obscuring protrusion and made the length of the unit adjustable for windows. Although this air conditioner was never produced, it marked a brave new direction for the company.[28] Radar technology for the defense industry was another growth area for the company. Vassos redesigned the naval radar indicator for RCA's Radiomarine Corporation of America. The indicator used radio waves to reveal objects from as close as eighty yards away to as far as fifty miles. It was in operation and marketed by RCA in the postwar era and used in the S.S. *Independence* in 1951 as well as in other ships.[29]

Vassos continued designing radios for the RCA International Division and worked on luxury products like the Berkshire series, high-fidelity, broadcast-quality entertainment systems featuring high-end equipment housed in midcentury-style furniture. Released in 1947 and marketed to wealthy consumers, these systems were designed by prominent designers of the day, including Lester Beall and Hollis Baker. Harry Olson of the RCA listening lab designed the technology behind the Berkshire products' high-fidelity speaker systems. The Vassos-designed instrument panel for the 1947 Berkshire series included a complex tuning dial and mechanism controls in gleaming satin-finish metal with black knobs. Vassos's challenge was to find a way to convey layers of detailed information in a clear way. His solution was to use a combination of push buttons and tuning knobs at various tiers. Under the dial scale window on the radio, the user could push buttons to select a station. The four large round knobs were clearly labeled and controlled (from left to right) volume, noise suppression, variable selectivity and sensitivity, and manual tuning. Fourteen push buttons below the knobs allowed the user to select the desired media mode, such as phonograph or television. Not surprisingly, however, this expensive customized system, with its gold-plated front, could not—and did not—last long on the market. Vassos was also involved in designing more widely marketed consumer market portable electronics, such as the sleek, metallic 1947 Globe Trotter eight-inch BX-6 radio with carrying case; the "filteramic" radios (Models 3RA61 and 1-XF-4), which promised to block static; and portable cassette tape recorders.

During his postwar work at RCA, Vassos developed styling concepts for such product series as the International line of receivers. The design group in Camden then translated and converted his ideas into working drawings. When Vassos designed displays for showrooms, the in-house staff made the actual drawings.[30] This arrangement allowed the designer time to work for several departments simultaneously. Indispensable in each department he advised, Vassos complemented the strengths of the in-house design team and collaborated with in-house designers like Stewart Pike. At the inception of new projects, the designers worked closely with engineers so they could exchange ideas. This was particularly important because Vassos worked on both concrete products and speculative plans, ranging from the redesign of Japanese portable transistor radios to the development of closed-circuit educational television to the forecasting of the future of home television.

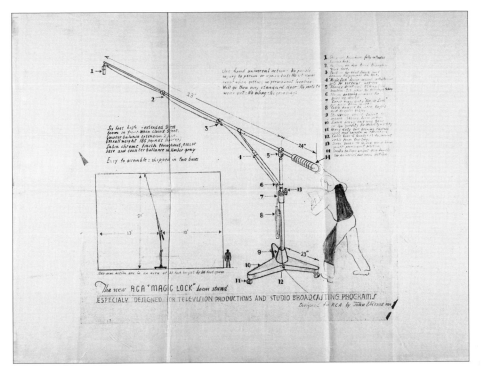

Design rendering for the "Magic Lock" Boom Stand K5-4A, circa 1948. John Vassos Papers, Archives of American Art, Smithsonian Institution.

"RCA Radar—enables ships to see through fog, darkness, storms." This advertisement from 1947 shows the Vassos-designed twelve-inch indicator in use. Private collection.

John Vassos designed the front panel for the Berkshire series of high-end radio, phonograph, and television cabinets launched in 1947. Courtesy of the Early Television Museum.

A publicity photograph of the RCA 501 solid-state computer designed by John Vassos, with a note from the office of the designer, circa 1958. John Vassos Papers, Archives of American Art, Smithsonian Institution.

An example of this reciprocity between engineering and design can be seen in Vassos's work on the 501, RCA's first solid-state all-transistor computer. The engineering department realized that the 501's exterior and functioning needed to be improved. Vassos employed his modular design strategy, framing the computer and its components as a system and not as individual devices. He completed work on the massive computer's freestanding integrated units in 1958.[31] Unfortunately, the 501 was copied by IBM (at least according to Vassos), which became the leader in the field with its 1964 release of the System/360, the first computer component system with truly compatible hardware and software.

In a 1964 memorandum responding to the question "What do you do here?" Vassos clearly summed up the division of his labor at RCA: "1/3 consumer products, 1/3 engineering, 1/3 corporate activity."[32] According to his colleagues, his most important role was as the "idea generator." In 1970, J. P. Taylor, vice president of marketing and a longtime RCA employee, recalled Vassos's most valuable contribution to the company as his creativity:

> As I think back on it, John, I believe that the ideas you gave me were more important than the design details. Today there are many illustrators who are adept with the air brush—but when it comes to ideas they are blanks. I shall always be grateful for the broad-visioned ideas you gave them. I don't know whether you realize that I used them in my writing and planning.[33]

For a consultant designer like Vassos, this was the best working arrangement, in that it allowed him to advise across department boundaries and to generate new ideas. His freedom enabled him to avoid what he felt were typical corporate distractions, such as battles for power and petty disputes. Overall, Vassos disliked corporate life. As he wrote, "There is something very unhealthy about it all, basically, most underlings (who do most of the work) are dominated by fear—the top echelon (who get their ass kissing) . . . most of them have mini-dictator tendencies."[34] His 1930s *Contempo* illustration depicting workers chained to their desks summed up his view of corporate employment's enslaving nature. He particularly did not like "team work," as he felt it interfered with his art and encouraged conformity. In a speech he delivered at a meeting of the Industrial Design Alumni Association, Vassos commented on management's suppression of the industrial designer's creativity through regimentation into "such systems as 'team work,' 'new products,' 'advance planning,' 'research and development'—divisions which rely upon the designer's talent, then promote the end result as a product of the 'department' and thus compromise the designer's individual philosophy."[35]

His personality enabled Vassos to develop and maintain strong relationships with clients over decades, despite his independence. He sustained lasting bonds with RCA's leadership and the company's founding family, in particular David Sarnoff and his son Robert Sarnoff (who took over the company in 1965). These relationships proved to be valuable anchors through turbulent times as the company changed strategies in the postwar years. David and Robert Sarnoff answered Vassos's frequent letters immediately and warmly. From their letters, it seems that they enjoyed having this dedicated "old-timer" from the earliest radio days on the crew. Vassos wrote to David Sarnoff to congratulate the company for photographing the moon in 1964,[36] and Sarnoff wrote back promptly, thanking Vassos for the "thoughtful letter." His RCA colleagues admired Vassos's opinionated style: "He's never been shy about expressing his views," one wrote. "He bought a Cadillac Eldorado in 1957—a wonderful looking car, except for those hideous soaring fins in the rear. The day he picked it up, he drove straight to the local body shop and had it de-finned."[37] Indeed, he railed against "so called gingerbread" car designs with "meaningless chromium plated bars, trim, and affected streamlining."[38]

Vassos worked on other leisure-time products and venues immediately after the war, including a jukebox for Mills Industries and United Artists movie theaters across the country. Jukeboxes, whose name came from *jouk,* a term of uncertain origin that meant to dance, were originally found only at unsavory places (known as jouk joints or juke joints) where young people danced to the rhythms of boogie-woogie. Once known as jouk organs, the coin-operated machines became popular in the early 1900s but did not reach the height of their use until the rise of new audiences in the postwar era. In the 1940s, jukebox manufacturers redesigned their products in an attempt to expand their use nationwide, particularly among

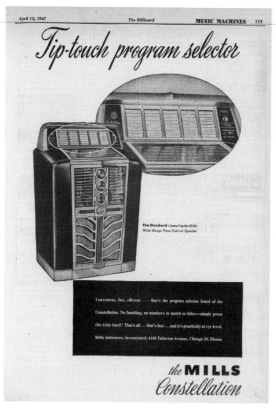

Tip-touch program selector

The Standard : *featuring the Mills Wide Range Tone Cabinet Speaker*

Convenient, fast, efficient . . . that's the program selector board of the Constellation. No fumbling, no numbers to match to titles—simply press *the title itself!* That's all . . . that's fast . . . and it's practically at eye level.

Mills Industries, Incorporated, 4100 Fullerton Avenue, Chicago 39, Illinois

the **MILLS** *Constellation*

"Tip-touch program selector." Advertisement for the Vassos-designed Constellation jukebox. *The Billboard,* April 12, 1947. Private collection.

This floor lamp, designed by John Vassos for the Egli Company, allowed for direct and indirect light at various heights and was created especially for use with a television. John Vassos Papers, Archives of American Art, Smithsonian Institution.

middle-class teenage audiences.[39] Chicago-based Mills Industries contracted Vassos to design its new Mills Constellation jukebox in 1946. The company paid Vassos an unprecedented $7,500 for his consultation.[40]

The styling did not go as smoothly as Vassos had hoped. There was disagreement over the color of the jukebox; the designer favored metallic blue but Mills preferred burgundy "or some other warm color."[41] Vassos relented and arranged for RCA to manufacture some of the Constellation components in Canada, choosing aluminum or form plywood for the console.[42] When it hit the market, Model 951 was a stunning machine, with forty song selections from twenty 45-rpm records; listeners could select six songs for twenty-five cents. The Constellation's tough aluminum cabinet protected it from the casualties of bar environments, such as alcohol spills and cigarette burns. It sat shoulder high for convenient viewing of the record selections. The jukebox was sold from 1947 to 1951, until Mills went bankrupt. With additional design features by Walter Lockwood Martling Jr., who designed the remote controls and speakers, the Constellation is now a coveted collector's item.

appealing open glass counters. He also redesigned the United Artists trademark, still in use today, by joining the *U* and the *A*.[49]

Vassos's involvement in theater redesign taught him sobering lessons about the disadvantages of being an outside consultant. In particular, he was enraged when Skouras's employees changed his work without his permission. This happened early in his contract at a theater in Elizabeth, New Jersey, and led to serious conflicts with the staff. Vassos explained in an apologetic letter to Skouras that this had happened before: "I have worked for years and am still working for big companies as a consultant at approximately the same type of job I did for you, George. In every instance the permanent personnel resent my presence. This is inevitable."[50] He had continuous clashes with the manager of Grauman's Egyptian Theatre; he received hostile letters, and eventually some of his bills went unpaid, leading him to stop working with the firm in 1954. Despite these frustrations, he and Ruth attended the gala opening of the redesigned Grauman's Egyptian Theatre.

Vassos continued creating large-scale public murals. This was a labor of love for the artist, who had earned his start at RCA with his mural-making skills and who enjoyed the challenge of translating written stories into wall art. As a product of the public art era of the 1930s, Vassos was strongly committed to this decorative form, although his painting style evolved from 1930s realism to simplified abstraction. His postwar murals were not social realist works such as he created at WCAU; rather, they were pared-down narratives of modernity that used line, color, and symbolic representation. His murals included one for the 1956 Dominican World's Fair in Ciudad Trujillo and a 120-foot mural at the luxurious Condado Beach Hotel in Puerto Rico. His 24-foot mosaic mural at the Lockheed Corporation's missile program research center in Van Nuys, California, depicted the conquest of space. He also consulted on the interior and exterior color design for Lockheed's massive aerospace campus. His mural *Cosmosynthesis* in the central lobby of the new RCA Building in Washington, D.C., presented the story of electronics, from wireless radio to television to the atomic age. In the mural, dramatically installed in a freestanding aluminum frame, Vassos suggested that the atom could both destroy and help human life. In 1960, Lyndon Johnson, then a U.S. senator, attended the opening of the building, where a demonstration of the new transistorized computer was part of the program.

DESIGN FOR THE HOME

Vassos returned to designing for RCA's world's fair exhibits, as he had done in the 1930s. For the Brussels World's Fair in 1958, the first world's fair in Europe since the war, Vassos designed an entertainment center that featured a modular design similar to that of his Living Room of the Future for the New York World's Fair in 1940, but with more colorful splashes to honor the emergence of color television. Color television had

This presentation of color television with a model family was designed by John Vassos and featured at the Brussels World's Fair in 1958 and at the National Home Furnishings Show at the New York Coliseum. John Vassos Papers, Archives of American Art, Smithsonian Institution.

not yet become the norm. Networks had aired limited programming "in living color" as early as 1953, and in the early 1960s NBC and CBS carried color shows regularly, but they were still experimental and not widely watched. Vassos created a colorful room that combined a blue-and-tan Mark Series color television with matching record player and stereo speaker, surrounded by bright-red record storage cabinets. He had recently shown his acumen with color in his work with architect Thomas H. Yardley on a prefabricated home called the Chromspun House of Color. This five-room ranch-style home, featuring vinyl floor coverings, was displayed at the National Home Furnishings Show in New York and traveled to department stores, including the J. L. Hudson Company store in Detroit.[51]

At the Brussels World's Fair, Vassos selected standard RCA Victor product lines for the L-shaped media recreation area, which was enlivened by large color blocks of vinyl placed over the integrated console unit spanning one whole wall. Instead of placing the television on an island by itself, as was typical of conventional television arrangements, he designed the console so it combined the storage space and television area and created a cohesive, harmonious horizontal line. Vassos again put the television at the center and added other forms of visual stimulation, such as an abstract painting and free-form sculpture, to place the console in a broader context.

This television room was high-end but also informal, unlike the club chair and cocktail environment associated with Vassos's early television room design. Television viewers no longer required formal attire; instead, this design celebrated an intensified family unity unique to the spacious suburban home. With dad anchored in a chair and mom sitting on the floor near the kids, the home entertainment center merged tradition and modernity.

Vassos had always been concerned with the placement of media machines in the home, but this issue became critical in the television-saturated postwar era. Vassos hoped to get RCA involved in prefabricated home construction. In a confidential memorandum about the "technically correct home," he described potential areas of media and communication in which RCA could profit. These "may be one-way (as radio, television and their developments) or it may be two-way as in personal telephone conversations or personal television two-way viewing," Vassos explained.[52] He deeply wanted RCA to be a leader "in this race to own the living room." In an impassioned letter to John Burns, then president of RCA, he explained, "RCA has the right to claim the living room, because no one else in the world has supplied so much pleasure and entertainment as has RCA through their facilities—NBC, TV sets, record players, our FM and other facilities."[53] Although television was playing a central role in domestic life by the early 1960s, Vassos argued that its unique audio and visual components were being ignored. He felt strongly that the placement of electronics in the living room needed careful consideration, as he wrote bitterly:

> Nobody has told the public where the television should be placed in the living room or where HiFi and other concepts are affecting acoustically and all the other pertinent details which deal with comfort and scientific arrangement. The living room is truly the center of entertainment and happiness and not a decorator's notion of some gimmick sugared with the aura of "gracious living" pushing further and further back the electronic . . . contributions of our era.[54]

As early as 1954, Vassos urged RCA to develop what he called an "Advanced Design Center" to provide long-range planning for media devices like recording machines and television receivers. Other major companies, such as General Motors and DuPont, strategically employed such planning centers. In a letter to Walter Watts, Vassos argued that advanced design should start immediately with the planning for the tape recorder, the home entertainment unit, and other domestic products.[55] He felt strongly that RCA should design televisions with narrow tubes for portability, add remote controls, and eliminate cumbersome cabinetry, among other features.

In the same letter to John Burns mentioned above, Vassos stressed the importance of creating a design center that could establish RCA's public leadership in design.[56] Later that year, in 1960, the company approved the Advanced Design Center plan, with television and miniature electronics as focal points. Vassos worked closely on the plan with Tucker Madawick, whom he knew from the American Designers' Institute. Madawick, a brilliant young designer hired by RCA in the late 1950s, was the team leader and later took credit for the formation of the Advanced Design Center.

The Design Center was not a physical place but a conceptual breeding ground for new ideas. Its mission was to cultivate visionary or "blue-sky" design, to stimulate thinking toward advanced solutions. The Design Center brought together designers, architects, and intellectuals to imagine the future of RCA television. The assembled "brain trust" included Melanie Kahane, Leonard Outhwaite, and Paul Rudolph, dean of the School of Architecture at Yale University and a major architect, whom Vassos recruited to join the group.[57] Following the team's extensive ideation sessions, the RCA industrial design department prepared concept sketches. The team's designs for thin large-screen televisions with crystal clarity foreshadowed the popular flat-screen television of today. They also imagined that these sets would be portable, for use in places like the office—as demonstrated by images of an executive enjoying a boxing match viewed in a folding briefcase on his desk. The Design Center also recommended miniaturizing components while providing better image quality. Portable and sleek, these televisions were envisioned in macro and micro, for wall and pocket, with few in-between sizes. These designs suggest an awareness of television's debt to both movie theaters and transistor radios.

Vassos's interior displays for the 1964 New York World's Fair RCA exhibition, where the company introduced color television, constituted his tour de force of home design for television. Malcolm B. Wells, who had designed other RCA buildings in Florida and in New Jersey, was chosen as the architect, and Vassos was the interior designer.[58] Vassos shaped the displays "to develop an interior of functional and aesthetic quality in the presentation of the RCA color TV story," including the selection of materials, furniture, and colors. He was well compensated for this job, receiving eight thousand dollars in addition to his regular retainer.[59] Vassos immediately established a relationship with the powerful New York urban planner Robert Moses, president of the World's Fair Corporation, to get approval for his expansive plans. As usual, Vassos had ambitious and strategic plans for the RCA Pavilion. He recommended that RCA immediately lease the plot next to the Soviet Union's pavilion. In his plan, RCA would symbolically challenge the communist nation to a technology duel, pitting the Soviets' recent conquest of space against RCA's most recent conquest—color television. As it turned out, the Soviet Union pulled out of the fair, but RCA secured a prime place across from the fair's main entrance. Indeed, with color television as a major fair display, and as with RCA's spectacular premiere of television at the 1939–40 New York World's Fair, Vassos saw a great opportunity to demonstrate his leadership in the field of home electronics planning.

Vassos designed a spacious "telerena—theater in the round" that featured a bandstand to greet visitors and a "crystal chandelier of color" made up of color televisions suspended from the ceiling.[60] To promote the company's splashy release of affordable color receivers, RCA decided against the color television chandelier in favor of placing three hundred closed-circuit televisions throughout the fair. In addition, RCA added a complete studio, where eight thousand visitors a day witnessed how television was produced as well as saw themselves for the first time on a color screen.

PROMOTING THE AMERICAN WAY

One of Vassos's largest-scale design commissions was for the country's most popular export—the American way of life. In 1955, with a budget of eight million dollars from Congress, the Eisenhower administration created the International Trade Fair Program to promote the United States abroad. Specifically, the program's stated objective was "the offsetting of communist propaganda around the world by a demonstration of American goods and the American pattern of doing business and how we want to cooperate with other countries."[61] By the end of the program's first year, the United States had participated in fifteen trade fairs all over the world, including in Paris, Vienna, Bogotá, Tokyo, Addis Ababa, Djakarta (now Jakarta), Karachi, and New Delhi. Extensive records of the fairs in the National Archives reveal the important ideological role of pavilion architecture in the seemingly neutral, entertaining environment of a trade fair. The program hired America's most prominent designers, including Donald Deskey, Peter Muller-Munk, Raymond Loewy, and John Vassos, to design pavilions for the trade fairs that represented and demonstrated the superiority of the American way of life. Vassos was tapped to design the American pavilions for both the Karachi and New Delhi fairs. With his extensive experience at RCA he was an ideal choice, as these fairs were to present television (and RCA) to audiences of many who had not yet experienced it. An urgent telegram to the U.S. secretary of state requesting that the State Department "contact John Vassos immediately" revealed his importance to the project.[62]

The Karachi and New Delhi Trade Fairs were almost back-to-back, with the Karachi fair running from September 9 to October 2, 1955, and the New Delhi fair running October 29 to December 15 (it was eventually extended to December 31). The U.S. Pavilion was relatively small in Karachi and featured the theme "For a Better Tomorrow," presented primarily in terms of television. Displays in the pavilion included the General Electric–sponsored House of Magic and an area highlighting U.S. economic aid to Pakistan.[63] In reviewing Vassos's work, Robert Warner, assistant director of the International Trade Fair Program, noted that he was

Vassos designed the U.S. Pavilion for the 1955 Karachi Trade Fair. John Vassos Papers, Archives of American Art, Smithsonian Institution.

impressed by Vassos, "a superb designer," and particularly by what he "did with an ugly warehouse."[64]

At the New Delhi Trade Fair, the U.S. Pavilion was one of the costliest, as U.S. government officials knew the fair would be "loaded with satellite countries."[65] Per the mission of the International Trade Fair Program, "an effective American showing in a given trade fair takes on a greater degree of urgency when a major Soviet bloc competition is present or threatened."[66] The U.S. Pavilion, the largest of the fair, occupied 100,000 square feet of central space.

Vassos faced many challenges creating the New Delhi structure, including a tight schedule, contract issues with builders, delays, and an overloaded interior with multiple exhibits. The largest exhibit, spanning 20,000 square feet, examined the peaceful uses of atomic energy through thirteen sections and included an atomic reactor.[67] To accommodate the many exhibiting parties, Vassos designed a sprawling, modern-looking single-story building. It was constructed of Indian concrete and brick as well as American steel, glass, plastic, and aluminum. A glass-walled television theater with massive RCA twenty-one-inch sets duplicated an American television studio.[68] The television sets aired live footage and entertainment from the fair, local Indian shows and events like weddings, and American programs such as *Kukla, Fran and Ollie.* The television exhibit was rated number one at the fair in a poll and, combined with the Atoms for Peace demonstrations, drew "millions of people jamming through the doors and turnstiles" who had never seen anything like it.[69] Vassos's glass-walled television studio, in particular, drew "people running from every pavilion. They stood on the sidewalk sixteen or eighteen or twenty deep to see their own people telecast."[70] Live performances of modern dance, with Martha Graham, and the big band music of Tommy Dorsey were also held at the pavilion.

Despite the popularity of the television and atom exhibitions, Roy Williams, director of the U.S. Commerce Department's Office of International Trade Fairs, was not pleased. Cost overruns plagued the project, which cost $606,544, more than double the planned budget of $250,000.[71] Williams complained that the building lacked the impressive height, dramatic exterior lighting, and open walls of the Soviet Union and China Pavilions. The U.S. Pavilion looked, he wrote, like "a massive wedding cake."[72] Indeed, polls confirmed that fair visitors greatly preferred the China Pavilion to the U.S. Pavilion, by a margin of two to one. Another supervisor, Robert Warner, then director of the Far East and Near East Office of International Trade Fairs, noted that "John Vassos's design is very impressive. Our building is modern and striking. . . . I think he did a wonderful job in New Delhi." He did concede, however, that Vassos's building was overly ambitious.[73] Despite this assessment, Vassos reaped wide publicity for his involvement in the trade fairs, appearing on NBC's popular *Today* television program with host Dave Garroway and in the international press.[74]

Beyond his government work, Vassos's success in design and his civic contributions began to be acknowledged by a wider audience of colleagues. He received numerous awards and honors, including the American Greek War Veterans Military Cross in 1947 and the Industrial Design Institute's Medal of Merit in 1955. In 1964, he received the Paidia Award from the Hellenic University Club. That same year, on January 22, Alexander Matsos, Greece's ambassador to the United States, presented Vassos with the Royal Cross of the Golden Phoenix. This honor, given at the direction of King Constantine II, was the highest award bestowed by Greece on people of nonroyal birth. It was given for Vassos's cultural and aesthetic contributions to upholding the Hellenic tradition and for his exemplary war record in World War II serving in Greece, North Africa, and the Middle East.

LEADERSHIP IN INDUSTRIAL DESIGN

Vassos was an influential leader who used his ample social skills and enormous energy to mobilize a national coalition of industrial designers. His dedication to the prominent industrial design professional society he helped found was a major aspect of

Logo of the American Designers' Institute, designed by John Vassos in 1938. Courtesy of Carroll Gantz.

Vassos's postwar life. In 1938, he became the chairman of the executive committee for the first professional organization of industrial designers in the United States, the American Designers' Institute (ADI). The American Furniture Mart, which wanted a close-knit group of designers to work with the furniture industry, financed the organization, which soon expanded to include all aspects of design related to home and institutional furnishings. The executive committee, which included Leo Jiranek, Alfons Bach, and Edward Wormley, oversaw the group's exhibitions and social activities. The steadily increasing roster of active members finally permitted the ADI to incorporate and become a self-supporting body. On July 12, 1940, the institute was granted a corporate charter.

Vassos not only helped lead the organization but also shaped its image. In 1938, he designed the ADI's seal, a powerful abstraction of a human hand holding a pencil, with the thumb drawn with a compass forming an ellipse. Vassos explained that the icon "symbolized the grasp and understanding that the designer has of his subject and the perfectly perpendicular pencil denotes the delicacy and refinement of the artist's effort."[75] The ADI's mission was to solidify industrial design as a legitimate profession by defining educational requirements, setting wage scales, and creating professional standards for design practice. In his first keynote address to the independent ADI, after being elected its chairman, Vassos urged members to be bold and original in their designs, even if management disagreed.

The organization flourished as industrial designers entered the field at a record pace. Members in 1945 included leaders in the field, such as Alfons Bach (also a Silvermine Guild member), Belle Kogan, László Moholy-Nagy, and Ben Nash. Regional leaders included Kem Weber in Los Angeles and Eva Zeisel and Walter von Nessen in New York. The ADI promoted its mission through educational events and public initiatives and was welcomed by museum and business leaders alike. Vassos served as president of the organization from 1938 to 1941 and was elected to its national board of trustees in 1948.[76] In 1951, the ADI went through a period of growth and change, absorbing the Chicago Society of Industrial Designers, moving its administrative headquarters to New York City, and changing its name to the Industrial Designers Institute (IDI).[77]

An established educational curriculum was essential to setting standards for the training of a new generation of industrial designers and creating credentialed boundaries around the profession, to ensure that only trained professionals could earn the title "industrial designer." To achieve this goal, in 1952 Vassos collaborated with Alexander Kostellow, the director of industrial design at the Pratt Institute, to create a four-year educational program. This program was eventually adopted internationally, setting the standards for industrial design education for decades.[78] The program had three coordinated phases—academic, design, and technology—with ten interdisciplinary units per year in wide-ranging fields, from sciences such as physics and mathematics to the humanities, including art history and literature, all meant to produce a well-rounded designer. It included the study of form, function, and human relations. In the first year students were introduced to two-dimensional design forms like line, plane, volume, value, color, and texture and three-dimensional elements like architectonics and tectonics.

Vassos, who had ample income from his industrial design business, devoted considerable time and energy to the organization he loved. He used his affiliations with RCA and Silvermine to expand membership and host educational events. Symposia he developed, such as the first 1954 "New Forces in Design" with John E. Arnold of MIT's mechanical engineering department and Seymour Robins of the Princeton University Perception Center, brought together designers, inventors, scholars, and engineers.[79] "Design Explosives," the IDI's third annual symposium in 1956, extended into four fields of knowledge—art, design, education, and psychology—to constitute a whole design practice. Vassos had considerable influence over the selection of speakers for the symposium. Elmer Engstrom, senior executive vice president and director of RCA, abstract painter Jimmy Ernst, and psychiatrist Wilson Scalon, clinical director of the Silver Hill Foundation, were among the people brought together to forge new connections for the field.

In 1944, fifteen leading industrial designers formed a new organization, the Society of Industrial Designers (SID), which challenged the authority of the ADI. The rival organization's founders included Walter Dorwin Teague, Raymond Loewy, and Henry Dreyfuss. The essential difference between the ADI, based in Chicago, and the SID, based in New York City, involved membership requirements. The SID limited its membership to professional designers who worked on a diversity of products for mass production, while the ADI had less rigorous standards for admission. The two organizations' fee structures reflected their differences. The hierarchical SID charged members according to their earning power, whereas the ADI charged the same dues across the organization. The entry requirements for the SID effectively kept the new organization's membership limited to fewer than one hundred. Although small, it was influential, and it was competitive with the ADI for client contracts. Vassos despised the snobbery of the SID, so he refused to join when invited in 1945.[80] He referred to SID members as a "clique" and was worried that the organization was hurting the field by creating new standards of industrial design services. Vassos disliked the SID's tactics and its attempts to dismantle the ADI by luring key members, like Alexander Kostellow, away from the group. He felt these were the same power-grabbing maneuvers found in big business. Vassos may have been behind a contentious 1945 article in the *Home Furnishing Review* that implied that SID members were "highhatting" the ADI.[81]

By 1963, despite the SID's prominent membership, the leaders of the organization, which had changed its name to the American Society of Industrial Designers (ASID), finally agreed to unite their efforts with their design colleagues in the IDI. Both groups reluctantly concluded that the two organizations were redundant and competed for the same people. After a year and a half of continuous negotiations, the final marriage between the two groups took place in 1965. The new organization also invited the Industrial Design Education Association to join, bringing educators into the organization's fold. This brought together the professional rigor of the ASID and the large numbers of the IDI. The name of the new organization was the Industrial Designers Society of America (IDSA). In honor of the leadership of each organization prior to the merger, Henry Dreyfuss was elected IDSA's president, and John Vassos was elected to serve as chairman of the board. The day after the lunch meeting solidifying the new organization, held at the Hilton Hotel in New York City, Dreyfuss wrote to Vassos to express gratitude for his leadership at the meeting, noting that the event "was the culmination of our joint thinking over these many years."[82] Always thinking ahead, Vassos replied with a long list of items that the organization needed to address, including securing copyright of the name and the chairmanship of the educational committee. The new organization represented more than 500 members and, as Dreyfuss proclaimed in his statement on IDSA's formation, signaled "industrial design's coming of age."[83] President Lyndon Johnson himself recognized the significance and promise of the new organization, noting in a letter to Dreyfuss that it "would provide creative leadership in combining function and aesthetics in our daily lives."[84] By 2015, IDSA had more than 3,200 members in twenty-eight chapters. Its website pays homage to John Vassos and the many other industrial designers who started the field and nurtured its growth.

Vassos emphasized that his goal as a designer was to "better and beautify American life."[85] This was clear in 1959, when he participated with other major design professionals in a panel discussion at the Museum of Modern Art in New York concerning two concurrent exhibitions about design. Arthur Drexler, who had recently taken over his post as department head from Philip Johnson, opened the exhibition *20th Century Useful Objects* at MoMA. Jay Doblin, a prominent industrial designer and educator, curated the *One Hundred Best Mass-Produced Products* exhibition at the Illinois Institute of Technology's Institute of Design, where he served as the director. Émigré designer László Moholy-Nagy had founded the Institute of Design in 1937 as a "New Bauhaus." It became officially incorporated into the Illinois Institute of Technology in 1952.[86] Vassos was one of the prominent industrial designers invited to select objects for the Institute of Design's exhibition. *Industrial Design* magazine brought these professionals together at MoMA to discuss the wide differences in the choices made for the exhibitions and the criteria of the selection. The discussion revealed Vassos's priorities as an industrial designer and his growing distance from the elite design establishment.

Although the curators' choices overlapped occasionally, their remarks during the discussion demonstrated stark distinctions and mutual disregard for each other's selection criteria, particularly in terms of the mass market. Drexler was critical of most mass-produced products, as "their design seldom rises above the vulgarity of today's high pressure 'salesmanship,'" although his exhibition included a few products like Marcello Nizzoli's Olivetti typewriter Lexicon 80 (1948) and a Necchi Mirella sewing machine (1957).[87] While Vassos conceded that marketing occasionally mediated the success of mass-produced products, such products could also be objects of beauty and functionality. He questioned the overall heavy emphasis on chairs and lack of consideration for electronics in Drexler's exhibition:

> I don't see any applications of mechanistic and electronic concepts. And even the historical comment was lacking. It is an esoteric exhibit, an exhibit dealing with the likes and dislikes of form. In a way, I almost felt it was a chair exhibit. The stress is so much on seating that one wondered if it weren't a scientific demonstration of the body's comfort in various sitting positions.[88]

Indeed, the designer concluded that the MoMA exhibition was missing a sense of design. It was lacking, he said, "any emphasis on the mass-produced unit which is intrinsic to our society and our objective—the thing that is well-designed with a feeling for the machine behind it."[89] Not surprisingly, Vassos's top pick for the Illinois exhibition was a utilitarian machine, Carl Otto's elegant 1953 Schick razor that incorporated a small motor and a "pleasing aesthetic sculptural form."[90] That exhibition's top ten designs included commercial favorites such as the 1953 Studebaker hard-top coupe and the Bell "500" phone. The show did include one chair—the Eames plywood and steel side chair, which Vassos noted was the first Eames chair that took into consideration the position of the sitter's head.

Vassos's personal life changed dramatically in the mid-1960s. Ruth died in 1965 of a blood clot in her brain. She had been living at the Green Meadows convalescent home.[91] Vassos sold their house in Florida in 1968. Despite his loss, he enjoyed the country life in Connecticut, especially upland game hunting with his Llewellyn setters. He participated in this sport all year long and appreciated how different field trials and breeding were from the hierarchy in his corporate job. "This sport is strictly democratic," he wrote. "You will meet a plumber, a banker, or top business executive in the field."[92] During this period Vassos also worked on large-scale colorful drawings for commercial clients, like the buoyant covers he created for *Tennis* magazine from 1971 to 1974. This artwork reflected Vassos's interest in figurative shapes in motion, which he had exhibited in his postwar murals. He also

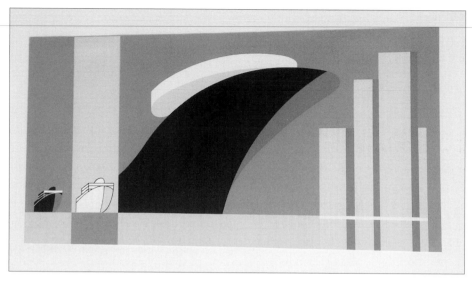

Art by John Vassos for the Skouras family, owners of the Prudential Line, circa 1974. Private collection.

designed holiday cards for Spyros Skouras's shipping company, Prudential Line, in the 1970s; the cards reflected the bold lines and geometric shapes of his 1930s work. He became more involved in civic affairs in Norwalk, Connecticut, designing the local train station and participating on local boards.

In the postwar period, Vassos shifted from designing consumer products to designing media technologies. He matured professionally and personally, and his wartime experiences gave him the confidence to lead his professional colleagues. He found success as a solo practitioner in the age of the large agency through his affiliation with RCA, which enabled him to have steady and prestigious work while avoiding the full-time employee role that he disliked. Vassos took a different path from most of his design colleagues by refusing either to become an in-house designer or to start a big agency. In doing so, he was able to keep his attention on the larger questions—planning, technology, and design—rather than on just packaging design, the realm of his contemporaries.

CONCLUSION
THE LEGACY OF JOHN VASSOS

John Vassos's prodigious career at RCA came to an end as the company entered a new era. In 1965, Robert Sarnoff, David Sarnoff's son, became president of RCA. It was a year of great expansion for the company, driven by the growth of color television. The phonographic market flourished, with sales rising to six million units. One of the first changes that Robert Sarnoff made was to alter the company's logo, which he associated with the "radio days" of the past. He sought to replace the old emblem, affectionately known as the "meatball"—the small familiar round icon featuring the letters *RCA* encircled, with the *A* trailed by a lightning bolt—and to do away with the Nipper trademark featuring the small dog listening to "his master's voice."

Vassos saw this changeover as an opportunity to gain favor with the new regime. He pitched several new logos to Sarnoff. In Vassos's remaking of the "meatball," the letters were enclosed inside a circle, as before, but the single circle became a double circle, suggesting a strong force holding the company together.[1] He modernized the company letters with a sans serif font and placed the iconic lightning bolt underneath them. He also added color to the lightning bolt, which previously was black or red.[2]

The designer had been thinking about RCA's logo for three decades. In 1945, Vassos proposed a new icon for the company—an electronic symbol he called Magictron. This gold-winged creature, which resembled a trophy or a statue of a Greek god, extended the company's Magic Brain theme and continued the association of the company with the godlike power of electricity. It was a typical Vassos design: visual and textual, emotional and graphic. Vassos retained both the lightning bolt element and the Magic Brain in this icon, which he felt symbolized all the manifestations of wireless technology.[3] The many drawings included in his proposal showed

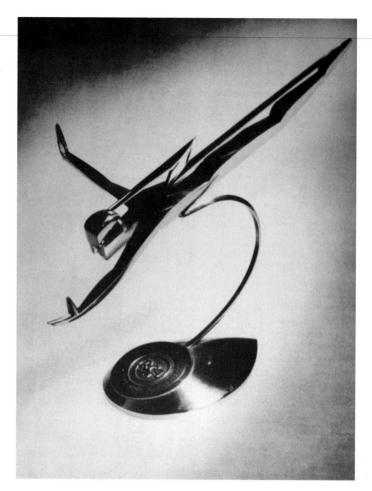

John Vassos proposed the Magictron as the new RCA trademark in 1945. Photograph by Marthe Krueger. Private collection.

the emblem's stylistic continuity with his earlier designs, including the radio and the electron microscope, while also embracing the television-saturated future.

Robert Sarnoff did not accept any of Vassos's proposed logos. Marking a fresh start under his new leadership, RCA announced the arrival of its new contemporary trademark on January 19, 1968. The bold design was created by the leading corporate design firm Lippincott & Margulies. RCA spent millions on the new design, which featured three computer-generated letters, intended to symbolize a rationalized, sophisticated communications company.[4] The impersonal letters suggested the power of a mechanized corporation in the computer age, beyond human fallibility. Indeed, principal designer J. Gordon Lippincott had coined the term *corporate identity* and claimed to have pioneered the integration of a company's name, logo, advertising, and packaging into a uniform marketing tool. The new trademark reflected the company's growth and diversification beyond broadcasting. RCA had moved past the lightning bolt and had entered the digital era of the computer.

Acknowledging his defeat, Vassos wrote to Sarnoff to congratulate him on RCA's new logo and its new program of identification. Feeling displaced by the company's choice to hire an outside firm, Vassos used the letter to somewhat defensively draw attention to his own past efforts to improve the company logo. First, he explained that he had wanted to change the lettering to block letters in the 1940s but was told he could not by the legal department. Second, he mentioned contacting Lippincott & Margulies to offer them advice about installing the new letters on RCA equipment.[5] Clearly, Vassos did not want to let go of his important role in the company, certainly not to a large corporate advertising firm like Lippincott & Margulies.

The new logo, autonomous and cold, signified a profound change in corporate politics. It marked a time very different from one when a mural painter could become a big company's lead designer and a worker could write regularly to the corporate founders. The logo design signified a shift for RCA under its new leader, whose conglomeration strategy eventually led to the company's decline. As N. R. Kleinfield noted in Sarnoff's obituary in the *New York Times,* under his leadership, RCA had become "a sprawling enterprise that also rented cars, wove carpets, published books, sold frozen peas and raised chickens."[6] The failure of new ventures such as videodiscs and business computers and the neglect of consumer electronics further contributed to the company's decline, and General Electric bought RCA in 1986. The transition to Robert Sarnoff's leadership marked the beginning of Vassos's retirement at RCA, and the end of an era.[7]

Vassos retired from RCA in 1971. In anticipation of the event, a retirement party was held on September 3, 1970, attended by Vassos's colleagues Elmer Engstrom (then CEO of RCA), Tucker Madawick, Wally Watts, and others. The invitation warmly called Vassos "the magic brain behind RCA design for thirty-eight years."[8] His industrial design colleagues recalled Vassos's contributions at RCA. One noted that his contribution was to create visual cohesion across product lines. It was Vassos who engineered the "New Look" of RCA broadcast equipment.

> Until then, our products looked as if they'd been manufactured at a dozen different factories. Some units were brown; others gray. Some had textured exteriors while others were smooth. John created a distinctive twin-toned color scheme—two shades of blue actually—that standardized everything we turned out, from the smallest studio camera to the largest transmitter, and stamped it unmistakably as RCA's.[9]

Retirement, however, did not stop Vassos from pitching design ideas to the company. Promoting what for him was the greatest era in design history, Vassos delivered a 1972 report titled "Art Deco: Its Origins and Evolution," offering what he called a fresh "revival program" for RCA. He proposed that the company bring back a softer-looking television cabinet with delicate legs, to offer alongside its Bauhaus-oriented modular systems. As Vassos wistfully wrote, "If this suggested program on Art Deco is adopted . . . [it] will give authenticity and nostalgia to a certain audience which can still remember."[10] He also continued his relationship with Tucker Madawick, now the company's division vice president of industrial design.[11] In 1975, he was honored again by RCA and its advertising agency J. Walter Thompson with a certificate acknowledging his contribution to the ongoing Magic Brain campaign. Marking a new phase in his life, the designer closed his New York office in 1975.

A lavish event at the Harvard Club in New York in 1973 with prominent Greek writer Basil Vlavianos presiding offered a template of his career. Dubbed a "testimonial dinner honoring John Vassos," the event was hosted by the American Society for Neo-Hellenic Studies. In chronological order, ten speakers each focused on an aspect of the designer's diverse career, bringing the multiple identities—the artist, the educator, the designer, and the strategist—together in an elegant compendium. Publisher John MacCrae spoke about Vassos's books and illustration style. Dean Aaron W. Warner of the School of General Studies at Columbia University addressed the significance of Vassos's teaching and design curriculum. Dr. James Kellis, formerly with the Office of Strategic Services, discussed Vassos's time in the Middle East during World War II. Martin Bennett, a retired RCA vice president, covered "the years at RCA with a Renaissance man."

Among his other honors, Vassos was nominated for an honorary degree at Pratt Institute in New York City in 1976. In his nominating letter to President Pratt, William Katavolos, the institute's chair of curriculum, compared Vassos to Leonardo da Vinci as well as to Benjamin Franklin:

> I myself in this year of our bicentennial celebration see a stronger bond to
> Benjamin Franklin, as an inventor, artist, author, statesman and steersman. I
> am at my limit when I attempt to outline [Vassos's] life and its impact upon
> us as educators and designers. . . . His legendary liaison with design in life,
> his deep sense of the radical in his service to conservative causes, his creative
> reach, has enriched us all.[12]

In the 1970s, as the history of the American industrial design profession became a focus of study, scholars increasingly approached Vassos for interviews. Jerry Streichler and Dianne Pilgrim, who were beginning to document the field for the first time, interviewed him. Arthur Pulos, Vassos's friend and son of Greek immigrants, collected the papers of the members of the first and second generations of industrial designers.[13] Vassos's work was being collected for museum permanent collections.

Renewed interest in art deco design brought requests for reproductions of his work. The book *Contempo, Phobia, and Other Graphic Interpretations,* published by Dover Books in 1976, reprinted a wide range of Vassos's work from advertising

Vassos with his great-niece Jayne Johnes at a retrospective of his work at the Silvermine Guild, circa 1978. Courtesy of Jayne Johnes.

and books and included an introduction by his friend P. K. Thomajan. This volume introduced Vassos's illustrations to a new generation, since his books had long been out of print.[14] In 1977, the *New York Times* featured an interview with the artist in which he discussed his work. The article, which was tied in with an exhibition at the Silvermine Arts Center featuring Vassos's book illustrations, gave Vassos the chance to express his artistic philosophy: "That the artist should paint a picture and that it should hang in the museum is fine and produces much pleasure, but the artist should also be able to design a road, a movie billboard or a giant transmitter. He should be able to function on both a metaphysical and utilitarian level."[15]

Vassos became increasingly interested in documenting his life. He realized that his story was important to a new generation, and so he began writing his autobiography (the work, although thoughtfully written, remains unpublished). Indeed, his life story is a tremendous tale, of a young Greek artist who achieved enormous success and influence within the largest electronics manufacturing company in the United States and founded the central professional organization of his field. Vassos produced about one hundred handwritten pages for his autobiography, which was to be published by Dover. He considered different clever titles for the book, including "From Bosphorus to Plymouth Rock," the lengthy "Beginning on the Bosphorus in the Early Teens thru the Turbulent Years to the Present," and "Vassos: A Legend—The Man and His Work." He sketched out a cover showing a man alone in an eerie, barren landscape, reminiscent of his 1920s drawings. The pages he completed covered his early life up until his involvement in the merger of the major industrial design associations around 1965. He came up with preliminary parallel section titles, such as "Dogs to Computers" and "Phobias to Fountain Pens." And he designed the layout of the intended typeset pages so as to emphasize the scope of his career. Vassos worked diligently and quickly, as he wanted to "get it down before my eyes close."[16] He dedicated the autobiography to Harry Stack Sullivan and Ruth Vassos, each of whom profoundly influenced his life. Other designers, such as Henry Dreyfuss and Raymond Loewy, built legacies through their agencies, which survived past their deaths, but Vassos had no heirs to his design philosophy. He rightly feared his story would be lost.

Contempo, Phobia, and Other Graphic Interpretations brought together Vassos's ample illustrations from advertising and books, but the designer was not satisfied.[17] He wanted his life story to be published. He sent pitch letters about his autobiography to likely publishers, emphasizing his relationships with famous people and his work on projects of national importance. Writing in the third person for added impact, Vassos summarized the story of a multifaceted man:

> A famous industrial designer and author-illustrator presents his life story in the most intimate, warm, and courageous style, in a book filled with adventure, action, and bold observation of our rapidly changing society and the complete upheaval of values and standards. It begins in the Bosphorus, in the mysterious city of Constantinople and continues through the First World War, pioneering a new profession in America, creating the first new school of illustration since Beardsley, right into World War Two, to the present.[18]

Indeed, Vassos's desire to be acknowledged for his contribution to the design profession remained unchanged. Such a pursuit of fame was certainly a trait of industrial designers who were heavily skilled in display and sales techniques, which they naturally applied to themselves.[19] Vassos always referred to himself as the celebrated modernist designer named as one of the top ten in America by *Fortune* magazine, even though that period was firmly over by the 1950s.

However, by the mid-1970s, with Ruth no longer serving as his editor and his health failing, his prose suffered. Most devastatingly to the artist, his eyesight was failing. Following hospitalization for eye surgery, he continued to work on his autobiography, writing in huge letters on massive sheets of lined paper. But it proved too difficult "to pick up the threads," since, as he wrote, "to begin all over again is like trying desperately to renew an interrupted love affair." In 1976, the state of Connecticut declared him legally blind at the age of seventy-seven, and he put the memoir project aside.[20] In his eighties, his health deteriorated. His sister Ivi and her granddaughter Jayne Johnes, an aspiring artist eager to learn from her charismatic

Uncle John, cared for Vassos. Although elderly, he enjoyed visiting the Silvermine Arts Center and spending time with old friends like Dik Browne, creator of the comic strip *Hägar the Horrible,* and dancer Marthe Krueger. Other prominent visitors at the designer's home included the actor and filmmaker John Cassavetes, the son of Vassos's old friends Nicholas and Katherine Cassavetes. Industrial designer Ray Spilman was a regular presence at the house. Jayne Johnes recalls that many wonderful meals of Greek salad and lamb chops followed by ouzo were served at the modernist table Vassos had designed in the 1930s.

John Vassos died on December 6, 1985, after a long decline complicated by diabetes. His obituary in the *New York Times* consisted of a short but dense paragraph. It listed his diverse accomplishments, noting that he "created the design for RCA's first color television camera and the Perey turnstile. . . . In addition, he streamlined the kitchen paring knife, made murals, designed American pavilions for various international fairs and illustrated fourteen books."[21] While the obituary only skimmed the surface of Vassos's many accomplishments, an extensive tribute to Vassos was held at the Connecticut-based Silvermine Arts Center, where Vassos had played a leading role from 1936 to 1955. The Silvermine exhibition beautifully captured the range of Vassos's career and honored him as a "world famous industrial designer." Artist, friend, and curator Carlus Dyer eulogized Vassos at this event, focusing on his contributions to the Silvermine Guild and praising his dedication to making the center a place "of quality and brilliance, freely accessible to all." Dyer noted that such generosity and dedication were "a way of life for John Vassos. They are indicative of his private and public motivation evidenced in all his ways as artist and influential leader."[22]

Despite the many accomplishments throughout his career that virtually defined the profession of industrial design, Vassos remains relatively unknown. No one had written his biography until now, nor has there been a solo exhibition of his work aside from one at the Hofstra University Library and the memorial exhibition at the Silvermine Arts Center.[23] Unlike other well-known pioneer industrial designers, Vassos had no large military contracts, no car designs, and no agency to carry on his philosophy, nor did he have a book describing it. In the era of in-house design, the most successful consultant designers worked with large international agencies, had large staffs, and maintained strong reputations. John Vassos Associates was the rare exception: a small agency with national reach. Vassos also was unique among industrial designers in that he had diverse strengths and worked in more than one arena, such as illustration and interior design, in addition to industrial design. Indeed, his career was not a transcendently successful one: it was an individual practice constantly being constrained and enabled by factors within his new profession.

Throughout this text, I have referred to Vassos as an industrial designer, a term that he actually hated. He argued: "As for us, we are belabored with a lousy name. Industrial design doesn't belong to us. It's a misnomer. Somebody said these people design for industry, so what are they—industrial designers. We ought to change that name."[24] He would have preferred "artist-designer," which Vassos described as "a polytechnic." This artist-designer loves human beings and "loves all of them to enjoy these things. Not the few and the rich."[25] Vassos revealed himself to be a man who was committed to a democracy of goods, who was fascinated with mass production yet also frustrated with consumer society.

One of Vassos's strengths was his ability to apply modern design elements to media components that had no prior accepted form. Like other stylists on the vanguard of industrial design, he was part elitist and part populist, and willing to temper functionalism with ornamentation. He educated others on the principles of modernist art and architecture when these ideas were just being introduced in the United States in the late 1920s. Beyond exterior styling, Vassos was concerned with the physical and psychological comfort of the user. He suggested the unification of broadcast equipment at RCA and added central control mechanisms to improve operations. He improved the interface on consumer media equipment so users could easily interact with their devices. Importantly, Vassos gave shape to the disembodied listening experience with easily readable interactive tuning mechanisms. He understood that the design of electronics, from the smallest radio to the most complex broadcast equipment, had to take into account the user's body and mind. The lessons he learned while writing *Phobia*, about the fears inspired by modernity, shaped his career and the products he designed.

Clients were drawn to his charismatic personality and wanted him to take total control of projects for them. Vassos was easygoing about billing and even accepted alternative payment plans, such as the stocks he took in lieu of cash as compensation for his mural at the Condado Beach Hotel in Puerto Rico. He preferred to handpick his clients, choosing ones with whom he had established ties through the Greek American community or through the American Designers' Institute. He sought above all to create lasting relationships based on mutual respect. For some clients, like United Artists, Vassos demanded too much creative control over his design projects, leading to conflict.

An urbanite, immigrant, and artist, he was sensitive to the world around him, with an intuitive sense of perception that shaped his use of lighting and awareness of detail. He responded viscerally to mass culture with both shock and horror, emotions most vividly expressed in his books *Phobia* and *Contempo*. He also responded with admiration and awe to the same mass culture, as revealed in his advertising illustrations and mural designs. His illustrations were not the measured response of the businessman but the emotional reply of the artist.

Vassos's design philosophy emerged from this ambivalent reaction to consumer society. Throughout his career, he sought to respond to the discomforts of modern life through design solutions. However, Vassos was no Luddite. He was excited by technical advancements, especially when applied to design. Thus, he offered solutions to the phobias caused by mechanistic society by paying close attention to the psychological needs and physical abilities of the user. For example, in his turnstile design Vassos removed sharp edges that might frighten commuters. Similarly, his Musicorner, featured at the 1939–40 New York World's Fair, used principles of modularity to make the entertainment unit seem like part of the house. Softening the edges by adding a flower box, he integrated complex machinery into the living room, like the television that could be mysteriously popped back into the module when not in use.[26] His miniaturized portable television sets and embedded screens were early models of the now ubiquitous mobile phone. Throughout his career, Vassos used modern design as a way of bringing machinery into the home and integrating it into the broadcast studio. He recognized that both the home and the office needed unique spaces carved out for new technologies that needed special casements.

In designing the ideal home, Vassos was successful because his styling was meticulous but also flexible. His enthusiasm for certain materials, such as Bakelite and tubular steel, waned, for instance, when he realized the limited applicability of these materials and also recognized that they were declining in popularity. He became more interested in the use of bright color as a way of unifying the electronic elements in the living room and of bringing the advances of color television to life. His color-saturated 1960s television corner, for example, drew the family's attention to the screen while surrounding them with modern art and modular furniture. He retained his commitment to component-oriented design, which he felt was the best way to convey the relationship of items from a product line, as expressed in his 501 computer system, designed with the user of the complicated system in mind. Vassos's emphasis on tactile user control is relevant today as car manufactures struggle to balance touch-screen and voice-activated car controls with "hard controls" like knobs. Car manufacturers rushed to make everything computerized, only to find out later that drivers prefer hard controls for sound-system volume, heating, and air-conditioning.[27] Vassos would remind us that the driver, not the car manufacturer, must determine the shape of the driving experience and that the knob is important!

Vassos's work on multiple media products and spaces of media consumption opens additional avenues of study for scholars, including fast-food restaurant design, the public reception of television in the 1930s, midcentury movie theater architecture, and postwar corporate murals. As the televisions in our homes increase dramatically in size and the ones in our pockets continue to shrink, we can benefit from looking back at early discussions of these screens' roles in our daily lives. Today, design has become a key element in the success of corporations such as Apple, but they were not the first to consider touch in media design. The career of John Vassos suggests that the earliest progenitors of broadcast media design have much to teach us about how technology is absorbed into our daily lives and becomes our "magic brain."

ACKNOWLEDGMENTS

This project has been in the works for more than a decade, so I have many people to acknowledge. It gives me great pleasure to express my thanks to them and to the institutions that made this book possible. Most of all, I am indebted to my graduate adviser, Will Straw, who offered sage advice, sharp editorial critique, patience, humor, and unwavering support from the very beginning. His dedication to rigorous archival research and cultural history has long been an inspiration. Other scholars at McGill University in the Department of Art History and Communications Studies who generously assisted me were Bronwen Wilson, Carrie Rentschler, Jenny Burman, and Aaron Vinegar. Special thanks go to media historian Jonathan Sterne, who helped shape my thinking about media technologies. Colleagues in my dissertation writing group who helped clarify early drafts included Wade Nelson, Geoff Stahl, Ger Zielinski, and Maria Jose Ferreira. I received early support and excellent advice from Alan Findeli, professor at the School of Industrial Design of the University of Montreal; Johanne Sloan, professor of art history at Concordia University; and Professor Haidee Wasson in film studies at Concordia University. This book is based on my doctoral dissertation, completed as part of my Ph.D. in the Department of Art History and Communications Studies at McGill University, and I am grateful to Karin Bourgeois, Maureen Coote, and Susana Machado for guiding me through the administrative process.

Generous grants from many institutions fueled this project. I am grateful for the support of the Culture of the Cities Project, an international research collaboration that brought together diverse scholars to study urban culture, and the support of the Social Sciences and Humanities Research Council of Canada. McGill University Alumni Association awards funded research trips to the Archives of American Art at the Smithsonian Institution in Washington, D.C., and to Syracuse University in Syracuse, New York, where the papers of John Vassos are housed. They also funded my participation in conferences, including the International Association of Media Historians conference at the University of Leicester, where I presented early versions of this research. I am deeply thankful for the generosity of the Archives of American

Art and the aid of the staff there, where I conducted much of the research for this book over the past decade. The Douglass Foundation Postdoctoral Fellowship at the Smithsonian American Art Museum in 2005–6 made it possible for me to continue my research in the archives. Ample thanks to my advisors Liza Kirwin at the Archives of American Art and Virginia Mecklenberg at the American Art Museum. Many archivists and staff members at the Archives of American Art were involved with this book and helped immensely, including Judy Throm, Anne Bayly, and Tessa Veazey. Wendy Hurlock Baker worked closely with me to obtain the many incredible images that greatly enhance this book, as did Marisa Bourgoin. My fellowship coordinator Amelia Gorelitz and Cynthia Mills made my year at the archives a productive one. Anne Collins Goodyear offered sage advice. Darcy Tell has been an incredible source of guidance and support over the years. Many curators at the National Museum of American History also provided their wisdom, including Peggy Kidwell, David Halberstich, Elliot Sivowitch, and Hal Wallace.

A research fellowship from the wonderful Wolfsonian Museum in 2006 granted me invaluable access to the museum's expansive radio collection and archives. I am thankful to executive director Cathy Leff, head librarian Frank Luca, and curator Marianne Lamonaca, and especially to curator Jon Mogul, who made sure my visit was productive and who has remained a friend. Thanks also to Amy Silverman at the Wolfsonian Museum, who facilitated my requests for images. The Fulbright U.S. student program funded my early research in Canada, and a teaching fellowship at Harvard University with Professor Alice Jardine deepened my understanding of mass media in 1950s America.

At the E. S. Bird Library at Syracuse University, where some of John Vassos's papers and artwork are held, I was ably assisted by Peter Verheyven, who shared his enthusiasm for and vast knowledge of the history of book publishing and of John Vassos's books. Nicolette A. Dobrowolski and Nicole C. Dittrich kindly assisted me with reproduction requests. Alexander Magoun at the David Sarnoff Library has been an incredible source of historical information about RCA and David Sarnoff, and he is always available when I need him. The David Sarnoff Library has moved from its Princeton location and is now housed at the Hagley Museum and Library in Wilmington, Delaware. I am thankful for the generous assistance of staff members there during research visits and also in obtaining rights and permissions to reprint illustrations in this book: Kevin Martin, Liz Fite, Jon Williams, and Lynsey Sczechowicz of the Audiovisual Reference Archives.

Others who helped me on this project were David Smith at the New York Public Library, Iain Baird at the Museum of Television, and Amber Paranick at the Library of Congress. My thanks also to Cindy Clair at the Silvermine Guild of Artists. At the Roland Park Library, interlibrary loan staff Jessica Faulkner and Julie Johnson helped me acquire rare books from across the country.

Museum curators and cultural historians assisted me in numerous ways. Steve McVoy at the Early Television Museum generously allowed me to use images from the museum's collection. Industrial designer and Vassos's IDSA colleague Carroll Gantz offered his memories of John Vassos in phone conversations and shared his ample knowledge of the history of industrial design. I am grateful to my colleagues at the Cooper Hewitt, National Design Museum, where my interest in John Vassos and industrial design history was formed. I want to thank particularly Gail S. Davidson, curator and head of the Drawings, Prints, and Graphic Design Department; Ellen Lupton, curator of contemporary design at the Cooper Hewitt; and Russell Flinchum. Stuart Ewen, distinguished professor of film and media studies at Hunter College, was my adviser in the Media Studies Department at Hunter College and shaped my thinking about American mass culture and industrial design in profound ways.

Jayne Johnes, John Vassos's great-niece, and John Johnes, his great-nephew, provided ample memories of "Uncle John" and shared a memorable meal with me at John Vassos's dining room table—food he had enjoyed, served with utensils he designed. Jayne Johnes has been an incredible source of enthusiasm and encouragement and generously provided many photographs from her personal collection. Antique radio collectors Steve Johnson of the website Steve's Antique Technology (www.StevenJohnson.com) and David Sica of the New Jersey Antique Radio Club have been great sources of knowledge and materials. At the National Endowment for the Humanities, the incomparable Steve Ross copyedited a late draft of the manuscript. My thanks to my colleagues at the National Endowment for the Humanities: Sonia Feigenbaum, Andrea Anderson, Clay Lewis, Karen Mittelman, and Jeff Hardwick, who offered excellent advice on publishing. At the Smithsonian American Art Museum, I was inspired by other fellows, including James Wechsler, Sergio Cortesini, Dorothy Moss, and Patricia Hills of Boston University.

At the University of Minnesota Press, former editorial director Richard Morrison challenged me to sharpen the book's focus and to expand my understanding of John Vassos in a wider context. My editor, Pieter Martin, deserves special thanks for the extraordinary amount of time and effort he put into the book; his close reading of the manuscript helped me write the book I wanted to write. Editorial assistants Erin Warholm-Wohlenhaus and Kristian Tvedten warmly and enthusiastically guided me through the process of image rights acquisition. My thanks to my reviewers Jeffrey Meikle, whose pioneering studies of industrial design history inspire my work, and industrial design scholar Carma Gorman for their incredibly valuable, thoughtful comments. I would like to give special thanks to Judy Selhorst, a masterly copy editor who greatly improved this text. I am also grateful to Gary Kass at the University of Missouri Press, Mary Christian, and Lynn Weber.

My family has been a major source of encouragement, especially my grandmother, the late Rose Shapiro. I am grateful to family members for their love and support:

my sister Gabrielle Miller, Dianne Schwartz, Harold Shultz, Nora Mandel, Geoff and Beth Taubman, Amy and David Lieberman, Betsy and Larry Shapiro, Shirley and Howard Shapiro, and Ellis and Marsha Caplan. My friends supported this project in many ways, and I thank Wendy Olsson, Rebecca Pernell, Athena Soupliotis, Marci Littman, Datsy Brijbasi, Ruth Wachspress, and the skilled Patricia Csank. Josie Raney kindly offered editing assistance, and Elmar Juchem helped with translation. My colleague and close friend Marie-Claude Rabeau in Montreal provided food, laughter, and valuable insight as well as translation assistance. Eugene Resnick, my dear friend, reviewed countless drafts over the years as the book evolved from dissertation to finished manuscript and offered his profound critical insight, expertise in history, and endless encouragement.

This book is dedicated to my twin daughters, Arielle and Maya, who were born during its gestation, and to my husband, Bruce Shapiro, my greatest support and love. Without Bruce, this project would not have been completed; his unsurpassed love, patience, and care made it possible.

NOTES

PREFACE

1. Telis Onassis to John Vassos, October 23, 1968, Correspondence Subject File "O," John Vassos Papers, Special Collections Research Center, Syracuse University Libraries (hereafter cited as Vassos/Syracuse).

2. Eight-track cassette recording of John Vassos speaking at award ceremony, Norwalk, Connecticut, March 25, 1970, Box 1, John Vassos Papers, Archives of American Art, Smithsonian Institution, Washington, D.C. (hereafter cited as Vassos/AAA). As I have noted, the John Vassos Papers at the Archives of American Art are uncataloged, and the files are in disarray. There is little thematic or chronological order to the boxes, and many materials are in misnamed files.

INTRODUCTION

1. John Vassos, "An Esthetic Evangelist," interview by David L. Shirey, *New York Times*, February 27, 1977.

2. Quoted in "Design as Commentary," *Industrial Design*, February 1959, 58.

3. Andreas Fickers, "Visibly Audible: The Radio Dial as Mediating Interface," in *The Oxford Handbook of Sound Studies*, ed. Trevor Pinch and Karin Bijsterveld (Oxford: Oxford University Press, 2012), 411–39.

4. John Vassos, "What Is the Industrial Designer?," manuscript draft, circa 1952, Box 12, "Writings," Vassos/AAA.

5. Charlotte Benton and Tim Benton, "The Style and the Age," in *Art Deco, 1910–1939*, ed. Charlotte Benton, Tim Benton, and Ghislaine Wood (Boston: Bullfinch Press, 2003), 19–20. These authors highlight the modern (rather than modernist) style that came to international prominence in the interwar years and can be seen in nearly every visual medium, from fine art, architecture, advertising, and interior design to household objects.

6. See Donald J. Bush, *The Streamlined Decade* (New York: Braziller, 1975).

7. Jeffrey Meikle, "Domesticating Modernity: Ambivalence and Appropriation, 1920–1940," in *Designing Modernity: The Arts of Reform and Persuasion, 1885–1945*, ed. Wendy Kaplan (New York: Thames & Hudson, 1995), 143–68.

8. John Vassos and Ruth Vassos, "Advertising," in *Contempo: This American Tempo* (New York: Dutton, 1929), n.p.

9. The author made this statement in a letter to Norman Bel Geddes, who was compiling information for an article about industrial designers, October 25, 1932, Box 7, Vassos/AAA. It is unclear if the *Fortune* article naming Vassos one of the ten most important industrial designers is the same one that has been attributed to George Nelson titled "Both Fish and Fowl," but much of the information provided is the same. "Both Fish and Fowl," *Fortune*, February 1934, 88.

10. Susan J. Douglas, *Listening In: Radio and the American Imagination* (1999; repr., Minneapolis: University of Minnesota Press, 2004), 9.

11. Susan Smulyan, *Selling Radio: The Commercialization of American Broadcasting, 1920–1934* (Washington, D.C.: Smithsonian Institution Press, 1994), 155.

12. John Vassos, "Why Not All-Electric Living-Units in the Home?," *Electrical Manufacturing,* October 1940, Box 2, "RCA Misc." folder, Vassos/AAA.

13. "Simplicity Keynotes Design of RCA Export Radios," RCA press release, n.d., Box 13, Vassos/AAA.

14. John Vassos, "The Dilemma of Modernism," 1931, 12, Box 2, Vassos/AAA.

15. Jeffrey Meikle makes this argument in *Twentieth Century Limited: Industrial Design in America, 1925–1939* (Philadelphia: Temple University Press, 1979), 40. Other designers associated with particular companies include Harley Earl (General Motors), Donald Dohner (Westinghouse), and George Sakier (American Standard).

16. Ray Spilman, article for "Contemporary Designers" series, 1989, Box 1, Vassos/AAA.

17. Carroll Gantz, e-mail interview with author, December 12, 2003.

1. DRAWING MODERNITY

1. Passport, 1924, Box 5, Vassos/AAA.

2. John Vassos, unpublished autobiography, handwritten draft, circa 1974, 1, Box 12, Vassos/AAA.

3. John Vassos document, in "Dawn of a New Age: The Immigrant Contribution to the Arts in America," accessed September 9, 2014, http://library.syr.edu/digital/exhibits/d/DawnNewAge/vassosgallery.html, Vassos/Syracuse.

4. Vassos, unpublished autobiography, 1, Box 12, Vassos/AAA.

5. Ibid., 1.

6. Ibid., 14.

7. Sidney Fields, "Only Human," *Sunday Mirror,* August 18, 1946, Box 14, Vassos/AAA.

8. Letter from London branch of the General Consulate of Belgium, August 3, 1915, Box 2, Vassos/AAA.

9. "John Vassos," *Athene,* Autumn 1947, 32, Vassos/AAA.

10. *Who's Who in America* application form, circa 1960, Box 23, Vassos/AAA.

11. Val Arms, "An Artist in New York," *National Herald,* October 4, 1942, E. P. Dutton & Company, Inc. Records, Special Collections Research Center, Syracuse University Libraries (hereafter cited as Dutton Records), "Vassos, John" folder.

12. A. C. Erisman (American Catalin Corporation) to John Vassos, July 17, 1933, Box 8, Vassos/AAA.

13. W. Blount Darden, letter to the editor, *Daily Press Times-Herald,* April 2, 1921, Box 2, Vassos/AAA.

14. Letter from the London branch of the General Consulate of Belgium.

15. Vassos, unpublished autobiography, 31, Box 12, Vassos/AAA.

16. Ibid., 15.

17. Ibid., 31.

18. Willis Birchman and James Flagg, *Faces and Facts by and about 26 Contemporary Artists,* privately printed, 1937, n.p., Box 12, "Autobiographical materials" folder, Vassos/AAA.

19. *Daily Nonpariel,* Council Bluffs, Iowa, July 19, 1930, Box 2, Vassos/AAA.

20. "Chronicle and Comment," *The Bookman,* January 1930, 529, Box 2, Vassos/AAA.

21. See Stuart Ewen, *Captains of Consciousness: Advertising and the Social Roots of the Consumer Culture* (New York: McGraw-Hill, 1976).

22. Vassos and Vassos, "Traffic," in *Contempo,* n.p.

23. Vassos, unpublished autobiography, 18, Box 12, Vassos/AAA.

24. Roland Marchand, *Advertising the American Dream: Making Way for Modernity, 1920–1940* (Berkeley: University of California Press, 1985), 142–53.

136. "Discuss Arts and Letters: Actors and Writers Speak before 250 Women at Luncheon," *New York Times,* January 10, 1931, Box 5, Vassos/AAA; "What Is Going On This Week," *New York Times,* October 18, 1931.

137. Helen Shalet to John Vassos, n.d., Box 7, Vassos/AAA. Shalet wrote to Vassos on stationery from the Pierrepont Hotel, inviting him to speak on women's rights. The event was covered in the newspapers.

138. For example, see "Local Notes," *New York Times,* October 7, 1928, which states, "At the Art Centre are now to be seen John Vassos's illustrations for Oscar Wilde's 'Ballad of Reading Gaol.'"

139. *John Vassos: Famous Illustrator and Modernist.*

140. Advertisement, *New York Times,* November 14, 1929, 7. Also see *New York Times,* November 5, 1930, where Vassos is listed as a speaker at the tenth annual Wanamaker Book Week event with other authors, including Russell Crouse and J. P. McEvoy. Draft text for the invitation reads, "Dear—. John Vassos will be host to a number of his friends . . . Wed. May 6 at 5pm." See Box 5, Vassos/AAA.

141. List of invitees and menu for party, 1931, Box 8, Vassos/AAA.

142. E. P. Dutton Publicity Department, letter to guest, 1931, Box 8, Vassos/AAA.

143. "Versatile John Vassos," *World,* Tulsa, Okla., May 31, 1931, Box 5, Vassos/AAA.

144. Clipping from *New York Evening Post,* October 14, 1929, Box 5, Vassos/AAA.

145. *John Vassos: Famous Illustrator and Modernist.*

146. All of these lectures are described in ibid. Also see John Vassos to Mr. James Pond, February 18, 1933, regarding speaking at the Explorers Club, Box 7, Vassos/AAA.

147. Many of Vassos's talks in the mid-1930s referred to this upcoming release. This was following the mediocre response to *Contempo* and Vassos's contract with Covici-Friede for *Phobia.*

148. "What Is Going On This Week," 38.

149. In agreeing to present a lecture at the Men's Club at Cranford, Vassos wrote, "I believe $25.00 will take care of my expenses." John Vassos to Orsamus Turner Harris, April 12, 1933, Box 7, Vassos/AAA.

150. Joseph Franken to John Vassos, January 16, 1933, Box 7, Vassos/AAA.

151. Rebel Arts to John Vassos, November 21, 1932, Box 7, Vassos/AAA.

152. Frances Pollack to John Vassos, March 14, 1930, Box 8, Vassos/AAA. In this letter, Pollack quotes a fee to Vassos of one hundred dollars.

153. Publicity photo, "Mr. Vassos with Mrs. Vassos and Rudy Vallee at E. P. Dutton Press Party in New York, 1928," Box 5, "Memorabilia, Photos (personal)" folder, Vassos/Syracuse.

154. "Likes Skyscrapers," *News,* Charlotte, N.C., August 3, 1930. The same picture was used in "As Wolf Kska Sees Vassos," *Star,* Wilmington, N.C., October 12, 1930, Box 20, Vassos/AAA.

155. "Greeks Protesting Athens Skyscraper," *New York Times,* July 8, 1930, Box 20, Vassos/AAA.

156. "Ancient Greece and Modern Skyscrapers," *Telegram,* Youngstown, Ohio, July 12, 1930 (which notes that a new edition of *Salome* will come out in the summer and announces the October publication of *Ultimo*), repeated in *Telegraph,* Macon, Ga., July 13, 1930; *Republican,* Waterbury, Conn., July 6, 1930; "Vassos Proposed Greek Skyscraper under Fire," *Star,* Wilmington, N.C., August 3, 1930; "Greek Designs Skyscraper," *World,* Tulsa, Okla., August 17, 1930; "Book Illustrator Plans Legion Home in Athens," *Gazette,* Cedar Rapids, Iowa, September 21, 1930; *Mayfield News,* Palo Alto, Calif., September 9, 1930. All clippings in Box 5, Vassos/AAA.

157. Among the places Vassos's images were reproduced, in addition to book reviews, were "Books Especially Prepared for Christmas Giving," *New York Times,* December 4, 1927, BR5; and, from *The Ballad of Reading Gaol,* "Conceptions by John Vassos," *Forum,* December 1929, 320. "The Market" was reproduced in the February 1930 issue of *Forum.*

158. Rose C. Feld, "Taking Heart against Our Perils in the Machine Age," *New York Times,* January 3, 1932.

159. For example, see the brochure *Modern Problems in Modern Art,* circa 1930, Box 1, "Illustration and Advertising" folder, Vassos/AAA.

160. Dutton to Vassos, "Royalty Earned and Deductions to 30 April 1933."

161. "Trilogy of John Vassos is $3.50 each and bound in a beautiful gift box, $10.50." Advertisement, *The Bookman*, December 1929, 17.

162. James M. Hutchisson, "Nathanael West, *Miss Lonelyhearts*, and *Contempo* Magazine," *Resources for American Literary Study* 24, no. 1 (1998): 84–100.

163. *Contempo* promotional materials, Box 8, Vassos/AAA.

164. Vassos's involvement with the magazine is chronicled in a series of letters between Vassos and Buttitta from July 2, 1932, to March 3, 1933, Box 8, Vassos/AAA.

165. Anthony Buttitta to John Vassos, July 2, 1932, Box 8, Vassos/AAA.

166. Anthony Buttitta to Milton Abernethy, July 2, 1932, Box 8, Vassos/AAA.

167. Elliott Beck MacCrae to John Vassos, October 19, 1932, Box 8, Vassos/AAA.

168. John Vassos to John MacCrae, January 19, 1934, Box 55, "Correspondence" folder, Vassos/Syracuse.

169. John MacCrae to John Vassos, January 19, 1934, Box 55, "Correspondence" folder, Vassos/Syracuse.

170. John Vassos to Dr. Tonka, n.d., Box 2, Vassos/AAA.

171. Vassos, "Telling Your Story in Pictures," 29.

172. *Springfield Republican*, December 8, 1929, Box 5, Vassos/AAA.

173. Bogart, *Artists, Advertising*, 8–13.

174. Carlus Dyer, draft of text for John Vassos Memorial Exhibition, March 1986, 2, Box 5, Vassos/AAA.

175. Ibid., 3.

176. John Vassos to Robert Sarnoff, September 10, 1957, Box 15, Vassos/AAA.

177. Vassos, unpublished autobiography, 54, Box 12, Vassos/AAA.

178. Ibid., 55.

179. Michael Shaw, "Exhibits and Studio Chips," *Philadelphia Inquirer*, February 5, 1936, Box 20, Vassos/AAA.

180. *The Silverminer: Devoted to Silvermine and Silvermine Life* (New Canaan, Conn.: New Canaan Publications, 1943). For photos from the *Social Democracy* exhibit at the Riverside Museum, New York, June 30–July 31, 1938, see Box 1, "Photos" folder, Vassos/AAA.

181. Quoted in Edward Alden Jewell, "Silvermine Guild Gives Art Display," *New York Times*, May 7, 1941.

2. BECOMING AN INDUSTRIAL DESIGNER

1. One may take 1927 as the seminal year when the term *industrial design* came into public use, as General Electric and General Motors added stylists to their staffs. Also in 1927, Vassos began working for Armand. Raymond Loewy's first industrial design assignment came in 1929, according to Arthur Pulos, "America's Industrial Design Genesis," *Innovation*, Spring 1991, 11.

2. Alain Lesieutre, *The Spirit and Splendour of Art Deco* (New York: Paddington Press, 1974), 22–25.

3. Steven Heller and Seymour Chwast, *Graphic Style: From Victorian to Digital*, rev. ed. (New York: Harry N. Abrams, 2001), 127.

4. John Vassos, Desk Stand for a Hand Telephone, U.S. Patent Des. 81,562, filed May 10, 1930, and issued July 1930.

5. Walter Storey, "Beauty Linked Firmly to Design: An Exposition Reveals How Art Is Applied to the Latest Products of the Machine," *New York Times*, April 1, 1934.

6. Paul T. Frankl, *Machine-Made Leisure* (New York: Harper & Brothers, 1932), 5.

7. J. Gordon Lippincott, *Design for Business* (Chicago: Paul Theobald, 1947), 100.

8. Sheldon Cheney and Martha Candler Cheney, *Art and the Machine: An Account of Industrial Design in 20th-Century America* (New York: Whittlesey House, 1936), 4.

9. Meikle, *Twentieth Century Limited*, 20–21.

10. Walter Dorwin Teague, *Design This Day: The Technique of Order in the Machine Age* (New York: Harcourt, Brace, 1940); Norman Bel Geddes, *Horizons* (Boston: Little, Brown, 1932); Henry Dreyfuss, *Designing for People* (New York: Simon & Schuster, 1955).

11. George Nelson, *Problems of Design* (New York: Whitney, 1957), 6.

12. Warren Susman, *Culture as History: The Transformation of American Society in the Twentieth Century* (New York: Pantheon, 1984), 271–85.

13. Adrian Forty, *Objects of Desire: Design and Society since 1750* (London: Thames & Hudson, 1986), 12.

14. Bush, *The Streamlined Decade*, 3.

15. For more on modern flatware in Europe and in the United States, see Ellen Lupton, "Modern Flatware and the Design of Lifestyle," in *Feeding Desire: Design and the Tools of the Table, 1500–2005,* ed. Sarah D. Coffin et al. (New York: Assouline, 2006), 190–245.

16. John Vassos to R. H. Riemenschneider (head of Walgreen's Pharmacy), February 18, 1933, Box 8, Vassos/AAA.

17. John Vassos to Carl Weeks, March 14, 1933, Box 8, Vassos/AAA.

18. Vassos to Riemenschneider, February 18, 1933.

19. Norman Bel Geddes, draft of a press release titled "Caption Material," File 381, Norman Bel Geddes Theater and Industrial Design Papers, Harry Ransom Humanities Research Center, University of Texas, quoted in Christina Cogdell, "The Futurama Recontextualized: Norman Bel Geddes's Eugenic 'World of Tomorrow,'" *American Quarterly* 52, no. 2 (2000): 193–245.

20. Kathy Peiss, *Hope in a Jar: The Making of America's Beauty Culture* (New York: Metropolitan Books, 1998), 100.

21. Peiss discusses Weeks's strategies, but not Vassos's. Ibid., 130, 164–66.

22. Vassos, unpublished autobiography, 20, Box 12, Vassos/AAA.

23. "A Tribute," *Broadcast News,* August 1934, 21.

24. Letters between Bourke-White and Vassos are held in Box 53, "Vassos," Margaret Bourke-White Papers, Special Collections Research Center, Syracuse University Libraries.

25. Benton et al., *Art Deco, 1910–1939,* 285, cited in Helen Searing, "Twentieth Century Art and Design," *Journal of the Society of Architectural Historians* 63, no. 1 (March 2004): 115.

26. Bourke-White's cover photograph of the Fort Peck Dam for the first issue of *Life* magazine, November 23, 1936, has been described in these terms; for analysis, see Wilson et al., *The Machine Age in America.*

27. Bogart, *Artists, Advertising,* 187–90.

28. John Vassos to Mr. Brown (Gray and Dudley Stoves), July 11, 1936, Box 8, Vassos/AAA.

29. Russell Flinchum, *Henry Dreyfuss, Industrial Designer: The Man in the Brown Suit* (New York: Cooper-Hewitt, National Design Museum, Smithsonian Institution, and Rizzoli, 1997), 73; Flinchum quotes Henry Dreyfuss, "Industrial Design Is a Profession," *Electrical Manufacturing,* October 1937. On the Wallace Silver Company's dismissal of Vassos, see John Vassos to Richard Bach, February 23, 1937, Box 8, Vassos/AAA. Vassos complained about Mr. Morris, the president of Wallace Bros. Manufacturing Company, in a letter to Roy Norr, December 10, 1934, Box 2, Vassos/AAA.

30. Vassos to Weeks, March 14, 1933.

31. John Heskett, *Toothpicks and Logos: Design in Everyday Life* (New York: Oxford University Press, 2002); Raymond Loewy, *Never Leave Well Enough Alone: The Personal Record of an Industrial Designer* (New York: Simon & Schuster, 1951), 133–41.

32. John Vassos to Thomas F. Stokes (B. F. Goodrich Rubber Company), March 17, 1934, emphasis added, Box 8, Vassos/AAA.

33. "1931 Industrial Art Show Eliminates Curlicues of 1929," *Business Week,* October 23, 1931, 22.

34. Edgar Kaufmann jr., *What Is Modern Design?* (1950), excerpted in *The Industrial Design Reader,* ed. Carma Gorman (New York: Allworth Press, 2003), 148.

35. Tony Fry, *A New Design Philosophy: An Introduction to Defuturing* (Sydney: University of New South Wales Press, 1999), 117.

36. Dreyfuss, *Designing for People*, 77.

37. John Vassos to W. T. Quimby (Quimby Pump Company), September 21, 1935, Box 8, Vassos/AAA.

38. John Vassos to Walter J. Barbecker (sales manager at the Shollhorn Company) to John Vassos, June 4, 1935, Box 8, Vassos/AAA.

39. John Vassos, "As the Walls Come Tumbling Down," typewritten manuscript, April 21, 1932, 2, "Writings, Essays" folder, Vassos/Syracuse.

40. An advertisement for a Paragon ticket punch is found in Box 8, Vassos/AAA. The bicycle was a project for which Vassos may not have been paid, which may account for why it was never produced; see John Vassos to Louis Weiss, February 15, 1933, Box 8, Vassos/AAA. The Quimby Company made screw pumps, centrifugal pumps, sewage ejectors, and sump pumps.

41. The Echo Elite came in both single-sided and double-sided versions. John Vassos, Harmonica, U.S. Patent Des. 116,069, filed April 1, 1939, and issued August 8, 1939.

42. Kim Field, *Harmonicas, Harps, and Heavy Breathers: The Evolution of the People's Instrument* (New York: Cooper Square Press, 2000), 29.

43. John Vassos to M. E., regarding Paragon ticket punch, October 8, 1934, Box 8, Vassos/AAA.

44. John Vassos, Bicycle, U.S. Patent Des. 112,889, filed November 10, 1937, and issued January 10, 1939; John Vassos, Bicycle, U.S. Patent Des. 113,584, filed December 13, 1938, and issued February 28, 1939.

45. John Vassos to Pierre Boucheron (Cutlery Division of Remington Arms), February 17, 1937, referring to a letter from Mr. Page of Savage Bikes, Box 2, Vassos/AAA.

46. Vassos's great-niece Jayne Johnes rode a version of the bicycle when she was visiting John Vassos at his home in Norwalk, Connecticut. Jayne Johnes, telephone conversation with author, January 23, 2014.

47. Norman Bel Geddes's metal stove for Standard Gas shares similar design features. See Meikle, *Twentieth Century Limited*, 101–2.

48. John Vassos, Cleaver Knife, U.S. Patent Des. 113,026, filed November 5, 1937, and issued January 24, 1939.

49. Dimitra Doukas, *Worked Over: The Corporate Sabotage of an American Community* (Ithaca, N.Y.: Cornell University Press, 2003), 131.

50. "Kitchen Paring Knife Is Now Streamlined," *New York Times*, August 26, 1937, Box 2, Vassos/AAA.

51. John Vassos to Bernice L. Maguire (Lord & Taylor), March 29, 1941, Box 8, Vassos/AAA.

52. Daniel Bacon (Perey Turnstiles) to John Vassos, December 10, 1929, Box 8, "Misc. 1934" folder, Vassos/AAA.

53. Henry Dreyfuss, "Everyday Beauty," *House Beautiful*, November 1933, 190.

54. *Perey Pioneer*, Perey Turnstile Company newsletter, circa 1934, Box 8, "Misc. 1934" folder, Vassos/AAA.

55. Perey Turnstile Company promotional materials, Box 2, Vassos/AAA.

56. Vassos, Syracuse speech, 34. Also see Keith O'Brien, "Turnstile," *New York Times Magazine*, June 7, 2013.

57. Vassos, "As the Walls Come Tumbling Down," 2–3.

58. *Perey Pioneer*, circa 1934.

59. John Vassos to P. L. Gifford (Perey Turnstiles), April 23, 1934, Box 11, Vassos/AAA.

60. *Perey Pioneer*, circa 1934.

61. Ed Hendrickson (Perey Turnstiles), e-mail communication with author, October 11, 2007.

62. John Vassos to Ross Treseder, January 23, 1933, Box 8, Vassos/AAA; Vassos, unpublished autobiography, 31, Box 12, Vassos/AAA.

63. John Vassos to A. L. Powell (General Electric), July 1932, Box 8, Vassos/AAA.

64. John Vassos to Mr. William Elliot (Packard Motor Car Company), December 8, 1932, Box 8, Vassos/AAA.

65. "What Does It Mean to Win the Modern Plastics Award?," circa 1939, Box 2, Vassos/AAA. Norman Bel Geddes also designed medals; for an example, his 1933 General Motors Jubilee Medal, see Norman Bel Geddes, Box 4, Vassos/AAA.

66. Deed of Gift to the National Museum of American History of the Smithsonian Institution, No. 18065, December 5, 1989.

67. John Vassos to Allan Brown (Bakelite Corporation), May 23, 1933, Box 2, Vassos/AAA.

68. John Vassos, Beverage Dispensing Device, U.S. Patent Des. 87,654, filed January 20, 1932, and issued August 23, 1932.

69. Treseder went on to become vice president of National Distillers. See Vassos to Norr, December 10, 1934.

70. Loewy, *Never Leave Well Enough Alone,* 206.

71. "Both Fish and Fowl," 88.

72. John Vassos to Ross Treseder, n.d., Box 8, Vassos/AAA.

73. Allan Brown to John Vassos, May 20, 1933, Box 8, Vassos/AAA. In addition to the Bakelite problem, the sterilizer Vassos produced in conjunction with the General Electric Lamp Company failed to work. A. J. Butolph (General Electric Lamp Company) to John Vassos, October 19, 1932, Vassos/AAA.

74. Ross Treseder to John Vassos, June 13, 1932, Box 8, Vassos/AAA.

75. "Over 30,000 Coca-Cola soda fountain dispensers have been built." Loewy, *Never Leave Well Enough Alone,* 206–7.

76. Treseder to Vassos, June 13, 1932; Ross Treseder to Alan Bemont (director of the National Alliance for Art and Industry), June 13, 1932, Box 8, Vassos/AAA.

77. *Sales Management,* August 15, 1934, 157; Jeffrey Meikle, *American Plastic: A Cultural History* (New Brunswick, N.J.: Rutgers University Press, 1995), 100.

78. Allan Brown to John Vassos, January 7, 1933, Box 8, Vassos/AAA. "They have chosen ten . . . and promised them . . . lots of publicity." John Vassos to Ross Treseder, January 28, 1933, Box 8, Vassos/AAA.

3. MODERNIZING THE HOME THROUGH RADIO

1. See Jonathan Sterne, *MP3: The Meaning of a Format* (Durham, N.C.: Duke University Press, 2012), 15. Sterne cites scholars working at the crossroads of interior and furniture design and radios and phonographs, such as Kyle Barnett, "Furniture Music: The Phonograph as Furniture, 1900–1930," *Journal of Popular Music Studies* 18, no. 3 (2006): 301–24; John Hartley, *Tele-ology: Studies in Television* (New York: Routledge, 1992); Danielle Schwartz Shapiro, "Modernism for the Masses: The Industrial Design of John Vassos," *Archives of American Art Journal* 46, no.1 (2008): 4–23.

2. Sara Ilstedt Hjelm, "Visualizing the Vague: Invisible Computers in Contemporary Design," *Design Issues* 21, no. 2 (Spring 2005): 71.

3. Forty, *Objects of Desire,* 200–206.

4. Vassos, "The Dilemma of Modernism," 9.

5. Advertisement for the National Alliance of Art and Industry event, 1933, Box 8, Vassos/AAA.

6. Ibid.

7. John Vassos to George Throckmorton, May 9, 1933, Box 8, Vassos/AAA.

8. John Vassos to Isaac Levy, May 18, 1933, Box 8, Vassos/AAA.

9. Orin Dunlap, *The Future of Television* (New York: Harper & Brothers, 1947), 19.

10. Alexander B. Magoun, interview with author, August 11, 2004, David Sarnoff Library, Princeton, New Jersey.

11. Forty, *Objects of Desire,* 204.

12. Vassos to Throckmorton, May 9, 1933.

13. Ibid.; George Throckmorton to John Vassos, May 12, 1933, Box 8, Vassos/AAA.

14. John Vassos to George Throckmorton, June 10, 1933, Box 8, Vassos/AAA.

15. John Vassos, "Report—RCA, Radiotrone Co.," 1933, 1, Box 8, "Misc. 1933" folder, Vassos/AAA.

16. Vassos recorded the details of his early work for RCA in a letter to Louis H. Engle at *Business Week*, March 23, 1936, Box 8, Vassos/AAA.

17. John Vassos to Ross Treseder, September 13, 1933, Box 8, Vassos/AAA.

18. John Vassos to George Throckmorton, August 26, 1933, Box 8, Vassos/AAA.

19. John Vassos, "A Half Century of Design," circa 1960, Box 2, Vassos/AAA.

20. Vassos, Syracuse speech, 10.

21. Vassos, "Report—RCA, Radiotrone Co.," 2.

22. John Vassos, "Radio Cabinet Design," *Electronics*, May 1934, 146.

23. Vassos, "The Dilemma of Modernism," 4.

24. Vassos, "Radio Cabinet Design," 146.

25. Vassos, "Report—RCA, Radiotrone Co.," 2.

26. John Vassos to George Throckmorton, January 13, 1934, Box 8, Vassos/AAA.

27. John Vassos to George Throckmorton, January 12, 1934, Box 11, Vassos/AAA.

28. E. F. Hainster to John Vassos, February 15, 1934, Box 11, Vassos/AAA. This letter explains that Vassos had received a raise from Mr. Throckmorton, increasing his salary by seven hundred dollars a month.

29. John Vassos, "Industrial Design at RCA—A Report Covering 1932–1970," circa 1970, Box 2, Vassos/AAA. "Mr. Stevenson, and Messrs. Nicholas and Vogel" are mentioned throughout Vassos, "Report—RCA, Radiotrone Co."

30. John Vassos, lecture on styling for training course, fall 1936, Lewis Clement Papers, 1938–1975, History of Science and Technology Collection, Bancroft Library, University of California, Berkeley (hereafter cited as Clement Papers).

31. H. L. Capron (Bamberger's Department Store) to Mr. Boucheron, September 5, 1934, Box 8, Vassos/AAA.

32. John Vassos, "Designing Export Radios," *Radio Age*, July 1949, 25.

33. John Vassos to David Munro, December 24, 1936, Box 8, Vassos/AAA.

34. John Vassos, "A Case for Radio Design," *Furniture Index*, May 1938, 16–18, Box 2, Vassos/AAA.

35. Vassos, "Why Not All-Electric Living-Units?," n.p.

36. Vassos, "Report—RCA, Radiotrone Co.," 2.

37. Ibid., 4–5.

38. John Vassos to George Throckmorton, August 3, 1933, Box 8, "Misc." folder, Vassos/AAA.

39. John Vassos to Allan Brown, June 14, 1933, Box 8, Vassos/AAA.

40. Allan Brown to John Vassos, June 16, 1933, Box 8, Vassos/AAA.

41. Meikle, *American Plastic*, 57.

42. Vassos, "Report—RCA, Radiotrone Co.," 4–5.

43. John Vassos to George Throckmorton, November 24, 1934, Box 11, Vassos/AAA.

44. Ibid.

45. The 96X model was chosen as one of the "most beautiful radios ever made" in a book by the same title by Peter Sheridan, *The Most Beautiful Radios Ever Made* (Atglen, Pa.: Schiffer, 2014).

46. Meikle, *American Plastic*, 57.

47. John Vassos to Richard Bach, September 3, 1934, Box 8, Vassos/AAA.

48. Ibid.

49. Vassos, "Radio Cabinet Design," 146.

50. Vassos to Levy, May 18, 1933.

51. John Vassos, "Design for Selling," *Sales Executives Club Weekly News Bulletin,* 1935, 1, Box 5, "Design for Selling" folder, Vassos/Syracuse.

52. John Vassos to Bernice Maguire (Lord & Taylor), March 29, 1941, Box 8, Vassos/AAA.

53. The 5Q6 was also offered in varied models 5Q6 and 5Q8.

54. "How to locate New York, N.Y., on the map of South America!," advertisement for Durez plastics, *Fortune,* May 1942, 33.

55. Meikle, *American Plastic,* 164.

56. Durez Molder company magazine, May 1939, 9, Box 2, Vassos/AAA.

57. Design drawings from the Vassos archive at the Archives of American Art show that he worked on streamlined phonographs with carefully placed control knobs, all resting on the top of the phonograph. These share stylistic similarities to Model VA-20 and Model VA-21 as listed in *RCA Victor Service Notes,* vol. 2, *Complete Index to RCA Victor Service Notes, 1938–1942,* 392-C, Hagley Museum and Library, Wilmington, Delaware.

58. A. Usher, "With RCA—North of the Border," *Radio Age,* July 1943, 20–23.

59. Vassos, "Designing Export Radios," 25.

60. Vassos, Syracuse speech, 12.

61. Betty Johnson and David Johnson, *Guide to Old Radios,* 2nd ed. (Wayne, Pa.: Wallace-Homestead, 1995), 96.

62. John Vassos to George Throckmorton, February 9, 1935, Box 11, Vassos/AAA.

63. Ibid., emphasis added.

64. Vassos, "Industrial Design at RCA," 8.

65. *Business Week,* May 30, 1936, quoted in Vassos, "A Half Century of Design," 46.

66. RCA's other stylists, W. B. Stevenson and Lynn Brodton, may have also given lectures, as their names are listed on the cover sheet for the training course, but I have not found any copies of their lecture outlines. See Clement Papers; also Box 11, Vassos/AAA.

67. John Vassos, fourth lecture for the training course in the fall of 1936, Box 11, Vassos/AAA.

68. "Outline of Mr. Vassos's Fourth Lecture for the Training Course, RCA Manufacturing Company, A Series of Lectures Given by John Vassos, W. B. Stevenson, and L. Brodton for the Training Course," fall 1936, Box 11, Vassos/AAA.

69. John Vassos to Thomas Joyce, August 20, 1936, Box 8, Vassos/AAA.

70. Gantz knew Vassos through his involvement with the Industrial Designers Society of America. Gantz, e-mail interview with author, December 12, 2003.

71. Paul Richardson, manager of radio and Victrola sales, quoted in "Improved electric tuning for all is a keystone of new RCA Victor standard line of domestic models," RCA catalog, 1937, Box 3, Vassos/AAA.

72. Poster of 1937 RCA Victor radio offerings, Box 3, Vassos/AAA.

73. Paul Richardson, manager of radio and Victrola sales, marketing document, n.d., Box 3, Vassos/AAA.

74. Vassos, "A Case for Radio Design," 16–18.

4. DESIGNED FOR ELECTRICITY

1. Meikle, *Twentieth Century Limited,* 117, citing "Main Street U.S.A.," *Architectural Forum,* February 1939.

2. Numerous articles published in this period connected design with commerce. See, for example, Storey, "Beauty Linked Firmly to Design."

3. Peter Gay, *Modernism: The Lure of Heresy, from Baudelaire to Beckett and Beyond* (New York: W. W. Norton, 2008), 324; Martin Filler, *Makers of Modern Architecture: From Frank Lloyd Wright to Frank Gehry* (New York: New York Review of Books, 2007), 35–48.

4. Neil Harris, *Cultural Excursions: Marketing Appetites and Cultural Tastes in Modern America* (Chicago: University of Chicago Press, 1990), 184.

5. Ruth Carriere to Mr. Gimbel, July 23, 1925, collection of Jayne Johnes.

6. "IDSA Mourns the Passing of Design Leader, John Vassos," *IDSA Newsletter,* January 1986, Box 1, Vassos/AAA.

7. Vassos, unpublished autobiography, 20, Box 12, Vassos/AAA.

8. Richard Cleary, *Merchant Prince and Master Builder: Edgar Kaufmann and Frank Lloyd Wright* (Pittsburgh: Heinz Architectural Center, 1999), 22.

9. William Leach, *Land of Desire: Merchants, Power, and the Rise of a New American Culture* (New York: Pantheon, 1993), 304.

10. Ibid., 306–7.

11. John Vassos to R. C. Kash (*Display* magazine), November 18, 1935, Box 8, Vassos/AAA.

12. Interior designers were not required to be licensed at the time. Vassos was involved in protecting the boundaries of his own profession, however, as one of the founding members of the licensing organization for industrial designers.

13. Vassos, "As the Walls Come Tumbling Down," 2.

14. Typewritten text of speech given at John Vassos's party, Rismont Restaurant, 1931, 2, Box 8, Vassos/AAA.

15. John Vassos to Ross Treseder, December 11, 1933, Box 8, Vassos/AAA.

16. One of the last Nedick's stands, on 34th Street between 7th and 8th Avenues across from Penn Station in Manhattan, closed around 2005.

17. Vassos, Syracuse speech, 11.

18. John Vassos, typewritten report, no recipient (probably to Nedick's, since it refers to drawings attached to the proposal), October 2, 1931, 2, Box 2, Vassos/AAA.

19. "John Vassos says . . . ," Bakelite advertisement, *Sales Management,* July 15, 1933, 75, Box 1, Vassos/AAA.

20. Quoted in "Interesting Lighting Gives Tea Room Distinction," *Lighting Magazine,* July 1931, 31.

21. Vassos, typewritten report, October 2, 1931, 1.

22. Quoted in "Interesting Lighting," 31.

23. Quoted in *Magazine of Light,* September 1931, 11, Box 1, Vassos/AAA.

24. Vassos, typewritten report, October 2, 1931, 1–3.

25. "Nedick's Seventh Avenue and 47th Street," *Transitions I.E.S.,* December 1932, 770, Box 5, Vassos/AAA.

26. Patricia Volk, "New York Observed: An Old Dog Comes Home," *New York Times,* January 19, 2003, http://nytimes.com.

27. John Vassos, typewritten description of Rismont project, circa 1931, Box 2, Vassos/AAA.

28. "Interesting Lighting Gives Tea Room Distinction," 12.

29. John Vassos, typewritten article, May 10, 1933, Box 2, Vassos/AAA.

30. Arthur J. Pulos, *The American Design Adventure, 1940–1975* (Cambridge: MIT Press, 1988), 411.

31. John Vassos, "A Small Modern Restaurant," *Pencil Points,* December 1931, 896.

32. U.S. Department of the Interior, *The Preservation of Historic Architecture: The U.S. Government's Official Guidelines for Preserving Historic Homes* (Guilford, Conn.: Lyons Press, 2004), 113–14.

33. Vassos, typewritten article, May 10, 1933.

34. Vassos, "A Small Modern Restaurant," 896.

35. "New Tap Rooms Hark Back to the Past," *New York Times,* December 10, 1933.

36. See Elaine S. Hochman, *Bauhaus: Crucible of Modernism* (New York: Fromm International, 1997), 177–78.

37. *John Vassos: Famous Illustrator and Modernist,* n.p.

38. John Vassos, typewritten note, n.d., Box 5, Vassos/AAA.

39. Glass slides, Box 5, Vassos/AAA.

40. *John Vassos: Famous Illustrator and Modernist,* n.p.

41. Terry Smith, *Making the Modern: Industry, Art, and Design in America* (Chicago: University of Chicago Press, 1993), 390.

42. Henri Lefebvre, *The Production of Space,* trans. Donald Nicholson-Smith (Oxford: Blackwell, 1991), 303. Also see Le Corbusier, *Towards a New Architecture* (New York: Architectural Press, 1946), 190.

43. Richard Bach began the industrial art program at the Metropolitan Museum of Art in New York and was an advocate of industrial design; see Meikle, *Twentieth Century Limited,* 20–21. Also see J. Stewart Johnson, *American Modern, 1925–1940: Design for a New Age* (New York: Harry N. Abrams, 2000), 11.

44. John Vassos to C. Austin Castle, February 17, 1933, Vassos/AAA.

45. John Vassos, "A Small Modern Apartment Designed by the Author for His Own Use," *Pencil Points,* October 1930, 789. This article has been reprinted in *Pencil Points Reader: A Journal for the Drafting Room, 1920–1943,* ed. George E. Hartman and Jan Cigliano (New York: Princeton Architectural Press, 2004), 274–78.

46. Walter Storey, "Modernizing the Walls of Our Homes," *New York Times,* February 16, 1930, 16, Box 2, Vassos/AAA.

47. Carma Ryanne Gorman, "An Acquired Taste: Women's Visual Education and Industrial Design in the United States, 1925–1940" (doctoral dissertation, University of California, Berkeley, 1998), 99.

48. Eliot Noyes, *Organic Design in Home Furnishings* (New York: Museum of Modern Art, 1941), 9, Box 3, Vassos/AAA.

49. This furniture is now at the Long Island home of Vassos's great-niece, Jayne Johnes.

50. Hal Foster, *Design and Crime and Other Diatribes* (London: Verso, 2002), 13–19.

51. Vassos, "A Small Modern Apartment," 789.

52. Beverly Gordon, "Woman's Domestic Body: The Conceptual Conflation of Women and Interiors in the Industrial Age," *Winterthur Portfolio* 31 (1996): 281–301.

53. Kristina Wilson, *Livable Modernism: Interior Decorating and Design during the Great Depression* (New Haven, Conn.: Yale University Press, 2004), 41.

54. See Gordon, "Women's Domestic Body."

55. Vassos, unpublished autobiography, 31, Box 12, Vassos/AAA.

56. Vassos also modernized Harry Stack Sullivan's office at his brownstone at East 64th Street in Manhattan; see Perry, *Psychiatrist of America,* 347.

57. Mrs. M. Levine (possibly Vassos's publicist) to John Vassos, October 6, 1932, Box 8, Vassos/AAA.

58. Vicki Goldberg, *Margaret Bourke-White: A Biography* (New York: Harper & Row, 1986), 141.

59. Vassos, Syracuse speech, 11.

60. "Office and Studio of Margaret Bourke-White, New York, NY, John Vassos, Designer," *Architectural Forum,* January 1932, 29.

61. For more on book design, see Henry Petroski, *The Book on the Bookshelf* (New York: Alfred A. Knopf, 1999).

62. Jayne Johnes, telephone interview with author, December 6, 2014.

63. Vassos, "Why Not All-Electric Living-Units?," n.p.

64. America at Home exhibit organizers to Walter Dorwin Teague, February 23, 1940, Box 363, "Designer's Room" folder, New York World's Fair 1939–1940 Records, Manuscripts and Archives Division, New York Public Library (hereafter cited as World's Fair Records).

65. America at Home exhibit organizers, inventory list, June 10, 1940, Box 364, World's Fair Records.

66. The location of the pavilion can be seen in "Today at the Fair—Complete Program and Map Guide," *New York Herald Tribune*, June 13, 1940.

67. America at Home rooms, credit page draft, May 8, 1940, to Mr. Vogelgesang, Box 363, World's Fair Records.

68. George Howe, "New York World's Fair 1940," *Architectural Forum*, July 1940, 31.

69. This figure comes from the file "Attendance," Box 364, World's Fair Records, which compares gate figures to attendance in the building. The lowest attendance figure for the exhibit was 12.5 percent, recorded between August 26 and September 1, 1940.

70. Notes on decorators, designers, and architects for series of special rooms in America at Home, circa 1940, Box 363, World's Fair Records.

71. John Vassos to Louise Bonney Leicester, February 28, 1940, Box 363, "John Vassos" folder, World's Fair Records.

72. Ibid.

73. John Vassos to Louise Bonney Leicester, March 22, 1940, Box 363, "John Vassos" folder, World's Fair Records.

74. Louise Bonney Leicester to John Vassos, April 9, 1940, Box 363, "John Vassos" folder, World's Fair Records.

75. John Vassos to Louise Bonney Leicester, April 14, 1940, Box 363, "John Vassos" folder, World's Fair Records.

76. Louise Bonney Leicester to John Vassos, April 17, 1940, Box 363, "John Vassos" folder, World's Fair Records.

77. "Jury for the Gold Seal Award," February 27, 1940, Box 363, World's Fair Records; also see scrapbook photo of TRK-12 indicating Gold Seal Award, circa 1940, Box 16, Vassos/AAA.

78. Shepard Vogelgesang to John Vassos, June 11, 1940, Box 363, "John Vassos" folder, World's Fair Records.

79. Box 232, World's Fair Records.

80. John Vassos, in *Directions* magazine, March 1941, 12, Box 1, Vassos/AAA.

81. John Vassos to Shepard Vogelgesang, April 25, 1940, Box 363, World's Fair Records. Also see Iain Baird, "Television in the World of Tomorrow," *Echoes*, Winter 1997.

82. Musicorner descriptive sheet, circa 1940, Box 364, "Inventory" folder, World's Fair Records.

83. Inventory Room 30, "Musicorner, Furnishings," circa 1940, Box 364, "Inventory" folder, World's Fair Records.

84. J. M. Williams, manager of record advertising and sales promotion at RCA, to Louise Bonney Leicester, August 9, 1940, Box 363, World's Fair Records. The description of Koussevitzky comes from the musicians' bios that James Stanley at RCA sent to Louise Bonney Leicester; they are found in Box 363, "John Vassos" folder, World's Fair Records.

85. Inventory Room 30, "Musicorner, Furnishings."

86. This is according to an article about the room titled "Designed for Living," *Victor Record News*, n.d., Box 1, Vassos/AAA.

87. Vassos, "A Small Modern Apartment," 792.

88. Vassos, Syracuse speech, 14.

89. Letter to *Architectural Record*, June 1940, 94.

90. Howe, "New York World's Fair 1940," 39.

91. List of corporations, Crosley Dist. Corp, March 14, 1940, Box 363, "Exhibitors General" folder, World's Fair Records; also see "A Radio for the Hunting Lodge designed by Russel Wright," March 26, 1940, Box 363, "Exhibitors General" folder, World's Fair Records.

92. Memo, March 26, 1940, Box 363, "Exhibitors General" folder, World's Fair Records.

93. John Vassos, "Report on Exhibition of Radio Music Rooms Mezzanine Gallery Number Three Rockefeller Plaza," November 3, 1934, 5, Box 8, "Misc. 1934" folder, Vassos/AAA.

94. Ibid.

95. Ibid.

96. Vassos, "Why Not All-Electric Living-Units?," n.p.

97. Ibid.

98. Ibid.

99. John Vassos, "Entertainment Unit Deluxe," *Furniture Index,* March 1939, n.p., Box 14, Vassos/AAA.

100. Ibid.

101. Pulos, *The American Design Adventure,* 196–97.

102. Hal Foster, "Prosthetic Gods," *Modernism/Modernity* 4, no. 2 (1997): 5–38.

103. "Designer of the Month: John Vassos," *New York Design Digest,* n.d., Box 2, "IDSA publications" folder, Vassos/Syracuse.

104. Virginia Conner, "Making Maximum Use of Minimum Space," *Architectural Record,* September 1940, 66.

105. Barbara M. Kelly, *Expanding the American Dream: Building and Rebuilding Levittown* (New York: State University of New York Press, 1993), 86–87.

106. Herbert J. Gans, *The Levittowners: Ways of Life and Politics in a New Suburban Community* (New York: Random House, 1967), 270–71.

107. Lynn Spigel, *Make Room for TV: Television and the Family Ideal in Postwar America* (Chicago: University of Chicago Press, 1992), 99–103.

108. Alfred Goldsmith to Dr. E. W. Engstrom with "Company-Confidential memorandum" attached, November 3, 1954, Box 3, "Correspondence" folder, Vassos/Syracuse.

5. VASSOS AND RCA

1. John G. Leitch, "WCAU—A Modern Monument to the Art of Broadcasting," *Broadcast News,* April 1933, 2–4, Box 4, Vassos/AAA.

2. Vassos to Throckmorton, May 9, 1933; Throckmorton to Vassos, May 12, 1933.

3. Vassos to Throckmorton, June 10, 1933.

4. Vassos, lecture on styling, fall 1936.

5. Peter Dormer, *The Meanings of Modern Design: Towards the Twenty-First Century* (London: Thames & Hudson, 1991), 51–52.

6. "A Series of Lectures Given by John Vassos, W. B. Stevenson, Lynn Brodton for the Training Course Fall 1936," RCA records, Box 10, Vassos/AAA.

7. See, for example, John Vassos, "Modern Broadcast Station Design," *Broadcast News,* December 1935, 22; in this article Vassos describes a streamlined building to which the "principles of horizontalism" have been applied. Also see John Vassos, "Modern Transmitter House," *Broadcast News,* April 1936, 16–17.

8. See the Hagley Museum and Library's news site for the David Sarnoff Library Collection Processing Project at http://www.hagley.org/sarnoff-library-project.

9. David Sarnoff, introduction in brochure *RCA Victor Presents for 1938, Luxury in Listening,* 1938, n.p., Box 9, Vassos/AAA.

10. Lynn Spigel, *TV by Design: Modern Art and the Rise of Network Television* (Chicago: University of Chicago Press, 2009).

11. Dennis P. Doordan, "William Lescaze and CBS: A Case Study in Corporate Modernism," in "William Lescaze and the Rise of Modern Design in America," special issue, *The Courier* 19, no. 1 (1984): 43–55.

12. Lynn Brodton, "Modern Design—Simplicity: New Forms Arise from Industry's Requirements," *Broadcast News,* January 1939, 9; John Vassos, "Designs Have Been Revolutionized," *Broadcast News,* July 1939, 15.

13. Forty, *Objects of Desire,* 200.

14. "Radio in the Palmy Days," *Broadcast News,* July 1932, 9.

15. Kristen Haring, "The 'Freer Men' of Ham Radio: How a Technical Hobby Provided Social and Spatial Distance," *Technology and Culture* 44 (2003): 734–61.

16. Douglas, *Listening In,* 69–70.

17. Donald Deskey designed the interiors of Radio City Music Hall in 1932.

18. On the relationship of radio to television programming, see Eric Barnouw, *Tube of Plenty: The Evolution of American Television* (New York: Oxford University Press, 1982).

19. Quoted in Smulyan, *Selling Radio,* 127.

20. Marchand, *Advertising the American Dream,* 268. Margaret Bourke-White's photographic murals depicting WJZ's towers were featured in the radio studios of NBC; see *Broadcast News,* August 1934, cover photo.

21. Brochure describing WCAU, circa 1933, Box 5, Vassos/Syracuse.

22. Kenneth W. Stowman, "A Visitor Tours WCAU," *Broadcast News,* April 1933, 10.

23. Ibid., 11.

24. Smulyan, *Selling Radio,* 139–42.

25. In 1960, Vassos created a series of murals depicting the development of electronics in the lobby of RCA's Washington, D.C., office. "Vassos Mural Unveiled in Washington," *Norwalk Hour,* May 26, 1960, 16, Box 2, Vassos/AAA.

26. Emily Thompson, *The Soundscape of Modernity: Architectural Acoustics and the Culture of Listening in America, 1900–1933* (Cambridge: MIT Press, 2002), 296.

27. Karal Ann Marling, *Wall-to-Wall America: Post Office Murals in the Great Depression* (Minneapolis: University of Minnesota Press, 1982), 31.

28. John Vassos, in Stowman, "A Visitor Tours WCAU," 11.

29. Brochure describing WCAU.

30. Vassos and Vassos, "Radio," in *Contempo,* n.p. Vassos did paintings on commission for RCA and NBC employees; John Vassos to R. C. Patterson Jr. (NBC), December 28, 1933, Box 8, Vassos/AAA. Also, Vassos agreed to "execute two copies of the Great God Radio" for Mr. R. J. Reid of WCKY, July 18, 1933, Box 8, Vassos/AAA.

31. E. W. Caldwell (president of the Science Forum of the New York Electrical Society) to Dr. Levy, May 27, 1933, Box 8, Vassos/AAA.

32. Erik Barnouw, *A Tower in Babel: A History of Broadcasting in the United States* (New York: Oxford University Press, 1966), 60.

33. Barnouw, *Tower in Babel,* 60. Also see Mary S. Mander, "Utopian Dimensions in the Public Debate on Broadcasting in the Twenties," *Journal of Communication Inquiry* 12 (1988): 71–88.

34. Smulyan, *Selling Radio,* 150.

35. Christopher H. Sterling and John Michael Kittross, *Stay Tuned: A History of American Broadcasting* (New York: Routledge, 2001), 119.

5. Helias Doundoulakis, with Gabriella Gafni, *Trained to Be an OSS Spy* (Bloomington, Ind.: Xlibris), 16–17.

6. Spigel, *TV by Design*, 100.

7. John Vassos to Ruth Vassos, November 10, 1943, Box 14, Vassos/AAA.

8. John Vassos to Ruth Vassos, January 8, 1944, Box 14, Vassos/AAA.

9. John Vassos to Ruth Vassos, March 9, 1944, Box 14, Vassos/AAA.

10. John Vassos, "Types at the Urinal," 1944, Box 14, Vassos/AAA.

11. William B. Breuer, *The Air Raid Warden Was a Spy: And Other Tales from Home-Front America in World War II* (Hoboken, N.J.: John Wiley, 2003), 154.

12. John Vassos to Ruth Vassos, May 24, 1944, Box 14, Vassos/AAA.

13. John Vassos to Ruth Vassos, October 27, 1943, Box 14, Vassos/AAA.

14. John Vassos, "Credo for Industry," *Linens and Domestics*, September 1946, Box 14, Vassos/AAA.

15. Donald J. Mabry, "The Rise and Fall of Ace Records: A Case Study in the Independent Record Business," *Business History Review* 64, no. 3 (Autumn 1990): 411–50.

16. Richard Osborne, *Vinyl: A History of the Analogue Record* (Farnham, England: Ashgate, 2012), 120–21.

17. "RCA Unveils Its New Discs, Denying It Is in a Trade War," *New York Times*, January 11, 1949, 29.

18. "List of Items Manufactured by RCA Victor Division," July 13, 1945, Box 12, Vassos/AAA.

19. The first model, which was expensive to produce and broke easily, was replaced in 1951 with a simplified version, but the overall shape remained the same.

20. John Vassos, memo to Mr. Barkmeier, Record Department, n.d., Box 12, Vassos/AAA.

21. Howard Baker (Psychological Laboratory, Johns Hopkins University) to the RCA Victor Company, February 21, 1949, Box 12, Vassos/AAA.

22. Phil Vourtsis (author of *The Fabulous Victrola*), e-mail correspondence with author, January 18, 2008.

23. Columbia Recording Corporation to John Vassos, December 20, 1940, Box 12, Vassos/AAA.

24. John Vassos to Tom Joyce, August 1, 1943, Box 14, Vassos/AAA.

25. Ibid.

26. RCA to John Vassos, March 26, 1946, Box 12, Vassos/AAA; W. W. Watts to John Vassos, February 23, 1949, Box 12, Vassos/AAA.

27. John Vassos to W. W. Watts, July 6, 1946, Box 11, Vassos/AAA.

28. Douglas Gomery, "Talent Raids and Package Deals: NBC Loses Its Leadership in the 1950s," in *NBC: America's Network*, ed. Michele Hilmes (Berkeley: University of California Press), 156.

29. Advertisement, *Radio Age*, April 1951, 19.

30. J. P. Taylor to Mr. Flynn, internal correspondence, June 30, 1958, Box 12, Vassos/AAA.

31. Vassos to Streichler, February 27, 1962.

32. John Vassos, memo, December 14, 1964, Box 12, Vassos/AAA.

33. J. P. Taylor to John Vassos, November 13, 1970, 1, Box 4, "Memorabilia" folder, Vassos/Syracuse.

34. Vassos, unpublished autobiography, 51, 52, Box 12, Vassos/AAA.

35. John Vassos, rough manuscript of speech, n.d., Box 10, Vassos/AAA.

36. John Vassos to David Sarnoff, August 2, 1964, Box 12, Vassos/AAA.

37. "Design for Living: Reminiscences of John Vassos," *Communicate: The Magazine of RCA*, circa 1980, 18, Box 12, Vassos/AAA.

38. John Vassos, "Speech for the 1936 Chicago Distributors Meeting," March 11, 1936, Box 11, Vassos/AAA.

39. Arthur Moore, "Jouk," *American Speech* 16, no. 4 (December 1941): 319.

40. Mills Industries Incorporated to John Vassos (letter containing contract), December 26, 1945, Box 12, Vassos/AAA.

41. Richard Law (Mills Industries) to John Vassos, August 23, 1946, Box 12, Vassos/AAA.

42. John Vassos to Charles Miller (regarding production of jukebox in Canada), May 20, 1946, Box 12, Vassos/AAA.

43. John Vassos, "Controlled Light," *Interiors,* February 1948, Box 2, Vassos/AAA.

44. Vassos was vice chairman of this organization, for which Eleanor Roosevelt was an honorary chairman; it was later identified as a Communist front. Government form, January 24, 1955, question 23, Box 13, Vassos/AAA.

45. Kevin Starr, *Material Dreams: Southern California through the 1920s* (New York: Oxford University Press, 1990), 99–100.

46. Bosley Crowther, "The Screen: 'Oklahoma!' Is Okay; Musical Shown in New Process at Rivoli," *New York Times,* October 11, 1955, 49.

47. Sheldon Hall and Steve Neale, *Epics, Spectacles, and Blockbusters: A Hollywood History* (Detroit: Wayne State University Press, 2010), 150–56.

48. John Vassos to George Skouras, June 25, 1949, Box 11, Vassos/AAA.

49. John Vassos to Pat DeCicco, February 11, 1950, Box 11, Vassos/AAA.

50. John Vassos to George Skouras, June 10, 1947, Box 11, Vassos/AAA.

51. Eleanor Coleman, "Color Takes Spotlight in Furnishings," *Chicago Sunday Tribune,* September 14, 1958, Box 12, Vassos/AAA.

52. John Vassos, "Development of a Technically Correct Home Environment," company-confidential report, attached to letter from Alfred Goldsmith to E. W. Engstrom, November 3, 1954, Box 3, Vassos/Syracuse.

53. John Vassos to John L. Burns, February 6, 1960, 2, Box 3, "Correspondence" folder, Vassos/Syracuse.

54. Ibid.

55. John Vassos to W. W. Watts, June 26, 1954, Box 3, "RCA" folder, Vassos/Syracuse.

56. Vassos to Burns, February 6, 1960.

57. John Burns, memo to Kenneth Bilby, cc: Vassos, August 3, 1960, Box 12, Vassos/AAA.

58. "RCA's World's Fair Exhibit to Serve as Official Color Television Communications Center," RCA press release, April 11, 1963, http://www.nywf64.com/rca02.shtml.

59. John Vassos, memo to Jim Toney (VP director of World's Fair RCA Pavilion), n.d., Box 14, Vassos/AAA.

60. "A Pavilion Concept for the Radio Corporation of America World's Fair—1964–1965," developed and designed by John Vassos and Thomas. H. Yardley, circa 1964, Box 8, Vassos/AAA.

61. Report from U.S. Department of Commerce Industry Conference on Trade Fairs, December 14, 1955, 8, Box 1, "Correspondences and Reports" folder, Record Group (RG) 489, National Archives at College Park, College Park, Maryland (hereafter cited as National Archives at College Park).

62. "Tokyo" to U.S. secretary of state, telegram, February 23, 1955, Box 1, "Design Contracts" folder, RG 489, National Archives at College Park.

63. Report, n.d., 23, Box 5, "USIA" folder, RG 489, National Archives at College Park.

64. Robert Warner to Roy Williams, October 4, 1955, Box 2, "Karachi" folder, RG 489, National Archives at College Park.

65. Roy Williams, report, December 14, 1955, 17, Box 5, "USIA" folder, RG 489, National Archives at College Park.

66. "Agreed Policy Guidelines for International Trade Fair Program," April 25, 1955, Box 4, "President's Emergency Fund" folder, RG 489, National Archives at College Park.

67. Leo Miller Associates, "U.S. Will Hold Largest Trade Exposition Abroad: John Vassos Designs Pavilions in India, Pakistan," press release, n.d., circa 1955, 3, Box 12, Vassos/AAA.

68. Ibid.

69. Williams, report, 22.

70. Ibid.

71. Ibid.

72. Roy Williams to H. C. McClellan, November 19, 1955, 2, Box 7, "New Delhi" folder, RG 489, National Archives at College Park.

73. Robert Warner to Roy Williams, September 19, 1955, Box 7, "New Delhi" folder, RG 489, National Archives at College Park.

74. Roy Williams to John Vassos, September 9, 1955, Box 7, "New Delhi" folder, RG 489, National Archives at College Park.

75. Industrial Designers Institute, press release, 1962, Box 10, Vassos/AAA.

76. "Design Institute Elects John Vassos a Trustee," *National Herald,* February 8, 1948.

77. Carroll M. Gantz, "History of IDSA: IDSA and Its Predecessors," accessed December 10, 2014, http://www.idsa.org/history-idsa.

78. John Vassos, speech at Syracuse University, given at the invitation of Arthur Pulos, August 28, 1962, 1, Vassos/Syracuse.

79. John Vassos, "New Forces in Design: Fairfield's First Symposium," *Fairfield County Fair,* October 21, 1954, Box 4, Vassos/AAA.

80. John Vassos to Egmont Arens, June 18, 1945, Box 4, Vassos/AAA.

81. "Design Profession Split by New Organization," *Home Furnishing Review,* July 1945, Box 4, Vassos/AAA.

82. Henry Dreyfuss to John Vassos, January 26, 1965, Box 4, Vassos/AAA.

83. Henry Dreyfuss, "The New Society," *Design Notes* 1, no. 1 (April 1965): 1, Box 4, Vassos/AAA.

84. Lyndon Johnson to Henry Dreyfuss, April 23, 1965, Box 4, Vassos/AAA.

85. "Design Institute Elects John Vassos a Trustee."

86. Franz Schulze and Edward Windhorst, *Mies van der Rohe: A Critical Biography* (Chicago: University of Chicago Press, 2012), 238–39.

87. "Design as Commentary," *Industrial Design,* February 1959, 58.

88. Ibid., 61.

89. Ibid.

90. John Vassos to Jay Doblin, February 11, 1958, Box 4, Vassos/AAA.

91. Ruth Vassos, death record, March 4, 1965, Box 2, Vassos/AAA.

92. Vassos, unpublished autobiography, 60, Box 12, Vassos/AAA.

CONCLUSION

1. John Vassos, memo to Chairman, Corporate Identification Committee, "A Proposal for Modernizing the RCA Trade Mark," February 25, 1967, 1–3, Box 3, "Designs-Trademark" folder, Vassos/Syracuse.

2. Ibid., 2.

3. Ibid., 3.

4. Margaret B. W. Graham, *The Business of Research: RCA and the VideoDisc* (Cambridge: Cambridge University Press, 1989), 12.

5. John Vassos to Robert Sarnoff, October 23, 1967, Box 11, Vassos/AAA.

6. N. R. Kleinfield, "Robert Sarnoff, 78, RCA Chairman Dies," *New York Times*, February 24, 1997.

7. Alexander B. Magoun, phone conversation with author, March 12, 2008.

8. Invitation to retirement party for John Vassos, Box 3, Vassos/AAA.

9. "Design for Living," 18.

10. John Vassos, "Art Deco: Its Origins and Evolution," January 1, 1972, Box 3, "Reports" folder, Vassos/Syracuse.

11. Tucker Madawick to John Vassos, October 21, 1975, Box 12, Vassos/AAA.

12. William Katavolos to Pratt Institute President Richardson Pratt, March 2, 1976, Box 12, Vassos/AAA.

13. Victor Margolin, "A Decade of Design History in the United States, 1977–1987," *Journal of Design History* 1, no. 1 (1988): 57.

14. Reflecting the growing awareness of Vassos's work, Dover reprinted *Phobia* in 2009.

15. Vassos, "An Esthetic Evangelist."

16. John Vassos, draft of preface for autobiography, August 12, 1974, Box 12, Vassos/AAA.

17. Actually, Vassos was not overly pleased with the Dover book, as he wrote in a letter to P. K. Thomajan: "In many respects, they don't realize that this is not a book of illustrations. The Phobia material alone brings it to a different category, but P.K. they are publishers." John Vassos to P. K. Thomajan, November 13, 1975, private collection.

18. John Vassos, draft of pitch letter for publishers, handwritten, circa 1974, Box 12, Vassos/AAA.

19. Rainey, *Institutions of Modernism*, 44.

20. Letter and declaration of legal blindness from the State of Connecticut, 1976, Box 14, Vassos/AAA.

21. "John Vassos," *New York Times*, December 10, 1985.

22. Carlus Dyer, draft of text for John Vassos Memorial Ceremony, March 1986, Box 11, Vassos/AAA.

23. Floor plans for the Silvermine memorial exhibition are held in Box 19, "Murals" folder, Vassos/AAA.

24. Vassos, Syracuse speech, 1.

25. Ibid., 2.

26. Peter Fuller, *Beyond the Crisis in Art* (London: Writers and Readers, 1980), 127.

27. John R. Quain, "Carmakers Take a Hint from Tablets," *New York Times*, January 2, 2015.

styles, providing, 88. *See also* Coca-Cola Company

Contempo (literary magazine), 48

Contempo (Vassos and Vassos), xiv, xv, 4, 5, 23–28, 38, 41, 220; cubist influence in depiction of human form, 24; disillusionment with American life after Wall Street crash, 23, 24–27, 40; exhibitions featuring images from, 43; illustration of "The Jew" in, 27, 28; recycling of images from, 51; reuse of "Radio" illustration for WCAU mural, 145; reviews of, 26–27, 233n147; sales of, 50; skepticism of modern culture in, 5; view of corporate employment's enslaving nature in, 195

Contempo, Phobia, and Other Graphic Interpretations, 216–17, 218, 252n17

Cooper Hewitt, National Design Museum, ix

corporate identity: RCA logo of 1965 and, 214

cosmetic industry, 61

Cosmosynthesis (mural), 53, 200, 201

counters, restaurant, xiv, 114–15

Covici, Pascal, 231n96

Covici-Friede, 30, 231n96, 233n147; publicity campaign for *Phobia,* 36

"Credo for Industry" (Vassos), 187

Crosley radio, 130

Crouse, Russell, 233n140

Crowther, Bosley, 250n46

cubism: influence on depiction of human form in *Contempo,* 24; as preferred style of murals, 144; in *Ultimo*'s cover, 30

"cultural front," 40

culture: consumer, 58, 112; mass, ix, 51, 220; New York as center of, 16. *See also* mass production

Curtiss, Arthur, 246n88

Dale, Carlotta, 141

Dance Center: cofounding of, 232n114

Dance Magazine, The, 4, 9, 12, 44

"Dancer's Reward, The" (Beardsley), 20

Darden, W. Blount, 3, 228n13

D.A. tooth powder, 66

Daugherty, James, 38

David Marcus Theatre (New York City), 199

Davis, Stuart, 172

de Chirico, Giorgio, 24, 118

Decicco, Pat, 250n49

decorative arts exposition in Paris (1925), 55–57, 110

Delaunay, Robert, 9

Delaunay, Sonia, 9, 16

democratic society: industrial design's democratizing effects and, 57

Denning, Michael, 40, 232n123

department store window displays, 109–11

Depression-era America: Great Depression, 40, 58, 119; hopefulness of, streamlined aesthetic embodying, 67; *Humanities* depicting contrasts between wealth and poverty in, 36–41

Desdegule, N., 230n64

design center: Vassos's recommendations to RCA for, 203–4

"Design Explosives" (symposium, 1956), 209

Designing for People (Dreyfuss), 57, 154

Design This Day: The Technique of Order in the Machine Age (Teague), 57

Deskey, Donald, 98, 109, 121, 205, 244n17

Devree, Howard, 232n110

"Dilemma of Modernism, The" (Vassos), xvi

dispensers, beverage, 77–79, 237n68

Display magazine, 111

Doblin, Jay, 184, 210, 251n90

Dogs Are Like That (Vassos), 18, 41

Dohner, Donald, 228n15

Dominican World's Fair in Ciudad Trujillo (1956): mural, 201

Donald Deskey Associates, 187

Doordan, Dennis P., 139, 244n11

Dormer, Peter, 243n5

Dorsey, Tommy, 128, 207

Douce, H. E., 230n72

Douglas, Aaron, 40

Douglas, Ann, 30, 229n40

Douglas, Susan J., xiv, 16, 140, 227n10

Doukas, Dimitra, 236n49

Dounce, H. E., 230n58

Doundoulakis, Helias, 249n5

Dover Books, 216, 217, 252n17

dreamlining, 67

Dream Phobias (dance performance), 36

Drexler, Arthur, xii, 210, 211

Dreyfuss, Henry, ix, xiv, 53, 57, 82, 98, 187, 209, 218, 235n10, 235n29, 236n53, 251nn82–84; on "cleanlining," 67; on designer's role in marketing, 66; ergonomics of designs, 154; as president of Industrial Designers Society of America, 210; on Vassos's turnstile design, 72

"Dromophobia: The Fear of Crossing the Street" (Phobia), ix, 31, 32

Drucker, Johanna, 229n29

DuMont, 148, 169

Dunlap, Orrin E., Jr., 173–75, 237n9, 247n23

DuPont Corporation, 203; Lucite plastic, 59, 60, 173, 174, 185

Durez plastics ad: featuring Vassos, 98, 100, 151, 239n56; Durez Molder brochure, 151

Dutton, E. P., 14, 16; Beatrice the Ballerina published by, 41; books donated for Musicorner by, 128; Contempo published by, 26; cultivation of elite book market, 16; Humanities published by, 36; popularity of Vassos at, 18–19; promotion of Vassos by, 4, 41–50; Salome and trilogy commission from, 14–23

Dyer, Carlus, 219, 234n174, 252n22

Dyer, Davis, 246n81

Eames chair, 211

Earl, Harley, 228n15

Echo Elite harmonica, 68, 69, 236n41

economy: Great Depression, 40, 58, 119; postwar, 186

Edison Magazine, 74

education: industrial design, 208–9; lectures aimed at teaching managers and sales representatives basics of design, 105–6, 149, 238n30, 239nn67–68, 243n6; lectures on interior design, 118

"Education" (Humanities), 40

Egli Company, 128, 196, 197

Eisenhower administration: International Trade Fair Program of, 205

Ekco Company, 83

Electrical Manufacturing, 88, 124, 132

Electrical Manufacturing Award: for electron microscope, 157

electric unit: integration of room's electrical devices into single, 130–34, 180, 181–82, 221; electricity as great unifier, 136

electronics: in America at Home Pavilion (1940), 128, 130; consumer demand in new electrified media age, predicting, 134; mechanical vs. all-electronic television systems, 165, 247n1; mural Cosmosynthesis depicting story of, 53, 200, 201; Vassos's influence on design of early, ix, xi–xii. See also "Musicorner" display; radio sets, design of; television sets

Electronics magazine, 84

electron microscope, 139, 154–57, 162, 246n68

Elegy in a Country Churchyard (Gray), 45

Elliot, William, 237n64

Ellmann, Richard, 230n57

"Emancipation" (Humanities), 27

Emerson Company, 83, 93, 130

emotional states: depicting, 17

Empire State Building: television transmission from, 166, 172; turnstile design at, 72, 73

Engel, Lehman, 36

England: radio design in, 83

Engle, Louis H., 238n16

Engstrom, Elmer, 209, 215, 243n108

"Enlightenment" (Humanities), 38

Entertainment Corner. See "Musicorner" display

entertainment unit deluxe, 131

Entin, Joseph B., 40, 232n122

E. P. Dutton Company. See Dutton, E. P.

equipment design and improvement at RCA, 138, 149–57, 245n45, 246nn76–79, 246n82; broadcast "consolette" mixer and op-7 mixer-preamplifier, 152–54; electron microscope, 139, 154–57, 246n68; ergonomics and, 150, 152–54, 156; 50-kilowatt 50-D transmitter and control desk, 150–52, 153; psychology used in, 150; studio equipment, 150–54, 191

Erewhon (Butler), 30

ergonomics, 63, 65, 72, 102–3; equipment redesign and, 150, 152–54, 156; physical and psychological comfort of user, 220–21. See also streamlining

Erisman, A. C., 228n12

Ernst, Jimmy, xii, 209

Esquire magazine, 4, 231n102; "A Case of Acrophobia" in, 36, 232n115

"Ethics" *(Humanities),* 40

Everything Is Hunky-Dory (Vassos), 53, 136

Ewen, Stuart, 4, 228n21

"Executioner goes down into the cistern, The" (Vassos), 18

exhibitions: new technologies in exhibition displays, 74–77; promotion through, 43. *See also* World's Fairs

Exposition Internationale des Arts Décoratifs et Industriels Modernes (Paris, 1925), 55–57, 110

Faber (publisher), 41

Fabrikoid: use of, 76, 115

Farnsworth, Philo, 165

fast-food restaurant design, 112–15; Nedick's, xiv, 77, 112–15, 146, 240n16, 240n18, 240n25

Faulkner, William, 48

fax machine, RCA, 128

fear: landscape of modernity in *Phobia* as backdrop for, 30–36

Federal Communications Commission (FCC), 176, 180, 248n34

Feiss, Carl, 125

Feld, Rose C., 233n158

Ferriss, Hugh, 28, 231nn90–91

Fickers, Andreas, xii, 227n3

Fiedler, Arthur, 128

Field, Kim, 236n42

Fields, Sidney, 228n7

Filler, Martin, 240n3

film: inspiration from, 6

Fitzgerald, F. Scott, 27

Flagg, James, 228n18

flatware, 235n15; Ultra line of silver-plate, 58, 66

Flinchum, Russell, 235n29

Florence Schick Gifford Hall complex, 52

font: Futura, 19, 48

Ford, Henry, 27

Forman, Murray, 247n19

form following function: equipment design and improvement at RCA, 149–57; for ideal radio design, 85, 102; for television design, 181. *See also* functional modernism/functionalism

Formica: at Nedick's, 114; use of, 74, 76. *See also* Bakelite Corporation

Fort Belvoir, Virginia: Vassos at, 183

Fortune magazine, xiv, 53, 61, 98, 100, 106, 218, 227n9

Forty, Adrian, 58, 81, 235n13

45 rpm products, 188–90; color coding vinyl of 45 rpm records, 189–90

Foster, Hal, 121, 241n50, 243n102

fountain pen: "Hundred Year" Lucite, 59, 60

Franken, Joseph, 232n117, 233n150

Frankl, Paul T., 57, 169, 234n6

French Line (ocean liner company), 7

Freudian psychology, 30, 34–35

Friede, Donald, 30, 231n96

Fry, Tony, 67, 236n35

Fuller, Peter, 252n26

functional modernism/functionalism, xiii, 66, 98, 105, 220; design philosophy of functionalism, 94, 134, 181; in interiors, 121, 124

furniture: collaboration between furniture manufacturers and radio/television manufacturers, 134; furniture cabinet phase of radio design, 81–82, 83; modular, 119–21. *See also* interior design

Furniture Index magazine, 90, 135

Futura (sans serif font), 19, 48

Gafni, Gabriella, 249n5

Gans, Herbert J., 243n106

Gantz, Carroll M., 106, 228n17, 239n70, 251n77

Garis brothers: Rismont Restaurant of, 115–17

Garroway, Dave, 207

Gay, Peter, 240n3

General Electric Company, 74, 145, 146, 148, 150, 169, 172–73, 205, 215, 234n1

General Electric Lamp Company, 237n73

General Motors, 203, 234n1

German expressionism, 35

Gesamtkunstwerk: concept of, 109

Gifford, P. L., 236n59

Gimbels department store, 110

Gluck-Sandor, Senya, 36, 232n114

Goldberg, Vicki, 122, 241n58

Golden Gate International Exposition: RCA field trial televisions at, 168, 173

Goldmark, Peter, 188

Goldsmith, Alfred, 243n108

Gomery, Douglas, 249n28

Gordon, Beverly, 121, 241n52

Gordon, John Stuart, 245n46

Gorman, Carma Ryanne, 241n47

Graham, Margaret B. W., 251n4

Graham, Martha, 207

graphic arts: defined in opposition to photography, 22; new image of graphic artist
as cutting-edge, 21. *See also* illustrator,
Vassos's development as

Grauman, Sidney, 198

Grauman's Egyptian Theatre in Los Angeles,
200; marquee at, 198; murals at, 53, 199;
restyling, 198–99, 201

Great Depression, 58; sensational modernism
during, 40; "small modern apartment"
appropriate to scaled-down expectations
of, 119. *See also* Depression-era America

Great God Radio (mural), 140, 141, 145, 148

Greek Letters and Arts Society, Columbia
University, 14, 15

Greek Relief Fund, 197, 250n44

Gross, Daniel, 246n81

Gross, Gerald, 229n43

Grunow radio with rotary tuning dial (1937),
102

Hagley Museum and Library, 243–8, 247–10;
collection, 73, 138, 141, 142, 147, 152, 153,
155, 158, 160, 170, 171, 175, 176, 180, 191,
239–57

Hainster, E. F., 238n28

Hall, Sheldon, 199, 250n47

Hansen, Harry, 231n83

Haring, Kristen, 244n15

Harlot's House and Other Poems, The (Wilde),
23, 48

harmonicas for Hohner Company, 68, 69,
236n41

Harper's Bazaar: advertisements in, 10–11

Harris, Neil, 109, 240n4

Hartley, John, 178, 237n1, 248n37

Harvard Club: testimonial dinner (1973), 216

Harvey, David, 33, 232n107

Hassam, Childe, 9

Hellenic University Club, 207

Heller, Steven, 55, 234n3

Hendrickson, Ed, 236n61

Heskett, John, 66, 235n31

Hillier, James, xvi, 139, 154, 156

Hjelm, Sara Llstedt, 237n2

hobby, das magazin der technik (German
magazine), 69

Hochman, Elaine S., 241n36

Hofstra University: exhibition at, 33, 219

Hohner Company: accordions, 151, 197;
harmonicas, 68, 69

Hollywood: anti-Semitic notions of Jewish
control of, 27; glamour and prestige,
associating radio with, 140. *See also* movie
theater restyling

home: interior design for, 118–24, 221; as
machine for living, 118, 119, 134; postwar
designs for, 201–5; as refuge, 119, 134–36;
"technically correct," dream of building,
136, 203; as theater for the self, 121–22;
as woman's sphere, Victorian ideology of,
121, 122. *See also* "Musicorner" display

home appliances, 191–92; streamlined
kitchen appliances and tools, 68–72

"Homo Sapiens" (*Humanities*), 38

Hoochchild, Mrs. Walter, 45

Hoover, Herbert, 57

Hopkins, Harry, xii–xiii, 3–4, 183, 186, 248n1

Horizons (Bel Geddes), 57

horizontalism: principles of, 243n7

House and Garden, 146

House Beautiful, 72

housing, prefabricated, 130, 202, 203

Howe, George, 130, 242n68

Huff, W. A. Kelly, 248n30

Hughes, Langston, 48

Humanities (Vassos), 4, 36–41, 232n119;
reviews of, 41; visceral violent illustrations
of, 40

"Hundred Year" Lucite pen for Waterman,
59, 60

Hutchisson, James M., 234n162

"I ask of you the head of Jokanaan" (Vassos),
17

IBM System/360 computer, 194

Icarus (Vassos), 13

iconoscope (picture tube), 165

idea generator: Vassos as, 194–95

IDI, 207, 208, 209

alliance of industry and design, 57; Vassos's comments on "esoteric chair exhibit" of, xii

museums: role in promoting alliance of industry and design, 57. *See also specific museums*

musical instrument designs, 197

"Musicorner" display (1939–40 New York World's Fair), xvi, 108, 124–36, 201, 242n83; description of, 128, 242n82; integrated "electrically energized units," argument for, 130–34, 136, 180, 181–82, 221; Leicester's invitation to Vassos to participate in America at Home Pavilion project, 126–27; materials used in, 128; media formats in, 128–29, 173, 180; modular cabinet, 124, 128, 129, 135, 182, 201–2, 221; music selections for, 128; negotiations over, 127–28; promotional literature for, 129–30; reproducibility and mobility of cabinets, 129–30

Nadeau, Luis, 230n54

Nash, Ben, 208

Nathan's Famous Brooklyn hot dog eatery, 112

National Alliance of Art and Industry: "Radio Style Clinic" (1933), 82

National Association of Broadcasters, 82

National Broadcasting Company (NBC), xv, 52, 145, 146, 207; color programming, 202; public telecasting by, 169

National Home Furnishings Show (New York), 202

"Nationalism" *(Humanities),* 38, 40

Neale, Steve, 199, 250n47

Necchi Mirella sewing machine, 211

Nedick's hot dog stand, xiv, 77, 112–15, 146, 240n16, 240n18, 240n25

Nela Park Magazine, 74

Nelson, George, 227n9, 235n11

Neo-American product line at RCA, 86

Nessen, Walter von, 208

Never Leave Well Enough Alone (Loewy), 66

New Amsterdam Theater in New York City: television broadcast of prizefight at, 181

Newark Museum, 57

New Deal, 40; programs, photography used to sell, 14

New Delhi Trade Fair (1955): U.S. Pavilion at, 205, 206–7

"New Forces in Design" (symposium, 1954), 209

New World radio (Colonial Radio Company), 83

New York City: as center of culture, 16; early drawings of, 5–6; Jazz Age in, 4; residence in, 3, 42, 43, 44, 118, 120, 121–22; Vassos's career in, xii–xvi. *See also* Radio Corporation of America

New York Design Digest, 134

New York Display Service, 2, 4

New Yorker magazine: Packard advertisements in, 7–8; review of *Ultimo* in, 30; TRK-2 television ad in, 170

New Yorker radios, xv–xvi, 96–98, 99, 100, 151; 5Q6, 96; 5QS, 96, 97; 6Q1, 96, 97, 98; 6Q8 and 6Q7, 96, 97; 7Q4, 96; Q–14, 96; Q–31, 96; Q–33, 96

New York Public Library's World's Fair collection, 126

New York Times, 44, 233n140; Dunlap's article on Phantom TRK-12 receiver, 173–74; Dunlap's coverage of television technology, 174–75; interview with Vassos (1977), 217; "Moby Dick" knife featured in article in, 72; Sarnoff's (Robert) obituary in, 215; on Vassos's apartment design, 119; Vassos's obituary in, 219

New York World's Fair (1939–40), 186, 201; America at Home Pavilion, xvi, 108, 124–36, 166, 242nn64–67, 242n69–70; attendance, 242n69; emergence of television at, 165, 172–76, 177, 247n16; Gold Seal Awards, 72, 102, 242n77; Land of Tomorrow, 172; RCA Pavilion, 126, 152, 172–76, 205; streamlining craze and architecture displayed at, 67; Trylon and Perisphere symbols of, 53; "World of Tomorrow," 52, 172. *See also* "Musicorner" display

New York World's Fair (1964): interior displays for RCA exhibition, 204–5, 250n60

Nipper logo (RCA), 161, 162, 163, 190, 213

Nizzoli, Marcello, 211

Nocturne circular glass radio (Spartan Company), 83

Norman, Donald A., 150, 245n52

Nova, Lou, 181

Noyes, Eliot, 241n48

obsolescence: planned, 67, 149; rapid, issue
of, 130

O'Clair, Robert, 230n57

"Odyssey of John Vassos, The" (publicity
brochure), 43

Office of Strategic Services, xvii, 50; other
prominent designers and architects working for, 184–85; Vassos's work for, 184–86

Oklahoma! (film), 199

Olden, George, 185

Old World style, 117

Olivetti typewriter Lexicon 80, 211

Olson, Harry, 192

Onassis, Aristotle, x, 227n1

One Hundred Best Mass-Produced Products
exhibition (Illinois Institute of Technology, 1959), 210–11

Orozco, 38

Osborne, Richard, 249n16

Otto, Carl, 211

Outhwaite, Leonard, 204

packaging: bottle design for Armand, 61–65;
promotional use of, 63–66; for recorded
music albums, 188–90

*Packaging the New: Design and the American
Consumer, 1925–1975* (exhibition), ix

Packard Motor Car Company: advertisements, 7–8, 9, 51; modern materials and
techniques in display for, 76–77

Paidia Award, 207

pain: urban scene infused with, in *Phobia*,
33–35

paintings on commission, 244n30

Paley, Sam, 137

Paley, William, 137

Paragon Company ticket punch, 68, 236n40,
236n43

paring knife, streamlined, 68, 71–72

Paris: decorative arts exposition (1925),
55–57, 110

Passimeter, Perey, 72–74, 75, 76

Patriot radio (Emerson), 83, 93

Patterson, R. C., Jr., 244n30

pavilion architecture at trade fairs: design of,
205–7

Peiss, Kathy, 61, 235nn20–21

Pencil Points (journal), 42, 53, 115; apartment
interiors in, 119, 120, 241n45; restaurant
designs in, 116, 117

Perey, John, 73

Perey Pioneer (newsletter), 74, 236n54

Perey Turnstile Company: turnstile design
for, xiv, 58, 72–74, 75, 76, 220–21,
236nn54–55, 236n59, 236n61

Perry, Helen Swick, 231n104

Peterson, Eldridge, 248n25

Petroski, Henry, 241n61

Phantom TRK-12 receiver, 173–74, 175

Philadelphia: CBS building in, 137; murals at
WCAU, 28, 53–54, 137, 138, 140–45

"Philanthropy" *(Humanities)*, 38

Philco, 82–83; Bel Geddes–designed consoles, 88; "dial-less" and "knob less" radio
fronts, 103–4; "Radio Music Room" exhibition at Radio City Music Hall (1934),
130

Phillips, Lisa, 169, 247n13

Phobia (Vassos), ix, xiv, 4, 5, 30–36, 106, 119,
146, 233n147; anxiety as central issue
of, 32; concepts influencing restaurant
design, 112; dangers of urban alienation
depicted in, 30–32, 33, 121; drawings for,
5, 30–36, 48, 162; exhibition featuring
works from, 45; goal of evoking subjectivity of German expressionists, 35–36; lessons learned while writing, 220; pictorial
elements of phobia, 32, 33–35; popularity
of, 36; psychology behind turnstile design
explained in, 73–74; publisher of, 30, 36

"Phobia—Its Whys and Wherefores" (lecture), 45–46

phonographs, 239n57; 45-J, 188; in Musicorner exhibition, 128; 9-JY, 189; pho-
nograph-radio consoles, 88; RCA Victor
Special model, 98–102

photography: in advertising, by 1930s, 13–14,
63, 64; designing product packaging for,
63–66; graphic art defined in opposition
to, 22; growth of, 21–22; persuasive power
of, 14; sensational, 22

Picasso, Pablo, 118

Pike, Stewart, 160, 192, 246n87

Pilgrim, Dianne H., 216, 231n91

pitch letters, promotional. *See* promotional pitch letters

Piver, 7

planned obsolescence, 67, 149

Plaskon material, 91

plastics, use of, 77–79; Durez, 98, 100, 151, 239n56; Lucite, 59, 60, 173, 174, 185; restaurant design and, 113, 114–15; in tabletop radios, xi, 88–96, 127. *See also* Bakelite Corporation

Plaza Hotel: "Abstract Ball," 9

PM (graphic arts magazine), 129

politics of *Humanities,* 36–41

Pollack, Frances, 233n152

Polyzoides, Adamantios, 44

postwar America, Vassos in, 183–212; design for the home, 201–5; designing for the leisure market, 186–88; leadership in industrial design, 207–12; movie theater restyling, 197–201; promoting the American way, 205–7; at RCA, 188–97

Pound, Ezra, 41, 48

Powell, A. L., 236n63

Pratt, Richardson, 216, 252n12

Pratt Institute, 209, 216

"Predicament of Modernism, The" (lecture), 45

prefabricated housing market, 203; Chromspun House of Color, 202; Musicorner's anticipation of, 130

Prince Albert (steamer ship), 1

printing methods, innovative, 6, 19, 229n53, 230n54

prison system: Wilde's indictment of Victorian, 22–23

private homes: designs for, 118–24

product design, 54. *See also specific products*

profit: relationship between form and, 57–58

Prohibition: use of Armand skin rejuvenator bottle as flask during, 61–65

projection system, Todd-AO, 199

promotional campaigns, Dutton, 4, 41–50; announcement of Athens skyscraper plan, 46–47; crossover achievement in

interior design and, 44–45; exhibitions, 43, 45; literary affiliations, 48; promotional brochure, 43, 45; publication of Vassos's illustrations in print media, 47–48; publicity photographs, 46, 47, 49; public speaking, 42–43, 45–46; results of, 50; staff members at Dutton involved in, 43–44; techniques of "authorial self-construction," 42

promotional pitch letters, 59–61, 82, 83–84, 235nn16–18; about autobiography, 218, 252n18; for Musicorner, 129–30

Proverb for It: 1510 Greek Sayings, A, 41

Prudential Line: holiday cards for, 212

psychiatry: Freudianism, 30, 34–35; *Phobia* as graphic presentation of fears and phobias, 30–36

psychology of consumers: equipment redesign and improvement at RCA using, 150; restaurant design and, 112, 114, 115; using design to lessen psychological distress of modern life, 32, 36; Vassos's understanding of, xiii, xiv, 32, 105–6; Vassos's understanding of, self-promotion in terms of, 61

public art era of the 1930s: murals as product of, 201. *See also* murals

public relations. *See* promotional campaigns, Dutton

public speaking, 42–43, 45–46. *See also* lectures

publishing: movement to New York from Boston and Chicago, 16. *See also* Dutton, E. P.

Pulos, Arthur J., 115, 216, 234n1, 240n30, 251n78

push-button tuning for radio, 103–4

Pyrex glass brick: use of, 157

Quain, John R., 252n27

Quimby, W. T., 236n37

Quimby Company, 236n37, 236n40

racism, 27–28

radar technology, 192, 193

radical change: capturing era on verge of, 20

radio: advent of widespread broadcasting in 1930s, 139–40; architecture and interior

(radio, continued)

design, 139, 157–60, 243n7; CBS building in Philadelphia designed for broadcasting, 137; growth of sales in 1930s, 82–83; importance of medium, 28; movement from battlefield and garage to living room, 139–40; perceived potential for disruption of domestic life, 81; television viewed as natural extension of, 175–76; tuning, issue of, 161; world improved by, theme of, 140

Radio Act of 1927, 145

"Radio Cabinet Design" (Vassos), 84

Radio City Music Hall, 130, 140, 244n17

"Radio" *(Contempo)*, 28, 244n30; on RCA Laboratories library bookplate, 144, 145; reuse as WCAU mural, 145

Radio Corporation of America (RCA), ix, x, 117; Advanced Design Center, Vassos's recommendations for, 203–4; aesthetic of corporate elitism, 140; Brussels World's Fair (1958) exhibits, 201–3; Camden, New Jersey, manufacturing plant, 76, 85, 99, 138, 148, 190, 192; company history, 145–46; conglomeration strategy under Robert Sarnoff, 215; corporate culture and philosophy, 164; Electronic Research Laboratory, 154; electron microscope, 139, 154–57, 246n68; 45 rpm products, 188–90; in-house equipment design and improvement, 138, 149–57, 191, 245n45, 246nn76–79, 246n82; under leadership of Robert Sarnoff, 213–15; Magic Brain campaign, 95, 161–64, 216; "meatball" logo, 161, 163, 213; murals at D.C. office, 50, 53, 200, 201, 244n25; musical recording division, 139; "Musicorner by John Vassos" and, 127, 128, 201; new logo in 1965, 213–15, 251n1; radio architecture and interior design, 139, 157–60, 243n7; RCA Pavilion at 1939–1940 New York World's Fair, 126, 152, 172–76, 205; RCA Pavilion at 1964 New York World's Fair, 204–5; responsibilities of styling department at, 85–86, 192; shaping RCA's identity across products, xvi, 139, 140, 148; styling team established at, 146–49, 150; Vassos as consultant to, xiv–xvi, 38, 54, 77, 79, 137–64, 238n16; Vassos as consultant to, areas of stylistic influence, 137–40; Vassos as consultant to, engineering department assignment, 190–92; Vassos as consultant to, hiring of, 84, 146, 147; Vassos as consultant to, postwar era, 188–97; Vassos as consultant to, radio designs by, ix, x, 53–54, 81–108, 192; Vassos's lasting relationships with RCA's leadership, 195; Vassos's pitch letter to Throckmorton, 82, 83–84, 137; Victor radio side of business, 83. *See also* TRK-12 RCA television

"Radio Eyes for Microbe Hunters" (advertisement), 156

Radio Living Room of Today, 173

Radiomarine Corporation of America, 192

radio sets, design of, ix, xi, 53–54, 81–108; accessibility of, xiii; "filteramic," 192; furniture cabinet phase, 81–82, 83; Globe Trotter eight-inch BX-6, 192; handmade craftsmanship of, 149; Model 6K10, 86, 87; Model 9K, 106; Model 96X, 91, 238n45; Model 21 0 (1933), 85; Model 811K, 86–88, 89, 161; Model 813K, 88, 161; Model Q641, 102, 103; at New York World's Fair (1940), America at Home Pavilion, 128, 130; pared down to its elemental features, xv–xvi, 86; phases of design, 81; plastic, xi, 88–96, 127; process of styling, 85–86; radio tuning dial and mechanism control, xii, 102–4, 192; role of radio in modern life and, xiv–xv; slide rule, or horizontal dial, 102; streamlining, 91, 107, 139; tabletop, 88–98, 106–7, 108; TRK-12 television as elegant, 168; U-26 and U-45 models, 88; Vassos's philosophy of radio design, 86, 93–96, 220; woods used to create texture, 96–98

"Radio Style Clinic" (March 20, 1933), 82

Radio Tempo, or *The Merging of Industry with Art in the Form of Music* (mural), 140, 142–45

Radio Travel-Log (RCA), 161

Rainey, Lawrence, 41–42, 229n44

Randall, Leslie, 52

Rasmussen, Nicolas, 156–57, 246n70

RCA. *See* Radio Corporation of America

RCA Building: at Rockefeller Center, 141, 146, 157; in Washington, D.C., 50, 53, 200, 201, 244n25

RCA International Division, 102, 164, 192

RCA Laboratories, 164

RCA Pavilion, 1939–40 New York World's Fair, 126, 152, 172–76, 205; Hall of Television, 173; radio tube shape of, 172, 176

RCA Pavilion, 1964 New York World's Fair, 204–5

RCA Victor Division: 45 rpm products, 188–90

RCA Victor dog trademark (Nipper), 161, 162, 163, 190, 213

RCA Victor Ltd., 164

RCA Victor Service Notes, 102

RCA Victor Special model phonograph, 98–102

Rebel Arts, 46, 233n151

recorded music: 45 rpm records and products, 188–90; limitations of 78 rpm record, 188; long-playing album (LP), 188

recording mixer: redesign of portable, 152–54

record player, 45 rpm, 188, 189. *See also* phonographs

redesigns: adding cosmetic details and artistry to full-scale, 58–59. *See also* equipment design and improvement at RCA

Reframing Abstract Expressionism: Subjectivity and Painting in the 1940s (Leja), 33

refreshment stand, movie theater: restyling, 197, 199–201

Reid, R. J., 244n30

Remington: shotgun designs for, 58

Remington-DuPont: "Moby Dick" knife, 71–72, 236n48

remote control, 88, 108

Renner, Paul, 19

restaurant design, xiv, 111–17, 240n16, 240n20, 240n25, 240n27, 240n31

Rex and Lobo (Vassos), 41

Richardson, Paul, 239n71, 239n73

Riemenschneider, R. H., 235n16

Rismont Restaurant and Tearoom, 44, 112, 115–17, 240n14, 240n20, 240nn27–28

Rivera, Diego, 38; mural in Rockefeller Center, 141–44

Riverón, Enrique, 49

Riverside Museum (New York City), Silvermine Guild exhibitions, 52–53, 234n180

Robins, Seymour, 209

Robinson, Boardman, 38, 110

Robinson, David, 52

Rockefeller Center: destruction of Rivera's mural at, 141–44; RCA Building at, 141, 146, 157

Rockwell, Norman, 6

Rohde, Gilbert, 121; Unit for Living, 126, 129, 130

Rolfes, Herbert, 247n18

Roosevelt, Eleanor, 250n44

Roosevelt, Franklin Delano, 172, 174, 183

Ross, Andrew, 162, 247n100

Royal Cross of the Golden Phoenix, 207

royalties on illustrated books, 16, 50, 229n46

Rudolph, Paul, 204

Rundle, Skeet, 190

Saarinen, Eero, 184

Sachs Quality Furniture: demonstration of television at, 174

Sakier, George, 228n15

sales culture of advertising, xiii

salesman: forms of psychological manipulation to be used by, 105–6; role of industrial designer as, 105; vocabulary to be used by, 105

Sales Management magazine: Bakelite ad in, 78, 79, 113, 240n19

Salome (Wilde), 46; controversy over, 19–20; different covers for various editions of, 19; illustrations for, 4, 14–23, 43, 48, 51; as openly anti-Semitic text, 27; playbill for 1926 production of, 14, 15; reimbursement for, 16; reviews of, 21; stylistic similarities/differences of Vassos and Beardsley editions, 20–21

Sargent, John Singer, 3

Sarnoff, David, 27, 107, 139, 166, 175, 190, 243n9, 245n50, 247n3, 248n35, 248n38, 248n40, 249n36; dedication of RCA Pavilion at 1939–40 New York World's Fair, 172; RCA's emergence as broadcast and media production giant and, 146, 166; on television, 177; on television, as natural extension of radio, 175, 176; Vassos's lasting relationship with, 195; Vassos's updating of, 150; during World War II, 186

Sarnoff, Robert, 52, 195, 251n5; new RCA logo and, 213–15

Scalon, Wilson, 209

Schick razor, 211

Schools and Training Middle East (OSS brochure), 184

Schulberg, Budd, 27

Schulze, Franz, 251n86

screen, television, 181, 221; foreseeing supremacy of flat, 182

Searing, Helen, 235n25

self, philosophy of the modern, 121

self-promotion, 59–61

sensational modernism, 40

set design, 3, 9, 12, 229n30

Severn, Margaret, 9

sexuality: in Vassos vs. Beardsley *Salome* illustrations, 20–21

Shalet, Helen, 233n137

Shane, Irwin A., 248n26

Shapiro, Danielle Schwartz, 237n1

Shaw, Michael, 234n179

Sheridan, Peter, 238n45

Sherry-Netherland hotel: advertisement for, 6, 145

Shirey, David L., 227n1

SID, 209–10

Signs of the Times, 74

Silvermine Arts Center, 52, 217, 218–19; tribute to Vassos, 219, 252nn22–23

Silvermine Guild of Artists, 48, 51, 52–53, 187, 209; *Social Democracy* exhibition, 52–53, 234n180; Vassos as president of, 52

Silvermine Music Festival, 52

"Silvermine Sillies" theatrical event, 51, 52

Sixth Sense, The (Vilan and Severn), 9, 146

Skidmore & Owings, 172

Skouras, George, 44, 197, 201, 250n48, 250n50

Skouras, Spyros, 197, 212

slide rule, or horizontal dial on radio, 102

Sloan, John, xiv, 5, 9

Slobdin, Roman, 129

"Small Modern Apartment Designed by the Artist for His Own Use, A" (Vassos), 120, 241n45

Smith, Terry, 241n41

Smithsonian Archives of American Art. *See* Archives of American Art, Smithsonian Institution, John Vassos Papers

Smulyan, Susan, xv, 228n11

Social Democracy exhibition, Silvermine Guild (1939), 52–53, 234n180

Social Statement Series (Silvermine Guild), 53

Society of Industrial Designers (SID), 209–10

soda fountains: beverage dispenser for, 77–79, 237n68

"Song of Love, The" (de Chirico), 24

Sorel, Felicia, 36, 232n114

sound: as function of radio, design determined by, 85, 86; rapid modernization of acoustical equipment and cultural shift in consideration of, 146

South America: radios marketed in, 96, 102

South Pacific (film), 199

Sparton Company, 83

Spigel, Lynn, 134, 139, 172, 243n107, 244n10

Spilman, Ray, 219, 228n16

Spirit of Radio, The (mural), 140

spread-band receiver, 88

spy training camp during World War II: Vassos as head of, 184

Stair and Andrew, 130

Stanley, James, 242n84

Stanley, Roy M., II, 248n4

Starr, Kevin, 250n45

Steichen, Edward, 14

Sterling, Christopher H., 244n35

Stern, Juliet Lit, 232n112

Sterne, Jonathan, 237n1, 246n94

Stevenson, William B., 148, 149, 239n66

Stokes, Thomas F., 235n32

Stone, Edward, 125

Storey, Walter, 119, 234n5, 241n46

Story of the Evolution of the Motion Picture Industry in the Perfection of Audio and Visual Achievement, The (mural), 199

stove, streamlined, 68, 70

Stowman, Kenneth W., 244n22

Strauss, Richard, 14

"Streamlined Convenience: A Minor Detail Becomes Important" (Vassos), 155

streamlining: futuristic aesthetic of, 58, 67–74, 140; mass production and, 67; of movie theaters, 197; Perey turnstile, 72–74, 75, 76; of radio architecture and interior design, 157; of radios, 91, 107,

139; of RCA's in-house equipment, 149, 152–53; "styling" in 1930s synonymous with, 67; in television design, 165, 169; in *Ultimo,* 9, 28

Streichler, Jerry, 216, 246n75

Streisand, Barbra, 50

Stryker, Roy, 14

Studebaker hard-top coupe (1953), 211

Studio, The (British magazine), 122

studio design, 140; history, 139; murals at WCAU, 28, 53–54, 137, 138, 140–45; radio architecture and interior design, 139, 157–60, 243n7

studio equipment designs, 150–54, 191

style: process of styling at RCA, 85–86, 192; styling team at RCA, 146–49, 150; wide-ranging application of, in industrial design, 66–73

subconscious: imaginative power of, 36; projection of individual's painful, in *Phobia,* 33; Vassos's style of illustration capturing subconscious life, 50

suburban consumerism, era of, 186–88; television room for, 203

subway stations: turnstile design for, 73–74

subway system drawings, 5–6

Sullivan, Harry Stack, xiii, xiv, 4, 44, 106, 218, 241n56; collaboration on *Phobia,* 32–33

Sunday News, 60

suppressive design, 58

surrealism: imagery in *Phobia* influenced by, 33

Susan and God (Broadway play): telecast of, 166

Susman, Warren, 235n12

Syracuse University, Vassos collection at E. S. Bird Library, ix, 2; Vassos illustrations from, 31, 34, 35, 37

tabletop radios, 88–98, 106–7, 108

tactile experience, xii, 221. *See also* ergonomics; knobs

Tampa, Florida: Vassos at Third Air Force at Franklin Field in, 183

Tashjian, Dickran, 231n91

Taylor, Coley, 230n67, 231n81

Taylor, Francis, 125

Taylor, J. P., 194, 249n30, 249n33

Teague, Walter Dorwin, xiv, 8, 53, 54, 57, 67, 82, 209, 235n10, 242n64; radio design of, 83

technology: postwar application to consumer products and housing materials, 186; power of, as adjunct to the body, 162; radar, 192, 193; redesign of RCA's major in-house, 138, 139, 149–57, 245n45, 246nn76–79, 246n82. *See also* electronics

"Telemobile" unit, 1939–40 New York World's Fair, 173

telephone for Bell Telephone Laboratories (1930), 56, 57, 211

telerena—theater in the round, RCA Pavilion (1964), 205

television broadcasts, 146; development of regular programming, 172, 178; early, 165–66, 247n1

television camera design, 191

television manufacturers, 169. *See also* Radio Corporation of America

television sets, ix, xi, 192; in America at Home Pavilion (1940), 130; challenges in design of, 166; color, 163–64, 201–2, 204–5, 213, 221; design issues at dawn of television age, xii; earliest ideas about television as extension of body, 161; exhibits at international trade fairs, 205, 207; family togetherness in "family room" in front of, 136; home design for, 128, 129, 201–3, 204; initial press coverage of, 174–75; intrinsic link to the home, in Levittown, 134; introduction of broadcast television at 1939–40 New York World's Fair, 165, 172–76, 177, 247n16; marketing, 177–82, 245n36; mechanical vs. all-electronic systems, 165, 247n1; Model TT–5, 96; in Musicorner, 128, 129; RCA Design Center and, 204; in RCA exhibit at Brussels World's Fair (1958), 201–3; RCA's "acucolor," 163–64; sales of, 178–80, 248n43; streamlining in, 165, 169; transition between radio and TV and, xv; TRK-5 and TRK–9, 169, 171, 174; TRK-12 RCA, xv, 126, 127, 157, 165–82, 171; TT–5, 168, 169, 171, 174, 179; Vassos's vision for future, 182

Tennis magazine: covers, 211

theaters, movie: restyling, 197–201

theater set design, 3, 9, 12

Thomajan, P. K., 40, 216, 232n126, 252n17

Thompson, Emily, 141, 244n26

Throckmorton, George, letters to, 40, 85, 190, 237n7, 238nn12–14, 238n18, 238nn26–27, 238n38, 238n43, 239n62, 243nn2–3, 245n47, 245n49, 247n5; promotion of design team within company, 149; Vassos on push-button tuning, 103–4; Vassos on use of plastics for RCA radios, 89, 91; on Vassos's first involvement with television, 166; Vassos's pitch letter to, 82, 83–84, 137

ticket punch, Paragon, 68

Today show (TV), 207

Todd, Michael, 199

Todd-AO: designing environment for, 199

Toney, Jim, 250n59

Toothpicks and Logos: Design in Everyday Life (Heskett), 66

topophobia, 112

trade fairs: promoting American way at international, 205–7, 250nn61–66, 251n67, 251nn72–74

trademarks. *See* logos

"Traffic Dance" (Vassos), 9

transmitter and control desk: 5-DX, 153; 50-D, 150–52, 153; technology of, shaping building's architecture, 157–59

transportation: revolution in, xiii; turnstile design for, xiv, 58, 73–74, 220–21; Vassos's drawings of, 9

Trauken, Joseph, 231n87

Treseder, Ross, x, 77, 79, 112, 236n62, 237n69, 237n72, 237n74, 237n76, 238n17, 240n15

TRK-12 RCA television, xv, 126, 127, 157, 165–82, 242n77; development of, 166–71; marketing, 174, 177–82, 247n10; at the 1939–40 New York World's Fair, 172–76, 177; Phantom receiver, 173–74, 175; promotional materials for, 169, 170–71

Trubenback, Conrad, 73

Tucker, C. W., 247n98

turnstile design, xiv, 32, 58, 68, 72–74, 75, 76, 220–21, 236nn54–55, 236n59, 236n61

20th Century Useful Objects (MoMA exhibition, 1959), 210–11

Udelson, Joseph, 169, 247n14

Ultimo (Vassos), 4, 6, 9, 28–30, 51; exhibitions featuring images from, 43, 229n48, 231n91; promotional campaigns and, 46, 47; reviews of, 30; sales of, 50

Ultra line of silver-plate flatware, 58, 66

"Uncertainty of the Poet, The" (de Chirico), 24

United Air Lines, 170

United Artists, 117, 195; commission to modernize movie theaters, 197–201; trademark, 201

United Fruit Company, 145

U.S. Air Force's camouflage division: Vassos's work with, 183–84

U.S. Department of Commerce Industry Conference on Trade Fairs, 250n61

U.S. Department of the Interior, 240n32

University of Toledo, 1995 exhibition, 40

Urban, Joseph, 3

urban growth: Vassos's critique of, 28–30

urban spaces: Vassos's skill in designing for, 74. *See also* turnstile design

user: taking perspective of, 154. *See also* ergonomics

Usher, A., 239n58

utopian design, 58

utopian social values of 1930s, 58

Valentine Theater (New York City), 199

Vallee, Rudy, xii, 46

Vassacopoulos, Apostolos (father), 1

Vassacopoulos, John Plato. *See* Vassos, John

Vassilovitch, Ivan (pseudonym), 41

Vassos, John, ix, 227n1, 227n4, 227n8, 228nn2–3, 228n12, 228n14, 229nn25–27, 229n33, 230n76, 231n96, 232nn117–19, 232nn129–30, 238nn12–30, 238nn32–40, 239nn51–52, 243n7, 243n93, 243n99, 245nn40–42, 245n59, 245n65, 246n87, 249n20, 249nn24–27, 249nn32–36, 249n38, 251nn78–80; affairs, 41, 232n130; anti-Semitism and, 27–28; artistic philosophy of, 217; autobiography (unpublished), 217–19, 228n2, 229n41, 232n130,

252n16, 252n18; awards and honors, 207, 216; background of, 1–4; blindness late in life, 218, 252n20; books by, 4, 41 career of, xii–xvi; on characteristics of designer, xiii; death of, 219; development as illustrator, xiii, 4–54; disadvantages of being an outside consultant, 201; dislike of corporate life, 195; Dutton's promotion of, 4, 41–50; empathetic approach of, xiv; failure of Coca-Cola beverage dispenser, 77–79, 237n68; goal as designer, 210–11; illustration style, 4, 6, 50–54; as industrial designer, rise of, 55–79, 234n4; integrated "electrically energized units," argument for, 130–34, 136, 180, 181–82, 221; interior design, domestic and business, 61, 109–36, 240n12; legacy of, xii, 213–21; letters of, 229n27, 232nn117–18, 232n125, 232n129, 234n170, 234n176, 235nn16–18, 235n28, 235n32, 236n37, 236n39, 236n43, 236n51, 236n59, 236nn62–63, 237nn7–8, 237n64, 237nn67–68, 237n72, 238nn12–14, 238nn17–18, 238nn26–27, 238nn33–34, 238nn38–39, 238n43, 238n47, 239n52, 239n62, 239n69, 240n11, 240n15, 241n44, 242nn71–73, 242n75, 242n81, 243nn2–3, 245n39, 245n47, 246n75, 247n5, 247n8, 247n98, 248n2, 248nn46–47, 249nn7–9, 249nn12–13, 249n24, 249n36, 250n42, 250nn48–50, 250nn53–56, 251n5, 251n80, 251n90; life after Ruth's death, 211–12; as man of contradictions, xvi; marriage, 3; meningitis, hospitalization with, 185–86; modernist style, defined, xvi, 50–51; name changes, 1, 2, 3; personality, xvi–xvii, 3, 106, 220; philosophy of radio design, 86, 93–96, 220; on place of design in our lives, xi; in postwar era, 183–212; process and priorities in designing, 73; RCA logos pitched by, 213–15, 251n1; retainers and compensation paid to, 84, 190, 204, 220, 238n28; retirement from RCA, 215, 252n8; self-perception as technician of human behavior, 106; sense of hopelessness and fear in modern society, 134–36; social network, 3–4; "technically correct home," dream of building, 136, 203; television sets for 1939–40 New York World's Fair RCA Pavilion, ix, 126; uniqueness of, 219; Upper West Side apartment, 42, 43, 44, 118; during World War II, 183–86, 207, 249nn7–10, 249nn12–14. *See also* *Contempo*; *Humanities*; *Phobia*; Radio Corporation of America; *Ultimo*

Vassos, Ruth, 3, 4, 46, 50, 51, 201, 218, 227n8, 249nn7–9; *Contempo*, collaboration on, 23–28; *Contempo*, perspective in, 5; death of, 211, 251n91; *Humanities*, collaboration on, 37, 38, 232n119; introduction to *Salome* playbill, 14; knowledge of husband's affairs, 41; *Phobia*, collaboration on, 32; promotional campaigns and, 46; *Ultimo*, collaboration on, 28–30; Vassos's wartime letters to, 185–86, 249nn7–9, 249nn12–13; window displays, 110

Verheyen, Peter D., 19, 230n55

Verne, Jules, 30

Victoria and Albert Museum, 2003 art deco exhibition, 24

Victorian era: *Ballad of Redding Gaol* as critique of prison system, 22–23; Beardsley's *Salome*, impact of, 19; feminine home of, 121, 122; modernist severance from, xiii; product displays of the 1930s in Victorian settings, 130

Victor Talking Machine Company, 146

Vilan, Demetrious, 9

violence, visceral, 40

Virginia War Service Committee (Newport News), 1

Vlavianos, Basil, 216

Vogelgesang, Shepard, 126, 242n78, 242n81

Volk, Patricia, 240n26

Vourtsis, Phil, 249n22

"Vox Humana" project, 85

Walgreen's Pharmacy: pitch letter to, 59

Walker, James R., 175, 247n1

Wallace Company, 58

Wallace Silver Company, 66, 235n29

Wall Street crash (1929): disillusionment with American life after, 23, 24–27, 40; "small modern apartment" design after, 119. *See also* Depression-era America

Wanamaker's, 6; Wanamaker Book Week (1930), 44, 233n140

Ward, Lynd, 40

Warner, Aaron W., 216

Warner, Robert, 205–6, 207, 250n64, 251n73

Warwick Galleries (Philadelphia), 52

Wassocopoulos, John. *See* Vassos, John

"Waste" *(Humanities)*, 37, 38

Waterman Company: "Hundred Year" Lucite pen for, 59, 60; pens designed for, 185

Watts, Wally W., 182, 190, 203, 215, 245n39, 248nn46–47, 249n27, 250n55

WCAU (radio station), 82; murals at, 28, 53–54, 137, 138, 140–45

Weber, Kem, 208

Weeks, Carl, 61, 66, 235n17, 235n21

Wells, Malcolm B., 204

West, Nathanael, 48

Westinghouse, 145, 148, 150, 172–73, 247n1

"We Want You to Enjoy Your Radio" (RCA), 161

What Makes Sammy Run (Schulberg), 27

White, Clarence, 63

"Why Not All-Electric Living-Units in the Home?" (Vassos), 131, 132–33

Wilde, Oscar: disdain for tradition and entanglement with themes of dangerous desire, 19; *Salome*, Vassos's illustrations for, 4, 14–23, 43, 48, 51; trilogy illustrated for Dutton, 16–23, 48

Williams, J. M., 242n84

Williams, Roy, 207, 250nn64–65, 251nn72–74

Wilson, Kristina, 122, 241n53

Wilson, Richard Guy, 231n91

Windhorst, Edward, 251n86

window displays, 109–11

Wolff, Irving, 85

Wolfsonian–Florida International University collection, 30, 76, 101, 167

women's rights debate, 42–43

woods: in radio set designs, 96–98; in television set designs, 167–68, 169

"Workers, The" *(Humanities)*, 39, 40

Works Progress Administration, 52

World's Fair Corporation, 204

World's Fairs: Brussels (1958), 201–3; Chicago (1933), 74, 77, 121, 247n16; Dominican, in Ciudad Trujillo (1956), 201. *See also* New York World's Fair (1939–40); New York World's Fair (1964)

World War I: Vassos's role during, 1–2, 5

World War II: Vassos's work for camouflage unit and OSS during, 183–86, 207, 249nn7–10, 249nn12–14

Wormley, Edward, 208

WRCA (fictional prototype for transmitter building), 157–60

Wright, Frank Lloyd, 109, 110

Wright, Russell, 93, 126; Winter Hideout in the Adirondacks, 126, 130

W2XBS broadcasting station, 172

Yardley, Thomas H., 202, 250n60

Yeon, John, 126

Zeisel, Eva, 208

Zenith dial, 102

Zielinski, Siegfried, 161, 246n91

Zim, Larry, 247n18

Zworykin, Vladimir, xvi, 247n1; development of all-electronic television, 165; electron microscope development and, 139, 154, 156, 162

DANIELLE SHAPIRO earned her PhD in art history and communications studies at McGill University, specializing in media and design history.